MERLEAU-PONTY

EXISTENTIALIST OF THE
SOCIAL WORLD

MERLEAU-PONTY

EXISTENTIALIST OF THE
SOCIAL WORLD

BY

ALBERT RABIL, JR.

COLUMBIA UNIVERSITY PRESS

NEW YORK AND LONDON

1967

Albert Rabil, Jr., is Assistant Professor of Religion at Trinity College.

This study, prepared under the Graduate Faculties of Columbia University, was selected by a committee of those Faculties to receive one of the Clarke F. Ansley awards given annually by Columbia University Press.

FOR JANET

who understands what is important

Merleau-Ponty's memory is still too vivid for anyone to be able to portray him; he will be more easily approached, perhaps, by one unknown to me. . . .

Jean-Paul Sartre, 1961

Preface

Maurice Merleau-Ponty was born in Rochefort-sur-Mer, France, on March 14, 1908. During the late 1920s he attended the most outstanding school in France for young men, the Ecole Normale Supérieur. Following the completion of his education, he began to teach in a *lycée*, continuing his studies in psychology and philosophy. Before the end of World War II he had written two important books combining his work in both fields; he emerged after the war as one of France's most promising young thinkers. In 1945 he was appointed Professor of Philosophy at the University of Lyon. In the tense atmosphere of the early postwar years, he focused his attention primarily on the political issues of the day, using as a forum the pages of *Les Temps Modernes*, a journal he and Sartre had jointly initiated after the war, and of which Sartre is still editor. In 1949 Merleau-Ponty came to Paris as Professor of Philosophy at the Sorbonne with a special assignment in child psychology. And in 1952 he became one of the youngest men ever appointed to the faculty of the Collège de France, filling the chair of philosophy occupied a generation before by Henri Bergson. He died in Paris on May 4, 1961, still a young man whose thought was "on the way."

The subtitle of this book, "Existentialist of the Social World," embodies the thesis that will be defended throughout. By "existentialist" I mean primarily Merleau-Ponty's preoccupation with the "lived" or "prereflective" world, the world with which we are in immediate contact and on which our reflective (or abstract) thought is based. He regarded it as the proper task of philosophy to create a method capable of describing this immediate contact without sacrificing its concreteness and its variety. The two poles of his thought are therefore "self" and "world." It is the clarification of the self to itself and to others at which his method and his descriptions aim; but it is the structures surrounding the self which make self-understanding a possibility. Merleau-Ponty's philosophy is thus a "social philosophy." Neither the subjectivity of the self nor the objectivity of the world but the relationship between them which continuously renders the self more than subjective and the world less than objective is the proper theme of philosophical analysis.

I believe that in Merleau-Ponty more than in any other philosopher one can find in dialectical tension the existentialist preoccupation with self-understanding and the social orientation of the politically minded and the reformer. The following pages attempt to describe this unique phenomenon, a "social existentialism," by analyzing its sources, by describing the new perspective that emerges through a particular vision of those sources, and by assessing the adequacy of that vision in relation both to the life of the man and to the ideas he propounded.

This book carries with it an enormous debt of gratitude to many persons, some of whom cannot even be named. I must begin by expressing my appreciation to my teachers at Duke University, Union Theological Seminary, and Columbia University, who have given me a vision of what historical scholarship means and who have inspired me with the will to attempt to follow their footsteps. I am also grateful for a Traveling Fellowship from Union Theological Seminary and for a Fulbright Grant which enabled me to spend a year in Paris, where the initial work on this project was begun. And I can say nothing less than that I was surprised by joy when the Graduate Faculties of Columbia University deemed this work worthy of an Ansley Award, making possible its publication.

There are some persons to whom the successful completion of this project was directly related and to whom I am happy to express my gratitude here. For the critical but always helpful suggestions of Professors Robert D. Cumming, John Macquarrie, Wilhelm Pauck, and Jacob Taubes, to whom a preliminary draft of this manuscript was submitted as a doctoral dissertation, I express my thanks, though it goes without saying that the views expounded here are the responsibility of the writer alone. To Mrs. Odessa Elliott, who suggested many stylistic improvements on an earlier draft, and to Miss Carol Steiman, who labored long over the bibliography, I am also indebted. Finally to my family, with whom and for whom it is a joy to work, I record here my thanks.

Hartford   ALBERT RABIL, JR.
August 4, 1965

Abbreviations

Citations to the following books and lectures by Merleau-Ponty, often referred to in the ensuing pages, will be given in the text itself. In cases where copyrighted translations exist, these have been used, though in some cases corrected. In all other cases translations are my own.

ACF   *Annuaire du Collège de France* (Summaries of Course Lectures, 1953-60).

AD   *Les Aventures de la dialectique*, 1955. English translation of chapter 1 in *The Primacy of Perception and Other Essays*, pp. 193-210.

EP   *Eloge de la philosophie*, 1953. English translation, *In Praise of Philosophy*, 1963.

HT   *Humanisme et terreur*, 1947. English translation of Part II, chapter 2, in *The Primacy of Perception and Other Essays*, pp. 211-28.

OE   "L'Oeil et l'esprit," 1961. English translation, *The Primacy of Perception and Other Essays*, pp. 159-90.

PC   *Les Philosophes célèbres*, 1956.

PP   *Phénoménologie de la perception*, 1945. English translation, *Phenomenology of Perception*, 1962.

PPCP   "Le Primat de la perception et ses conséquences philosophiques," 1946. English translation, *The Primacy of Perception and Other Essays*, pp. 12-42.

RE   *Les Relations avec autrui chez l'enfant* (Course Lectures, 1951-52). English translation, *The Primacy of Perception and Other Essays*, pp. 96-155.

S   *Signes*, 1960. English translation, *Signs*, 1964.

SC   *La Structure du comportement*, 1942. (Reissued in 1949; page numbers differ in the two editions; references here are to the 1949 edition). English translation, *The Structure of Behavior*, 1963.

SHP   *Les Sciences de l'homme et la phénoménologie* (Course Lectures, 1951-52). English translation, *The Primacy of Perception and Other Essays*, pp. 43-96.

SNS   *Sens et non-sens*, 1948. English translation, *Sense and Non-Sense*, 1964.

VI   *Le Visible et l'invisible*, 1964.

Sources of Quotations

The quotations which appear at the beginning of the chapters come from the following sources:

CHAPTER I

"Le Primat de la perception et ses conséquences philosophiques," 146; tr., 36-37

CHAPTER II

Phénoménologie de la perception, 199; tr., 171

CHAPTER III

Signes, 161; tr., 128

CHAPTER IV

Eloge de la Philosophie, 49; tr., 34
Eloge de la Philosophie, 83; tr., 62

CHAPTER V

Sartre, *Being and Nothingness*, pp. 439, 485
Phénoménologie de la perception, xv; tr., xix
Sartre, "No Exit," in *No Exit and Three Other Plays*, p. 47
"Le Primat de la perception et ses conséquences philosophiques," 133; tr., 25

CHAPTER VI

L'Express, October 9, 1954, p. 3

Contents

PART II

The Evolution of a Social Philosophy: 1945-1955

PART III
Transformations and Continuities: 1950-1961

PART IV
Old and New Perspectives on Some Philosophical
Problems: 1945-1961

PART V
Epilogue

PART I

The Beginning of
a Philosophical Adventure: 1935-1945

I

A Critique of Psychology
and Its Philosophical Significance

Philosophical awareness is possible only on the basis of
science. It is only when one has conceived the world of
the natural sciences in all their rigor that one can see
appear, by contrast, man in his freedom.

Merleau-Ponty

Revolt Against Rationalism

Prior to the completion of his first book, *La Structure du comportement*, in 1938,[1] Merleau-Ponty published only three articles.[2] Each of these articles was a book review, but Merleau-Ponty used two of the occasions to put forward his own
hopes for French philosophy. Indeed, the books he chose to
write about are indicative of these hopes. For all of them are
phenomenological studies, that is, descriptive analyses of aspects of experience grasped by reflection as they are *lived*
rather than as they are known by scientific reason. Scientific
reason here means the understanding of reason in a science
or philosophy which either considers man to be an object in
nature like every other object or considers nature to be constituted by the human mind. Merleau-Ponty, along with others
of his generation like Sartre and Jean Hyppolite, was in revolt
against this kind of rationalism. He was convinced that his
teachers could not take account of a world in which nature is
not itself geometrical and human society is not a community

of reasonable minds.[3] Sartre with characteristic verve, does more than simply suggest this split between the generations. He writes:

Futile and serious, our teachers ignored history. They replied that [our] questions could not be posed, that they were badly posed, or—and this was a habit in the writing of the period—that "the answers were in the questions." To think is to measure, said one of them who did neither the one nor the other. And all [of them said]: man and nature are the objects of universal concepts.[4]

This is the philosophical context in which Merleau-Ponty's first book appeared. As he says: "Among contemporary thinkers in France, there exist side by side a philosophy, on the one hand, which makes of every nature an objective unity constituted vis-à-vis consciousness and, on the other, sciences which treat the organism and consciousness as two orders of reality and, in their reciprocal relations, as 'effects' and as 'causes'." (SC 2, tr. 4) His own intention is to understand "the relations of consciousness and nature: organic, psychological, or even social,"[5] without either reducing man to nature or nature to reason. He wants to describe the relationship between man and nature in such a way that the continuities as well as the discontinuities between them will be revealed, and in so doing to overcome the artificial split in science, in philosophy, and in the relationship of science and philosophy. His initial approach was influenced by a group of German psychologists who came to France in the early 1930s and who were attempting to integrate empirical psychology with a phenomenological method in philosophy.[6] It is not surprising, therefore, that The Structure of Behavior begins with a critique of empirical psychology, especially behaviorism as represented by John Watson, and that it offers an alternative description intended to render the data more intelligible. This description is based on an appropriation, though in modified form, of Gestalt psychology, which leads finally to a new philosophical perspective.

Critique and Reorientation of Psychology

Ivan Pavlov (1849-1936) was one of the founders of experimental psychology. Although he never attempted to construct a psychology on the basis of his physiological studies, he hoped that others would use these studies to do just that. Pavlov assumed a fundamental continuity between man and nature, between what goes on inside the human body and what goes on outside it. John Watson (1878-1958), who used Pavlov's physiology as the basis for an empirical psychology, carried Pavlov's reduction to the extreme when he argued that consciousness was unnecessary as an explanatory hypothesis and could be ignored. Pavlov never went this far.[7]

The physiological basis of Watson's behavioristic psychology was the theory of the reflex arc. The reflex arc describes the channels through which stimuli reaching the body from outside are carried through the body and cause a reaction. A stimulus is received by a sense organ (or receptor). Sensory or afferent neurons[8] conduct the received stimulation to the central nervous system. Motor or efferent neurons then conduct the stimulation from the central nervous system to the effector (a muscle or gland) causing a reaction. Since most bodily actions are complex (i.e., require many reflex arcs acting in conjunction), connections are posited between reflex arcs which "adjust" (stimulate or inhibit) the reflexes to one another so that a coordinated action ensues.[9] This theory led to two conclusions which Merleau-Ponty challenges. The first is that the body is a "sum of parts" which are coordinated at every instant, and that each part of the sensory apparatus is sensitive to *only* one form of stimulation.[10] Second, the body becomes a passive agent, reacting and adjusting to external stimuli which act as "causes." There is, therefore, no distinction between man and nature.[11]

Let us look first at the one-to-one correlation between stimulus and reaction. Merleau-Ponty describes many results of experimental pscyhology which do not fit this pattern. A good example is Köhler's experiment with a monkey, designed to test the behavioristic theory. If a monkey is placed in a dark room into which a spot of light is beamed, he will turn toward the light. According to behaviorism this is not to be explained in terms of any intention of consciousness but rather by the light itself which acts on certain motor muscles to cause a reaction. The light therefore is decomposed into a series of points of excitation which act on various motor mechanisms. All these partial processes, external to one another, are adapted to respond in a given way by a preestablished correlation between certain organs or receptor apparatus and certain effector muscles. The nervous action is thus nothing but the putting into play of a great number of autonomous circuits. But if, as Köhler did, one connects the internal eye muscles of a monkey with the nervous tissues which command the external muscles, and then connects the latter to the nervous tissues which command the internal muscles, and finally places the animal in a dark room and beams a spot of light into it, the result will not be that the animal turns *away* from the light (as behaviorism would require), but rather that he turns toward it. (SC 39, tr. 38-39) In other words, the animal *adjusts* to a whole new situation. Variations in the stimulus can take place while the reaction remains constant, and (as in our example) variations in the connections of the nervous tissue can lead to the same reaction. (SC 31, tr. 31) There is no one-to-one correlation but a variety of possible combinations, the explanation of which would require, on the basis of the assumptions of the stimulus-response pattern, a theory as complicated as the description of the heavens in Ptolemaic cosmology. If the adequacy of a scientific theory depends on its ability to account for the phenomena, then behaviorism fails, both because the stimulus cannot be defined independently of the organism and because there is no constancy in the pattern of relations between stimuli and reactions when they are defined in behavioristic terms.

Merleau-Ponty does not say that the stimulus-response pattern does not exist. He limits it, however, to laboratory (i.e., pathological) experience.[12] In normal life, what we *observe* is the adjustment of the organism through *body intention*. The body is not simply a *passive* agent which adjusts to external stimuli, but also an *acting* agent which organizes the world around it. Hence, causality must be described in *circular* rather than in linear terms. If an organ in an animal is removed, others will assume its function. A man suffering from hemianopia does not believe that his visual field is really only half what it should be, but only that his vision is bad. In each case, there is an adjustment to a new situation through body intention. (*SC* 40-42, tr. 40-41) This circular process is what the gestaltists call "form" (= structure), and it may be described in three statements: first, the nervous system is a field of forces which includes both external and intraorganic factors at once; second, these forces tend to equilibrium according to certain modes of distribution and obtain from the body movements in accord with this equilibrium; and third, the movement as executed provokes modifications in the state of the afferent system which in turn provokes new movements. This dynamic process assures the regulation of behavior. (*SC* 48-49, tr. 46) Gestalt psychologists, however, regarded this adjustment of structures in physical terms.[13] What is needed is a description of form which takes account of "circular causality." Merleau-Ponty suggests three levels on which this reciprocity can be expressed.

First, "a lesion, even localized, can determine structural disorders which concern the whole of behavior, and analogous structural disorders can be provoked by lesions situated in different regions of the cortex." (*SC* 66, tr. 62) A lesion cannot be strictly localized because it depends on the response of the whole organism to a problem posed by its milieu; hence symptoms will vary with the questions raised. For example, lesions do not prevent immediate experience but they do prevent reflection on this experience. In cases of pathological inability to read, the sick person can read his name as a word but not the individual letters which compose it. Within a group of words he can pronounce a particular word but not its letters, or he can pronounce a particular word but not that same word if it is isolated. What he loses is a certain level of action. Pathological functioning thus points to a new *signification* of behavior. Structure is therefore a general function of the organization of behavior. (*SC* 66-76, tr. 62-69)

Second, "nevertheless, nerve functioning cannot be treated as a global process where the intervention of any of the parts would be of equal importance. The function is never indifferent to the substrate by which it is achieved." (*SC* 76, tr. 69) A lesion in one part of the brain affects language, in another part, perception, etc. Hence the place of the lesion affects functioning also. This does not mean that the regions are the seats of modes of corresponding thought, but rather that they are the privileged means of realization in the respective cases.[14]

Third, "consequently, place in nerve substance has an equivocal signification. Only a mixed conception of localizations and a functional conception of parallelism can be accepted." (*SC* 79, tr. 72) Local excitations are distributed to the whole organism and reorder its behavior. Hence localizations are local but also functional (i.e., related to the whole organism). Moreover, there is a parallelism between nervous activity and the operations of consciousness. But the correspondence is not one-to-one, as in older psychology and physiology. Parallelism must be understood structurally and functionally. (*SC* 79-84, tr. 72-76)

These are the factors relating to the integration of experience. Merleau-Ponty takes three experiences—spatial perception (*SC* 84-88, tr. 76-79), chromatic perception (*SC* 88-94, tr. 79-85), and language (*SC* 94-97, tr. 85-88)—and attempts to apply the principles set forth to a new view of these phenomena. Let us take chromatic perception as illustrative of his line of reasoning.[15] The chromatic value assigned to an excitation depends on the chromatic structure and not simply on the local excitations. For example, gray paper on a yellow background appears blue; the background is as important as the local excitation (the gray paper) in the perception of blue.[16] Moreover, the ensemble depends also on the spatial structure, i.e., the colors we assign to things often depend on their spatial arrangement. For example, when a gray ring is resting on a background which is half green and half red and the whole ensemble is perceived, it appears gray; but when a strip of paper or a wire is laid across the ring at the point of separation between the red and green background, then half the ring appears reddish and half appears greenish. This occurs because in the first part of the experiment the forces of cohesion which held the ring together were strong enough to block out other stimulations, while in the second part of the experiment the ring had become nonhomogeneous, and other stimulating forces took command. Changes in chromatic perception, therefore, depend on changes in the arrangement of the whole field and cannot be comprehended at all in terms of a one-to-one correspondence of afferent and efferent neurons. On the basis of these examples physiological psychology appears to be riveted in the particular; it takes account only of the forces acting in a local situation ("figure") but ignores the general context ("ground") in which these forces act.

Outline of a New Metaphysical Anthropology

If we consider the *philosophical* implications of the critique just completed, we see that the problem lies in treating various orders of reality as *substances* imposed upon one another. Thus nature (the physical), the body (the physiological), and mind (the psychical) are three orders of reality which cannot be integrally related to one another. Behaviorism—and even

Gestalt psychology—reduced all of the orders to the physical so that consciousness added nothing in the explanation of behavior. Introspectionist psychology, on the other hand, described consciousness without relating it to the physical world. Both materialist and spiritualist explanations of behavior are reductive. The problem is to give a philosophical explication of the structure of behavior which will not be subject to the criticisms that can be brought against idealism and materialism. What is necessary for this task is an "enlarged reason" which can deal with the lived world without reducing it to mind or matter, without bifurcating it, and without declaring it unintelligible.[17]

But how can we describe the relationships between organisms and their environments without being reductive? Merleau-Ponty proposes to do so by treating behavior as a *structure* which emerges in various ways for reflection. From this perspective behavior is visible at several levels. There is first the level of the *syncretic forms*. At this level, behavior is related to certain types of situation or to certain complexes of special stimuli. The whole complex is required for a reaction. For example, a starfish will react only to stimuli which simulate those of its natural habitat. Its *whole* response to a situation is that of "instinct." On this level of existence the organism is imprisoned in its natural conditions. Some organisms live only on this level, but all act "instinctively" under certain conditions.[18] Second, there is the level of *unmovable forms*. When "signs" appear which are not determined by instinct, we can assume that they are based on structures relatively independent of the materials in which they are realized. A configuration appears which stands out from its material base. For example, an animal has been taught to run a maze along which there is a white curtain and at the end of which he finds a reward. He shows awareness of a "situation" when he is given a shock upon reaching the end of the maze, for following the latter experience he will no longer run the maze parallel to the white curtain. He has perceived a relation between the white curtain and the shock at the end. It is this configuration and not the reward which explains his actions.[19] There is finally the level of *symbolic forms*. In animal behavior signs always remain signs and never become symbols. An animal that has been taught to leap from one chair to another will not do the same if it is provided with a stool and an armchair or two stools. But for a person this is not the case. One who can use a typewriter or an organ can improvise, that is, type words never seen before or play music never seen before. In the same way we can decipher texts of unknown or forgotten languages. These examples of symbolic action point to the fact that it is through the analysis of the internal structure that external signification is measured. Symbolic power is the power to analyze this internal structure; this is precisely what the animal lacks.[20]

We have now reached an important turning point. For not only has it been shown that reductive explanations, whether based on mental or material premises, are invalid, but it has also been asserted that the interactions between organism and environment at each level must be understood as various ways of *belonging-to-the-world*. Can our experience of the *lived* world be described in such a way as to justify this conclusion? Merleau-Ponty proposes to answer this question by describing the manner in which the world is *perceived* at various levels. In particular, he considers the physical, the vital, and the human orders of perception.

Consider *physical forms*. On the one hand, physical laws cannot be regarded as belonging to individual things in nature; they belong to stable groups and apply to the "field" in which the components of this group are related. Therefore, laws are in reality structures. But these structures are not, as Gestalt psychology believes, *in* nature itself. They belong to the field in which things interact with one another. Physical forms are not a physical reality; they are objects of perception in the form of an ensemble of laws, and they make knowledge of nature possible. The intelligibility of the physical order depends on a perceptive world in which structure is given to an observer, but in which the structure belongs neither to the observer nor to the thing observed. It belongs rather to the world in which both are related. (SC 147-57, tr. 137-45).

When we turn to the perception of organic structures, or the *vital order*, we can no longer speak of laws in the physical sense, for now we are dealing with the *behavior* of organisms. We must speak instead of "norms," inasmuch as the "circular" relationship between an organism and its environment is of a different type from the relationship obtaining in physical nature. As we saw earlier in the example of chromatic perception, it is not the material properties of the stimuli which determine the response of the organism, but rather their vital significance. Thus, whereas with physical systems we can speak of a unity of correlation, with organisms we must speak of a unity of signification. (SC 157-73, tr. 145-60)

In the *human order* the perception of meaning precedes all else, for perception always aims at human intentions rather than at objects, and these intentions are seized as the realities of the world we experience. That they are the first realities is illustrated by the fact that a baby knows its mother through a lived relationship long before it knows what she looks like; and a child speaks a language in which no prior knowledge could assist him. But if this is the character of the human order, then there can be no question of a consciousness separated from and prior to behavior (action); nor can consciousness be defined wholly in terms of cognition (understanding, judging), since there are many ways of intending an object (willing, fearing, desiring, etc.). Man is not defined by the rational structures he has created (social, political, economic), but by his ability to *create something more* beyond what has already been established. In other words, man is defined by the projection of his intentions into the world. But if the mental component of human behavior cannot be separated from action, then neither can any other component, for example, the vital. At the human level these components disappear as such and are integrated into a unified organism. (*SC* 174-98, tr. 160-84)

What has this analysis of the perception of the lived world in its various dimensions revealed about *the nature of perception itself*? Merleau-Ponty suggests several conclusions, all of which are much more thoroughly described in *Phenomenology of Perception*. They provide a convenient transition from his study of behavior to his study of perception proper.[21] In the first place, to grasp something in perception is to grasp it perspectivally. And this means that every perception, while it is a contact with the world as a reality, is never coincident with what is grasped. Nothing perceived is ever exhausted in the perception of it, even though it is the thing itself that is perceived. Thus the world transcends us. But we also transcend the world, since our perception is a continual organization of the world. In perception the world is revealed as both in itself and for us *at the same time*. It is the way in which we are originally in contact with the world. The character of perception, then, appears to be "ambiguous": we are in contact with things, but we cannot coincide with (i.e., exhaust) those things; we are rooted in truth (since we are in contact with the real), but error and hallucination are always possible (since the real always escapes us to some extent).

Perception takes place through the body, which is the projecting instrument of our intentions into the world. When we perceive it is not through the eyes or through the mind or through any other bodily organ. It is through the unity of these. The body is not an object or a sum of objects (or parts); it is a unified field, just as is the world of objects which it perceives. The body, together with the objects perceived, constitutes the entire "field" of perception. But the body is not identifiable with the objects it perceives. There is a unity of perception but also a distinction between the body and perceived objects, inasmuch as I can never take a distance from my body as I can from other objects. Any object in my field of perception can be absent without annulling my perception of the field; but I am always present to my body.

Several questions suggest themselves here. If perception is always "ambiguous," how can we account for a perceptual "synthesis" of the world? If such a synthesis is possible, on what basis is it possible? Can the body become the ground of an intersubjective world, that is, do we have reasons for assuming that what is perceived by one body can be perceived by another in the same way, or have we returned by a different route to the solipsism of which idealism is guilty? These are the questions, among others, with which *Phenomenology of Perception* proposes to deal. But before we turn our attention to that work, let us look at some of the questions underlying Merleau-Ponty's critique of psychology and the vision of the world based upon this critique.

Some Critical Considerations

In one recent textbook of psychology E. G. Boring says:

The only reason for mentioning these four schools (Introspection, Behaviorism, Functional psychology, and Gestalt psychology) in this book is that the student hears about *behaviorism* and *Gestalt psychology* and has a right to be told what they are and that they are no longer important as schools. What was good in all the schools is now simply part of psychology.[22]

The attitude behind this statement bears comparison with that expressed in Merleau-Ponty's critique and reorientation of psychology. Professor Boring would doubtless agree with Merleau-Ponty's critical strictures regarding the inadequacy of introspectionism and behaviorism. What he would reject is the contention that these shortcomings call for a new *philosophical* interpretation of psychology. He believes, in fact, that psychology will progress toward unification as it *sheds* its philosophical heritage.[23] And both he and Wolman, to whom I have also referred, declare that the only kind of truth that matters in psychology is scientific truth. Now if this meant simply that psychology must be based on the use of a scientific method, then no one, least of all Merleau-Ponty, would disagree. But if "scientific truth" is taken to mean that psychological experimentation leads to a unified system and that this system can and will render the human order intelligible in the same way that physics has rendered the natural order intelligible, that is another question entirely. Wolman, who contends that there is no distinction between the "natural sciences" and the "social sciences," means precisely this. The model of scientific truth in psychology is, in his view, that of physics. This is a reassertion of the "empiricist" attitude in the sense in which it is criticized by Merleau-Ponty. This attitude implies that a science which deals with the relationship between man and nature can be as exact as a science which deals with nature alone. Or, to put it another way, human freedom is a figment of our imaginations, based on the fact that the data thus far collected are inadequate to dispel the illusion of freedom; ultimately psychology will show that man is what nature is. But this, to say the very least, is a highly questionable assumption. It is ironic perhaps that the book in which Wolman asserts the identity of the natural and social sciences is entitled *Contemporary Theories and Systems in Psychology.* The fact that such a book was called for in 1960 is an indirect verification of Merleau-Ponty' contention that a science dealing with human and physical nature together must admit of more than one level of explanation, and that these levels cannot be wholly "reduced" to one another. In other words, psychology must give up the idea that it can be a "natural science" in the strict sense.[24] Much recent psychological literature, as well as that in many other social sciences—and even in the natural sciences—suggests that the significance of human freedom as a "causal" factor is coming to be recognized in science itself.[25]

No doubt this question will be debated for a long time. And in this debate Merleau-Ponty will stand on the side of those who, believing in the application of a "scientific method," nevertheless maintain that the clarification of empirical data requires an interpretation which will *always* be philosophical, because no interpretation can grasp an eternally true essence. Every interpretation is "contingent," that is, not wholly "scientific." The important thing, as Merleau-Ponty sees it, is not to become *rigidly* scientific, but to maintain an openness which will allow the data to speak and be understood.

II

A Phenomenology of Perception

No one is saved and no one is totally lost.

Merleau-Ponty

The Proper Sphere of Philosophy: The Lived World

In *Phenomenology of Perception* [1] Merleau-Ponty attempts to return from the world constructed by men, whether on the model of physics or on the model of the human mind, to the lived or experienced world. [2] Contact with this lived world takes place through the perceptions of the body-subject which emerged at the end of Merleau-Ponty's analysis in *The Structure of Behavior*. *Phenomenology of Perception* is not only a description of this original contact between body and world but also the unfolding of a vision of reality on the basis of which this contact can be made intelligible to reflective consciousness.

It is Merleau-Ponty's contention that the lived world he proposes to describe has never been adequately dealt with by empiricism or by intellectualism, the two major currents in modern Western thought. By empiricism Merleau-Ponty means atomism in philosophy and behaviorism in psychology (which was discussed in the preceding chapter). Philosophical atomism is deficient because it attempts to break experience into parts, for example, impressions and qualities, which are never perceived in isolation from their larger figure/ground context. Moreover, in attempting to relate the data of experience through the "association of sensations," atomism makes the world a conglomeration of substances and thereby renders experience inexplicable. When, for example, a hunter and rabbit appear in a field there are spaces between them, and the entire context is perceived together. It is impossible to "substantialize" the objects and the spaces between them which constitute their context. (Cf. S 95, tr. 76) Nor can memory rescue empiricism here, for memory cannot explain why the pattern evokes one response and not another; and when it is said that perception responds to the pattern memory recalls, then the work memory is supposed to do is already done. Moreover, memory is unable to take account of illusion. Both atomism and behaviorism share a common error: each attempts to explain our experience of the world as science explains physical nature. But our experience of the world is not *first* as science depicts it. We must get behind these "explanations" in order to describe human behavior. (*PP* 9-30, tr. 3-22)

By "intellectualism" Merleau-Ponty means idealism in philosophy and introspectionism in psychology (which was referred to in the preceding chapter). In philosophical idealism consciousness is a universal constituting agent. The world does not exist in itself but only for a consciousness, and further, is completely comprehended by consciousness; there are no opaque corners, nothing hidden. If empiricism errs in not seeing that we need to know what we are looking for, intellectualism errs in not seeing that we must also be ignorant of what we are looking for. For if the world is completely present to us, if perception coincides with what is perceived, nothing new can ever appear.[3] "Attention," which requires an alternation of our perceptual field, will never be aroused. Furthermore, the categories employed by intellectualism to explain experience are deficient. For example, "judgment," which in intellectualism supplies what is missing in sensation, cannot explain hallucination, the difference between "seeing" and "thinking one sees." Moreover, perception cannot be regarded as coinciding with understanding, since what is always the same to understanding (e.g., a square) is not so to perception. (*PP* 34-63, tr. 26-51)

The significance of this critique is clear: neither philosophical nor psychological tradition does justice to the world we experience. Either the thinker is an observer of a world from which he can remove himself, or the world is an object of consciousness. Both traditions thus appeal to an *absolute*, either an absolute truth external to the thinker or an absolute consciousness. Neither takes account of finitude or gives it any positive value. But after all it is finitude which describes human existence. How do we uncover the finite world? If empiricism and intellectualism are based on *cognitive* categories (scientific or mental), then in order to uncover a more fundamental level of existence we must turn our attention to the *precognitive* givens of experience which are defined, not by our knowledge of them, but by our *behavior* in relation to them. It is this behavior with which perception is concerned. What will be the problem of perception in dealing with this world? If, on the one hand, it is true that the world cannot be viewed as the association of sensations as empiricism believes, then perception must open onto a world which is *already patterned*. Perception begins with a sedimentation from the past; its task is not to "explain" the world but to describe the world that is already there in terms of its own givenness. But if, on the other hand, the world is not already given to judgment or understanding as intellectualism supposes, then perception must open onto a world which is also *in the act* of assuming a structure. The problem of perception is the problem of accounting for this simultaneous openness to a phenomenal field and its presence in us. (*PP* 64-77, tr. 52-63)

How are we to resolve this problem? Two conclusions reached in *The Structure of Behavior* provide a point of departure. The first is that since "scientific explanations" do not "explain" behavior, we must give up any attempt to see the relation between subject and object in strictly "causal" terms and adopt instead the notion of reciprocal determination of each by the other. Merleau-Ponty introduces the word "motivation" in *Phenomenology of Perception* in place of the term "circular causality" used in *The Structure of Behavior*. Motivation is one of those "fluid" concepts designating the release of one phenomenon by another, "not by means of some objective efficient cause ... but by the *meaning* which it holds out. ..." [4] Meaning here refers to the existential significance of an action, to the coalescence in an act of a determinant past and a free or spontaneous present. The synthesis of these factors is in the body which we discovered in *The Structure of Behavior* to be the point at which subject and object meet. Thus, an analysis of the role of the body in behavior will lead us toward the desired resolution of the problem of perception.

The Body and the Lived World

If it can be shown that the body cannot be rendered intelligible in terms of traditional thought either as a subject or as an object (and here it is traditional psychology and physiology which is meant), then there will be good reason for asserting that the body must be regarded as belonging both to the subject and to the object *at the same time*. We can best do this by noting the consequences of regarding the body either as a subject or as an object. If, on the one hand, the body is regarded as a *subject without a milieu*, then its behavior in many cases is unintelligible. Take, for example, the case of anosognosia, the refusal to accept the loss of a limb. A psychological explanation is necessary since the person refuses to recognize the absence of the limb. But if the nerves to the brain are severed the phantom member disappears; hence physiological factors enter into the situation also. Neither psychology nor physiology alone can explain this phenomenon, since between the presence of the limb to the subject in one case and its absence from the subject in the other there is no intermediate ground. But the situation is different when the body is viewed *existentially*, that is, as belonging to a world. Anosognosia then becomes the refusal of an actual condition for an imaginary one, the acceptance of an impersonal world through the repression of an existing situation. The limits of the physical and psychical factors *within the subject* can never be precisely determined, but his existential relation to the world which they designate can be described. (*PP* 87-106, tr. 73-89) The results are just as unfortunate if, on the other hand, the body is regarded as a *milieu in itself*. This happens both in introspectionist psychology which, in treating the body as a psyche, uncovers the contents of consciousness rather than experience of the body; and in behaviorism which, in regarding the body as an object like all other objects, fails to recognize the presence of a psyche. (*PP* 106-13, tr. 90-97)

Behind these various attempts to separate subjectivity from objectivity is the desire to make the body yield *knowledge,* whereas the function of the body is not primarily to know but to *act.*[5] The body is a project, a surging forth in the midst of a given milieu. It organizes this milieu by synthesizing its own action with the sedimented or given world which surrounds it. Thus the action of the body is the point of contact between the world already given and the world coming to birth. And as such it reveals at any moment the manner in which we are existing in the world. That this is so may be shown by an analysis of the body's relationships to the world. (See *PP* 114-19, tr. 98-103)

Let us look first at the space of the body in relation to the space of the world about it. My body "inhabits" a space of its own; it is not an object "in" space as are other objects of which I make use—this much we saw in the preceding chapter. And when the body must serve as an object of action as well as its subject, then its ability to act is greatly curtailed. A case of psychic blindness serves to illustrate the point. The patient is unable to make abstract movements; for example, he cannot move his arms or legs as ordered out of context by the doctor, but he can move them rapidly in a particular situation to which he is accustomed (e.g., performing his job of making wallets). Concrete movement takes precedence over abstract movement. Why? Because in a concrete movement the body is *projecting* toward an object, and so long as the body acts it does not have to be located; it is immediately given. But when the patient is required to make his body the milieu of action, he can no longer readily locate its parts. To the extent, then, that the body ceases to be projective, it ceases to have a "world." The sick person is not transformed into an "object." He remains a subject, but one whose world is extremely contracted. His world no longer readily suggests a meaning for him; it has lost its spatial physiognomy and its temporal thickness. The "intentional arc" through which consciousness aims at the cognitive, appetitive, and perceptual life "goes limp" in illness and the unity of existence is lost.[6]

The example of sexuality, taken from the affective rather than from the natural world, also illustrates our way of existing in the world. It is incorrect to say that all existence has a sexual significance; rather should we say that every sexual phenomenon has an existential significance. When a girl (as in a case reported by Binswanger), prohibited by her mother from seeing the young man she loves, loses her appetite, voice, and sleep, she reveals a refusal of existence which all these functions symbolize. Similarly, when a man who has had a quarrel with his wife leaves in a drawer a book she had given him and is unable to locate it until they are reconciled again, he discloses his way of being in the world. In forgetting where the book was he was shutting off from his life everything related to his wife. Sexual existence thus reveals that the body can either accept or reject (though not abolish) its world. We must be careful, however, not to reduce sexuality to existence. For sexuality influences existence, often in imperceptible or unconscious ways. The true situation is that there is a mutual influence of existence upon sexuality and of sexuality upon existence which makes it impossible unambiguously to label an intention or action "sexual" or "non-sexual." [7]

Speech affords a third illustration of our existing in the world. One would think that in this case thought precedes action. But if we study the experience of a child, for whom the essence of a thing is its name, we shall see that things are not first recognized and then named, but that to name is to recognize them. There is, to be sure, a thought present in this original grasping of language, but the thought does not precede the grasping itself. Take the example of an orator making a speech. When he speaks and when we listen, there is no margin of thought beyond the expression itself. Only when the speaker has finished does thought about what has been said begin. The fundamental way of representing language is to utter it; the meaning is contained in the uttering itself. It is of course true that one can transform speech into a reflection or discussion regarding what has already been said; but to do so is to fall into banality.[8] Genuine speech is the expression of the body's action in relation to the world.[9]

Thus we may conclude that "the experience of our own body ... reveals to us an ambiguous mode of existing." The relation of the subject to his world cannot be completed in terms of causal connections; therefore the body is not an object. Similarly, awareness of the body is not a thought; therefore its inherence is never wholly clear or transparent. In the final analysis the body cannot be "known" at all except through the life we live out in it involved in the world. (PP 231, tr. 198; see VI 189) This theory of the body is, as Merleau-Ponty says, already a theory of perception. But before we describe precisely how this is the case, let us look into the historical roots of Merleau-Ponty's discussion of the body.

The Significance of the Body in Modern Thought[10]

There has been a remarkable preoccupation with the problem of the body in twentieth-century French philosophy.[11] Bergson, Marcel, Sartre, and Merleau-Ponty have each developed important ideas regarding its function. But what is even more remarkable is that none of the later thinkers acknowledged any of his predecessors in working out his own position, despite the fact that there is a perceptibly cumulative effect in the development of their descriptions. However, despite this absence of acknowledged influence from one to the other, it is possible to trace lines of influence as well as (in some cases) factors leading to the attenuation of influence.

Bergson's description of the role of the body opens his study of *Matter and Memory*.[12] The world, he begins, is full of images (= things), all of which operate upon one another on the basis of constant laws, a perfect knowledge of which "would probably allow us to calculate and to foresee what will happen in each of these images."[13] The world, in other words, opens before us as a plenitude of images, all of which rigidly adhere to the laws of nature and whose past, present, and future are therefore contained within them. Nothing new could enter such a world. There is one image, however, which is different from all the rest: the body. The body always interposes itself between the excitations received from without and the movement about to be executed from within. "All seems to take place," Bergson writes, "as if, in this aggregate of images which I call the universe, nothing really new could happen except through the medium of certain particular images, the type of which is furnished me by my body."[14] But what is it that happens? Does the body "represent" the world as a mental creation? This cannot be the case, since the brain and the nervous system are themselves material images, and they can be removed without removing the totality of images we call the world. Hence the body cannot create the world through a mental representation. What, then, is the nature of the "really new" introduced into material images by the body? It is *movement*. The body, although in other respects like the images which surround it, is different in that it can *act upon* the other images. It must be defined then as *a center of action*. Through perception the body acts upon other images (albeit with a limited degree of freedom), bestowing movement upon them and receiving this movement back again.

At first glance, there are striking affinities between Bergson's description of the role of the body and that of Merleau-Ponty. For both, the body is the point of contact between a "material" world and a "mental" representation of the world. For both also the body is first of all an instrument through which we *act* upon the world; it is an expression of a degree (or different degrees) of human freedom. However, there is a significant difference between them, for while Bergson was interested primarily in establishing the *theoretical necessity* of this third dimension, Merleau-Ponty was concerned as well to elucidate its *meaning* descriptively. This is to say that Bergson did not become an existentialist. Nor did Merleau-Ponty, during the years he was writing his first two books, believe that Bergson's analysis was moving in the same direction as his own. My reasons for reaching this conclusion must wait until chapter 7, when they can appear in their proper context. But if this conclusion is correct, then the most that can be said with respect to influence is that, while Merleau-Ponty may have been aware of the presence of these ideas in Bergson, he was not indebted to Bergson for the manner in which he elaborated them.

The case of Gabriel Marcel seems to be different. For while, as in the case of Bergson, his analyses of the body are never

cited by Merleau-Ponty, the "existentialist" direction of
Marcel's analysis is the outstanding feature of his position.
For Marcel the nature of the body became the key by which
he was able to move beyond idealism to a "concrete" philosophy of existence.[15] His earliest reflections are attempts to
distinguish between the body as an object physically given
and as a psychical object immediately known through reflection.[16] Although he does not mention Schopenhauer by name,
the terms in which his thought is cast suggest that he was
familiar with Schopenhauer's description of the metaphysical
significance of the body.[17] For according to Schopenhauer
the body is given in two entirely different ways. It is given
first as "an idea in intelligent perception, as an object among
objects and subject to the laws of objects." But it is also given
"as that which is immediately known to everyone, and is
signified by the word *will*." [18] When Schopenhauer speaks of
the body as an "object," he means that it is a phenomenal
object in the Kantian sense. The body is my idea of the body,
just as the world is my idea of the world. And when he speaks
of the body as "will" he means that the body is "real in a sense
in which no other object is real," since will is for Schopenhauer
the thing in itself.[19] It is in the second sense that the body has
a privileged metaphysical status. As the "objectification of the
will" the body as it acts is an expression of the will itself, and
the individual parts of the body are an expression of the
various aspects of the will.[20] Thus it is through the body that
the individual knows the world, indeed, assumes that there
are other bodies similar to his own. The body, in short, becomes the means by which will is universalized.[21] However,
the body is only a preliminary objectification of the will; it is
transcended by the subsequent intellectual apprehension of the
will through aesthetic contemplation and ultimately through
renunciation of the will. Thus for Schopenhauer the body
does not have a conclusive, but only a provisional, metaphysical status. It is the basis for our original opening onto

the world but not for what is finally the most significant opening.

When Marcel speaks of the body as an "object," he does not mean that it is a phenomenal object; it is a real object which belongs to an "objectified" world. As such, it is to be contrasted with the body given immediately in reflection as no other object is. As for Schopenhauer, so for Marcel in his earliest reflections, the body as immediately present is still an object present to the *mind*, albeit in a manner different from other objects. But Marcel soon recognizes that even this is an abstraction, and that the body is in some sense present *prior to* reflection. Thus, whereas for Schopenhauer the body remains a mental object (in one case phenomenal, in another case noumenal), Marcel gradually reaches the conclusion, in his reflections on the difference between the two ways in which the body is apprehended, that the body as immediately present to me is *beyond objectification* insofar as it is the *foundation* for reflection. It would be more true to say that "I *am* my body" in the sense that "I *live* my body" prior to any reflection. Whenever reflection enters to treat the body as an object, then I am *abstracted from myself*, I become an object to myself, that is, nothing. The body, therefore, is the root of personality and individuality, the ultimate referent of a concrete philosophy. As such, it cannot be thought about or grasped as other objects can. To objectify it is to rob it of its individuality; the world loses concreteness.[22]

The emphasis Marcel places on the concrete world opened up by the body and on the intimate connections between my "self" and my body is certainly congenial to Merleau-Ponty's frame of reference. Merleau-Ponty may have paid little heed to Marcel's analysis of the body because he rejected Marcel's philosophy on other grounds,[23] and that may be why, as in the case of Bergson, having rejected Marcel's general viewpoint, he seldom referred to him except in a critical vein. But it is also possible that Merleau-Ponty found deficient, from his point of view, the structures in terms of which Marcel's analysis of the body's relations to others was couched. For in Marcel's view man's relationship to God is the paradigm for his relationships to other men. Hence, all his descriptions of the body's proper relations to others aim at a *personal* world. And this personal world, though "concrete," is not the *whole* of the "existential" world envisioned by Merleau-Ponty's analysis of the body.

Whether for these or for other reasons, when Merleau-Ponty twice had occasion in 1951 to discuss the problem of the body in modern thought, it was to some modern psychologists and to a few French writers, not to Bergson and Marcel, that he gave credit for the most profound descriptions of the body. In a lecture course he made the following remark about the genesis of his idea of the body, though he hardly elaborated beyond these cryptic references:

If my body is to appropriate the conducts given to me visually and make them its own, it must itself be given to me not as a mass of utterly private sensations but instead by what has been called a "postural" or "corporeal" schema. This notion, introduced long ago by Henry Head, has been taken over and enriched by Wallon, by certain German psychologists, and has finally been the subject of a study in its own right by Professor Lhermitte in *L'Image de notre corps*. (*RE* 23, tr. 117; see also *ACF* 1953, 146-48)

In a lecture in Geneva, during the same year, Freud was singled out as the psychologist whose analysis, at least in his later years, described a process—largely unconscious—in which the mind passed into the body and the body into the mind. The Freudian understanding of the unconscious aspect of this process Merleau-Ponty describes as a knowledge which we do not wish to recognize, and he believes that in saying this Freud was on the verge of discovering what he had himself characterized as "ambiguous perception." (*S* 291, tr. 229-30) Even more significantly, perhaps, Merleau-Ponty notes that this understanding of the body-subject passed into modern literature even before Freud's influence was felt, and he cites, Gide, Proust, Valéry, and Malraux as writers who struggled with its implications. He does not say why they became concerned with it, but notes that when they did the result was an obsession with themselves as body-subjects in relation to other persons. Insofar as they attempted to recognize what was unique in themselves, others confronted them through feelings of torment, envy, or anxiety. Merleau-Ponty cites this example from Valéry, which certainly anticipates Sartre:

> You capture my image, my appearance; I capture yours. You are not *me*, since you see me and I do not see myself. What I lack is this me that you see. And what you lack is the you I see. And no matter how far we advance in our mutual understanding, as much as we reflect, so much will we be different. . . . (Quoted in S 294, tr. 231-32)

The important point here is that the body became the means of revealing a social world for these writers. Merleau-Ponty does not follow Valéry, as Sartre did, in defining the social world as one in which men are related to one another primarily by virtue of their alienation from one another. But he was aware of a literary tradition which attributed philosophical significance to the body.

The first metaphysical description of the role of the body from within an explicit "existentialist" framework was that of Sartre. Sartre's descriptions of the body are contained in Part III of *Being and Nothingness*, that is, in his philosophy of the social world. He contends that Hegel, Husserl, and Heidegger all failed to solve the problem of how as a subject I can be related to others as subjects.[24] Four conditions must be met if the other is to be constituted as a subject: first, the other cannot be proved since he is outside my experience (i.e., I cannot experience the subjectivity of the other); second, the starting point is the Cartesian *cogito* (i.e., the other is constituted in the inmost depths of my being); third, the other cannot be first of all an object for me if there is to be a world;

and fourth, the other must therefore appear in the *cogito* as an internal negation of myself, as "not-being-me." These conditions are met in the "look",[25] through which I experience fear, shame, and pride. Take, for example, the experience of the "look" as it discloses shame. When I am looking through a keyhole and another catches me in the act, I feel shame. But what I actually have felt is the other as the negation of myself; he has revealed my subjectivity to me without revealing his own. Thus the *basic relationship* between myself and the other is *alienation*. Alienation accounts for there *being* a world.[26]

It is into this framework that Sartre places the three ontological dimensions of the body. The body is first of all lived; I "exist my body" in the sense that it is my means of access to other objects. Hence, although my body is immersed in the world it also transcends the world by virtue of projects through which it makes the world an object.[27] The body is, second, "for-others." The significance of this relationship is twofold. On the one hand, it means that I grasp the other as an object. For example, I judge his "character," thus objectifying from my point of view what from his point of view is something always being transcended. On the other hand, the other as object is qualitatively different from things as objects, for in objectifying the other's body I become more conscious of my own subjectivity.[28] The final ontological dimension of the body is its alienation from itself when it encounters the other. In the experience of the "look," for example, when the other catches me unexpectedly, he makes me aware that I am for him an object, thus alienating my body from me.[29]

If we compare Sartre's descriptions of the body with those of Merleau-Ponty, we shall find that the differences are as striking as the similarities. In the first place, while for both Sartre and Merleau-Ponty the body is the means through which we act upon the world and is therefore the privileged point of our access to the world, for Sartre its revelatory power is secondary to an initial experience of alienation, whereas for

Merleau-Ponty any experience can be an initiating experience. We have discussed spatiality, sexuality, and speech as three examples. Thus it is not accidental that Sartre presents his descriptions of being-in-the-world *prior to* his description of the body, while Merleau-Ponty describes the body as *emergent with* the world, i.e., as opening us onto a social world. Related to this is the fact that while for Sartre every human project reveals subjectivity, for Merleau-Ponty every human project reveals *inter*subjectivity, a copresence with others. Furthermore, there is a distinction in Sartre between those experiences which reveal objectivity and those which reveal subjectivity, while for Merleau-Ponty all experiences involve an "ambiguous" intermingling of subjective and objective elements which makes an absolute distinction between them impossible.[30] Finally, while Sartre defines pathological illness as the body alienated from itself by the other and aware of its alienation, for Merleau-Ponty pathological illness means the refusal of an ambiguous world in favor of a reduced world in which subject and object are absolutized in much the way Sartre has absolutized them.

Perception as Being-in-the-World

"The theory of the body is already a theory of perception," Merleau-Ponty states in opening Part II of *Phenomenology of Perception*: "the world as perceived." What this means is that "every external perception is immediately synonymous with a certain perception of my body, just as every perception of my body is made explicit in the language of external perception.[31] Just as the body is not only centered in itself but also projected outward from itself toward objects, so is the perceived world simultaneously what it is in itself and what it is for the one who perceives it. The world as an object has the character of being also for the subject, and conversely, the subject as a body has the character of being also for the world. It is this intermixture which we must try to describe in analyzing perception of the world.

To begin at the beginning, what is the meaning of sense perception? It is a "form of communion" between the body and the world. (*PP* 346, tr. 212) Diseases of the frontal cortex illustrate this in revealing the effect sensory excitations would have on muscular tonicity if those excitations were not integrated into a situation. For example, the gesture of raising the arm is modified according to whether the visual field is red, yellow, blue, or green. Red and yellow produce smooth movements, while blue and green produce jerky ones. Sensations thus designate the *physiognomy of the world,* its living significance for us. How are we to describe this significance? First of all, we must recognise that sensations refer to a structured world and are part of a general background against which perception takes place; they are perceived only in relation to objects they inhabit. They *belong* to objects and when we perceive them it is because they stand out from objects which radiate their qualities. At the same time, there is a distinction between various sensations, although no strict demarcation between them can be established, since in some sense it is true, as Cézanne observed, that we "hear colors" and "see hardness." [32] But this double character of the perceived object means that it will always transcend any perception of it. There can be no "final" synthesis of the perceived object; it will always be capable of being perceived in a multiplicity of ways. In order for perception in this manner to be possible the body-subject must supply a unity of the body image but one which is, at the same time, as open and limitless as the perceived object. And this turns out to be precisely what the body-subject does. For within the body the senses are distinct from one another, but they combine in various ways to form a unity of perception. For example, a man born blind knows through touch what the branches of a tree are and what an arm is. The world has a certain structure for him. But after an operation restoring his sight, he marvels that there is such a difference between a tree and a human body. Vision has not just added something to his world but has changed its structure. Now this synthesis which the body-subject effects vis-à-vis the object can only be described in terms of the *intentional activity* of the body in relation to the world. The body and the world are synthesized not as in natural science but as a body for an object and an object for a body. In other words, the synthesis is *contingent*; it indicates an openness, a temporal thickness. Ultimately it refers us to time, to history. (*PP* 240-80, tr. 207-42)

What, next, is the meaning of the perception of space? Space perception does not refer to physical space or to geometrical space, for perceived space does not belong only to the object or only to the subject; it belongs to both at once. Perceived space is existential space. Take, for example, the perception of our *environment*—the immediate world which surrounds us. If inverted glasses are placed on a subject, the world at first will appear upside down, but eventually it will right itself. Space is thus *orientated* in relation to the body-subject who perceives. And the body is always present where orienting action is called for, whether we are conscious of its orienting activity or not (and indeed, in our first contacts with the world—as infants—we are not aware of orientations that are taking place). Consider further the perception of *depth*. When we see an object at a distance we see its apparent size. But the perception of apparent size depends on a prior experience of an undistorted world. The same is true of all the dimensions of space perception: height and depth, vertical and horizontal, near and far. Each of these is an abstract designation "for one single form of being in a situation, and they presuppose the same setting face to face of subject and world." (*PP* 309, tr. 267) The perception of *movement* reveals the same existential quality. When we perceive an object moving, movement inhabits the object itself. Otherwise, when we are standing in a garden and watching a stone move through the air, there would be no difference between saying "the stone is moving" and "the garden is moving." When we say the stone is moving, this means that our gaze is anchored in the garden and is attracted by the stone. Motion and immobility are thus moments in the organization of the perceptual field and both are embraced by it; only against a background of immobility can motion stand out. It is the body which organizes the field, which determines the object in motion by perceiving it. Thus, in all three phenomena considered, we see that space perception "is a structural phenomenon and is comprehensible only within a perceptual field which contributes in its entirety to motivating the spatial perception by suggesting to the subject a possible anchorage." (PP 325, tr. 280) In any perception space can be contracted. Space is contracted at night, for example, when there are no outlines; darkness is a pure depth without foreground or background. The unreality is lessened if we are in a confined space (e.g., our room), for then we can retain the setting of daytime by groping around the room for familiar objects. Space is also contracted for the sick person, for whom there is a shrinkage of possibilities of action. But, though contracted, lived space is always present; it can never be removed. When space is viewed in an existential manner then there is no need to explain away or deny what is lived by the schizophrenic or by a mythical (primitive) consciousness or in dreams. Each of these ways of experiencing the world is possible only on the basis of a lived space which cannot be denied without denying the world in which they are anchored. (See PP 392, tr. 340) Space perception, existentially conceived, therefore removes us from the dilemma of having to say either that everything is meaningful or that everything is absurd. We can say instead that meaning is always present, no matter what else may also be present. Space perception thus leads us back to the lived world in which meaning is anchored.[33]

But, if it is possible to describe an anchorage of the body in the lived world and the multiplicity of perspectives there, is it equally possible to account for the *unity* of the perceived world? How can we account for perceptual constancy? If we consider the phenomena of light and color in the lived world, then we can observe that light is a means of expressing the unity of the perceptual field; the field will appear differently as light changes. Color finds its place in the visual field in relation to the light which surrounds it, and the same is true of other qualities that we perceive. Thus we arrive at the deeper meaning of the organization of a field: our perception is animated by a logic which assigns to each thing its determinate character in relation to all other objects in the field, while canceling out all stray data. And this whole operation is sustained by the certainty of the world. "In this way we finally see the true significance of perceptual constancies. The constancy of color is only an abstract component of the constancy of things, which in turn is grounded in the primordial constancy of the world as the horizon of all our experiences." [34] This does not mean, however, that the structure the body gives to the world exhausts the structure of the things perceived. To perceive something does not mean to coincide with it; the object perceived, in fact, always outruns perception of it (as we saw in the preceding chapter). Thus, the body does not constitute the things themselves; it takes up things already internally constituted and makes them its own. But this means that the syntheses of perception are *partial*. Something of what is essential to the object is left behind by the body. In fact, any particular aspect of the perceptual field (visual auditory, etc.) can be removed without abolishing the perceptual field. But if the syntheses of the body are partial in this way, if the perspective views of perception can never exhaust the object perceived, then how can a synthesis come about? This can only happen *in time*. I shall discuss the significance of temporality later. Suffice it to note here that temporal syntheses are contingent; they unfold, undergoing transformations in the process. Acceptance of the idea of temporal syntheses, therefore, is at the same time a recognition of the fact that it is impossible to reach absolute certainty regarding any perceptual synthesis, just as it is impossible to remove all certainty (i.e., the world). To live, to be involved in the world, is to live in the midst of both truth and error, but always within a context in which the two are not ultimately confused or distinctions made impossible. (*PP* 345-97, tr. 299-345)

Finally, this way of being in the natural world is also the manner in which we inhabit the *human* world. In fact, as soon as I have sensory functions, a visual, auditory, and tactile field, I am in communication with others, I begin to see the body of the other as a theater of a process of elaboration. This, however, does not solve the problem of my relation to the other. For unless and until a reciprocity has been established between us there is only alienation. But how can this be established? Consider my internal relation to the other. I am not for another person what I am for myself, nor is the other for me what he is for himself. Considered internally, we can be for each other in mutually understandable or compatible ways only if coexistence is experienced on both sides. If, for example, there is more love on one side than on the other in a love relationship, then one person feels free while the other feels that his life is flowing away into the freedom which confronts him in the other. Love must be mutual if it is to lead to genuine coexistence. But this is precisely the problem: how can I, from my point of view, see from the point of view of the other? Are we not enclosed in solipsism? And this problem, which arises from within my perspective, is not resolved if that perspective is generalized. It would be resolved in that case only if my perspective were that of God, which it is not. The sole resolution to this difficulty is to recognize that *the social world is also primordial*. It is already there, given, prior to my attempts to account for reciprocity. The human world, like the natural world, leads us back to the lived or existential world. (*PP* 398-419, tr. 346-65; see also *RE* 20-26, tr. 114-20)

Now if an analysis of the body and of the world—both human and natural—returns us to the lived world, and if it is true that this lived world is defined by motivational relations between subject and object such that the synthesis between them is always both present and absent, definite and indefinite, can our descriptions claim the assent of rational thought? Are we simply trying to describe what is beyond thought and thereby falling into irrationalism? This would be the case only if we could not establish that what we have said has no other foundation than our own authority. Does it have such a foundation? Where shall we look for it? Let us look for it first in consciousness. Can consciousness serve as the foundation of the world? In order to do so it must be able to constitute its world. But this is precisely what it cannot do. We have already seen, for example, that consciousness finds a world constructed before it in which it lives. We have also seen that consciousness cannot give us the absolute certainty of things perceived in such a way that it could serve as their foundation; truth and error are part of consciousness, and both are possible only on the basis of the world. Hence, the world precedes consciousness, or rather, consciousness comes to birth only in the presence of a world. But if consciousness is first of all a project of the world (an action), how does thought about the world ever begin? This can only happen *in time*, in a field which unfolds before consciousness. It is therefore to time that we must look for the foundation of perception. (*PP* 423-68, tr. 369-409)

What is time? It is literally the *presence of the world*. When I reach out to the world through my project, my past is present in my reaching, just as is the future toward which I project. Hence past and future are both here and now in the present; both spring forth when I reach out toward them. They are never, however, *wholly* present. A past may cease to play its part in the present and a future may cease to project meaning. For example, Van Gogh's paintings enter into my present because of the impression they have made upon me. But if they cease to be viewed they will be relegated to one sector of historical time and belong no longer to a past projected into the present. Similarly, the new future I envision in projecting my revolutionary attitude may cease to appear new, nullifying the meaningfulness of my revolutionary project (and we shall see that this actually happened to Merleau-Ponty). Thus time is a synthesis of the world, but a "transitional synthesis" in which the multiplicities of ways of being in the world are assembled and disassembled. It is both a foundation and an opening. In time, then, we find the foundation for the view of the world set forth in the preceding analyses. Above all, time is the matrix in which I can be mutually present to others. Two consciousnesses (as we have seen) can never be mutually present to one another, but two temporalities can (even though it is true that the other person never exists for me in the way I exist for myself), "because each one arrives at self-knowledge only by projecting himself into the present where both can be joined together." [35]

Temporality points to freedom, because freedom is defined as a project undertaken in time; it is an *action*. But it is a project which is always in some respect limited by a situation. For example, I am in the middle class or the working class long before I am conscious of myself in this respect. As a situation of oppression or exploitation congeals around me, my relations to others are defined. Thus, in the Russian Revolution of 1917 the peasants joined the workers, not because they envisioned a new social order but because they saw that their interests were those of the workers. At the same time, however, no situation "causes" anything to happen. Revolutionary conditions may be present without leading to a revolution. What actually takes place depends on the intentions, the projects of men. Freedom, then, is to be acted upon by and to act upon the world at the same time. (*PP* 517, tr. 453) It is creation against the background of the unfolding of time.[36]

This is the vision of the world as it is presented in *Phenomenology of Perception*. Before we raise the critical questions involved in this vision, let us look at Merleau-Ponty's version of being-in-the-world in relation to that of Heidegger, who coined the expression.

Merleau-Ponty and Heidegger: Two Views of Being-in-the-World

According to Heidegger, *Dasein* is in-the-world in two ways: first, as a being qualitatively different from other beings in the world [37] and second, as related to the world first through precognitive experience.[38] On the basis of this point of departure Heidegger hopes, like Merleau-Ponty, to overcome the body-mind dualism stemming from Descartes. The direction of their analyses, however, is quite different, as we can see by a comparison of the critique each offers of Descartes. According to Heidegger, Descartes defined substance as that which was completely self-sufficient. In terms of this definition, only God (as thinking being) is, ontologically speaking, a real substance. The world, or any given object within the world (extended being), is only an ontic or an ontico-ontological substance. Therefore, Descartes failed to clarify either the meaning of Being [39] or the nature of the world.[40] According to Merleau-Ponty, Descartes' error was to posit a thinking subject which was "timeless" in the sense that it was certain of itself prior to all contact with the world, and which was therefore the universal constituting power of all being accessible to it. There is no way, after this, to escape the conclusion that my mind is God! In other words, a world is never con-

stituted. (*PP* 426-28, tr. 372-73) Heidegger's critique reveals
that his primary concern is to clarify the nature and structures
of *being*, while Merleau-Ponty intends instead to clarify the
nature and structures of the *world*. Since, however, in *Being
and Time* Heidegger approaches the structures of being
through *Dasein's* privileged "opening to being," his descriptions of being-in-the-world are directly comparable to those of
Merleau-Ponty. There is a similarity between the two, for
example, in their respective descriptions of the relation between the body-subject (*Dasein* for Heidegger) and the world.
Heidegger describes *Dasein* as involved with things ready-
to-hand prior to *Dasein's* knowledge of them.[41] Understanding
is a reflection on this precognitive given which assigns meaning
to it.[42] Reflection reveals that things are clear insofar as they
stand out from a background and obscure insofar as they remain hidden from us.[43] Their givenness is thus a simultaneous
presence and absence through which our world is oriented.
Heidegger emphasizes, as does Merleau-Ponty, that the lived
distance between *Dasein* and things is not based on *Dasein's* reflection or constitution, but rather "comes before
Dasein."[44] There is a further similarity in their views of time.
Merleau-Ponty in fact draws heavily on Heidegger's analysis
of time in his discussion of temporality; and even though he
criticizes Heidegger's view as an orientation toward the
future, while his own is an orientation toward the *present*,
there is actually little difference in the outcome of the
two views.

The differences between Heidegger and Merleau-Ponty
are more pronounced in their respective analyses of the ways
in which men are related to one another in the world. Heidegger asserts, as does Merleau-Ponty, that *Dasein* is in-the-
world primarily "with others," because only another *Dasein*
can clarify the being of *Dasein*. But as his analysis proceeds,
it becomes apparent that "being-with" (*Mitsein*) is necessarily
an impersonal relationship through which *Dasein* falls into

the anonymity of "the they" (*das Man*).[45] Therefore "being-with" is by definition an inauthentic mode of being. One becomes authentic, in Heidegger's view, only by *standing out from* others, by refusing anonymity. The primary means through which this is accomplished is taking upon oneself the anxiety of being which threatens one (and especially the anxiety of death). However, since this affirmation of oneself is something that is necessarily done by oneself (i.e., alone), Heidegger's analysis reaches the curious conclusion that it is not by "being-with" but by being *against* others, that *Dasein* achieves authenticity. Heidegger's world, in the final analysis, is not a social world at all. It is similar to Sartre's world in which men are alienated from one another. No such meaning can be attributed to Merleau-Ponty's view of "mutual presence," as we have made clear. In later essays Merleau-Ponty cricicized Heidegger for failing to describe the actual experiences through which the opposition of men to one another is overcome (*SNS* 138, tr. 69), and for believing that *Dasein* could grasp his essence or being without taking account of all the mediating factors of experience which lead continually to modifications of that essence (*SHP* 55, tr. 94). To refuse one's determination by the world in the fullest sense of the word is only another form of refusing to be in-the-world. It is, in fact, to "explain" the world, to act as if one were a transcendent spectator.[46]

Some Critical Questions

Ferdinand Alquié was the first to designate Merleau-Ponty's position a "philosophy of ambiguity." [47] The phrase has been used since that time by several writers although not in the same sense in which Alquié uses it. By Merleau-Ponty's ambiguity Alquié means a philosophical attempt to state simultaneously the positions of empiricism and intellectualism and thereby to ignore the problems which they raise by dissolving each position as a philosophical possibility. The process by which Merleau-Ponty achieves this feat is a description of the conjunction of empiricism and intellectualism as "lived" rather than known. However, Alquié reasons, if the lived precedes the known, and if thought cannot be separated from the lived, then the lived never can be questioned by reason. And in this case the problems of reflection indeed are eliminated because they are never posed. If Sartre's world is the adolescent world of contradictions, Merleau-Ponty's world is that of childhood in which no problems exist! Ambiguity is simply substituted for analysis. Alquié's critique involves several points. First, he seems to be saying that a philosophy which confines itself wholly to description is condemned simply to observing and reporting on experiences without being able to reflect on them critically. Such reflection requires detachment from what has been experienced. But such detachment depends in turn on resolving the question of how reason is possible. In other words, in order to be able to "describe" in the full sense of the word, one must have an adequate theory of rationality. Otherwise, description never becomes problem-oriented and philosophy never appears. Alphonse de Waelhens remarks in Merleau-Ponty's defense that phenomenology does not attempt to explain but to describe, and that in describing the functioning of reason Merleau-Ponty perhaps comes closer to "explaining" reason than do other philosophers who concentrate on its nature.[48] Nevertheless, Alquié has his finger on a critical problem which emerges from *Phenomenology of Perception,* namely, whether Merleau-Ponty has adequately formulated a *method* on the basis of which his descriptive philosophy could be taken up and elaborated by others.

Despite his recognition of a problem that is certainly left after one has read *Phenomenology of Perception,* it must be said that Alquié does not accurately communicate what Merleau-Ponty intends by "ambiguity." It is not an oscillation between empiricism and idealism but an actual description of the "interworld" which stands in opposition to both. Perhaps Al-quié had in mind here Bergson, who did try to "dissolve" the antitheses of realism and idealism by positing a middle world between the two. However, for Merleau-Ponty this third dimension is not merely the means to a theoretical solution of a problem; it is the subject of his descriptions. It is incorrect to say that Merleau-Ponty does not actually open up an "ambiguous" world with his descriptions.

Edward Ballard, also centering his attention on the relation of the precognitive to the cognitive, argues, not as Alquié that the two cannot be separated but that Merleau-Ponty cannot move from one to the other without contradiction.[49] For if the precognitive source of the natural world remains precognitive, it is outside the realm of knowledge altogether. If on the other hand it becomes cognitive, it can do so only by virtue of concepts which are already operative in the natural world. In other words, either the precognitive is incommunicable or it is communicable only on the basis of a natural world of cognition, in which case the precognitive disappears. This criticism could mean that the precognitive can be thought but only in relation to cognitive categories *supplied by the reflecting subject*. Now Merleau-Ponty could agree, as he said later in defending *Phenomenology of Perception*, that "the unreflected comes into existence for us only through reflection." (*PPCP* 138, tr. 30) What he could not sanction is the contention that the subject *supplies* the categories. He insists that they come from the world itself. But, if this is granted, there is no contradiction in saying the subject reflects on the basis of what is precognitively given, since the precognitive possesses structure. The criticism could also mean, however, that the precognitive *cannot be thought at all* because once it is thought it is no longer precognitive; hence it is impossible to return to the primordial world. Here the critique might be met on the empirical level. Has Merleau-Ponty described such a world or not? Ballard contends that Merleau-Ponty has no criterion by which he can be certain that he has really described an experience of the precognitive world.

This same point is made with greater force by Eugene Kaelin He suggests that Merleau-Ponty's language is often vague and that his arguments are buttressed more by examples (taken from physiology and psychology) than by philosophical reasoning; and further, that the notion of "motiviation," the descriptive term for interactions whose boundaries cannot be specified, is hardly defined by Merleau-Ponty.[50] Kaelin does not believe that these difficulties are, in principle, insurmountable, but that Merleau-Ponty must clarify the boundaries of experience so that, for example, the difference between the sedimented knowledge of the past and the free creative additions of the present is brought to light.[51] He must show how the analysis of a primary or original experience can yield a primary (rather than a secondary) intuition.[52] And he must show how there can be a communication of primary experiences between persons.[53] Kaelin suggests a way out of this last difficulty, on the basis of some of Merleau-Ponty's analyses of art. [54] Only after we have dealt with the development of Merleau-Ponty's philosophy can we determine the extent to which he resolved these issues, certainly raised by his early books.

Still another problem suggested by Merleau-Ponty's existential descriptions is their universality. Alphonse de Waelhens, for example, believes that Merleau-Ponty comes very close to saying that the truth of things is exhausted by the significance they have for men.[55] Stephan Strasser points to a similar problem when he suggests that Merleau-Ponty's belief that even the laws of mathematics are inseparable from men involves a relativism of truth which would vitiate the universal significance of any phenomenon.[56]

This implicit relativism and world-centeredness in Merleau-Ponty naturally leads to the question of the necessity for an ultimate foundation beyond the world. A number of Roman Catholic philosophers have argued (from different perspectives) that Merleau-Ponty's philosophy requires the affirmation of an "absolute" or "being" in order to make his position coherent.

Joseph Moreau's critique is the farthest removed from Merleau-Ponty's own standpoint.[57] Using Malebranche as a representative of critical or transcendental idealism, he argues that access to an intelligible material world is possible only if there is a principle of intelligibility through which we can approach it. This being the case, our original relation to the world is not precognitive at all, but rather cognitive; and therefore, truth must be the perfect filling of intentions (i.e., absolute certitude) if it is to be adequate.

Other critics remain more within the perspective from which Merleau-Ponty was thinking. Stephan Strasser provides the general framework for all of these when he discusses, without mentioning Merleau-Ponty by name, the necessity of affirming dependence upon something transcending the world as imperative for one who maintains that there is meaning.[58] Remy Kwant believes that Merleau-Ponty's failure to affirm such dependence was the result of his preoccupation with precognitive experience and its correlate, the body-subject. Had he dealt more with the question of the universality of experience, Kwant maintains, he would have been required to focus his attention more directly on the human spirit which transcends the body-subject. In other words, a truly humanistic philosophy must point beyond itself to "being".[59] Finally, Alphonse de Waelhens, arguing from the standpoint of existentialism, says that philosophy cannot remain in the immediate without soon becoming contradictory. The only resolution he sees to the problem of "mysterious affinity," raised by Ballard and Kaelin, is the affirmation of an absolute within relativity. He would not agree with Moreau (whose book was written much later) that the introduction of the absolute would involve an absolute certainty; rather would it involve the affirmation of an absolute meaning which is the point of departure for the most radical questioning possible.[60]

Many of the questions raised by *Phenomenology of Perception* were dealt with to some extent by Merleau-Ponty's later essays. It is a curious fact that, although his later writings were available to most of the critics cited above, none made adequate use of them. Virtually all of Merleau-Ponty's interpreters have concentrated on his second book. I shall demonstrate that, as a basis for critical evaluation of his thought, this is a mistake.

III

Search for a Method

There is not a philosophy which contains all philosophies; philosophy as a whole is at certain moments in each philosophy. To take up the celebrated phrase again, the center of philosophy is everywhere and its circumference nowhere.

Merleau-Ponty

Readers of Merleau-Ponty's early philosophy have seen the most diverse influences at work in his thought. One recent American interpreter believes Hegel and Bergson are the most obvious influences discernible in Merleau-Ponty, with Bergson's influence especially predominant in *Phenomenology of Perception*,[1] while a second finds Hegel and Husserl most important, though of these two he believes Hegel's influence most significant.[2] French commentators invariably point to Husserl as the shadow in which Merleau-Ponty stands, but one sees Husserl's influence shared by Descartes,[3] while another sees it towering alone above all others.[4] Finally, a Belgian philosopher of no little ability believes that Merleau-Ponty is indebted to both Husserl and Hegel, but nevertheless gives a great deal more attention to Merleau-Ponty's relation to Sartre and Heidegger.[5] This difference of opinion should lead us to suspect that finer shades of distinction need to be employed in interpreting Merleau-Ponty's early philosophical method. We shall see, as we turn now to the genesis of Merleau-Ponty's method, that this is indeed the case.

Husserl's Phenomenology: Its Intentions and Its Outcome

Husserl stands at the beginning of the phenomenological movement in Germany and, in the most profound sense, in France as well. It is therefore imperative that we begin our discussion of the genesis of Merleau-Ponty's method with an analysis of the development and implications of Husserl's phenomenology.

Many have been led to conclude that Husserl's philosophy consists of several directions of thought which can be appreciated independently of one another. Thus some saw in his critique of psychologism in 1900 a fruitful avenue for a new realistic philosophy, and considered the *Ideen* I of 1913 a reversion to idealism.[6] Others (including Merleau-Ponty) found the philosophy of the *Lebenswelt* at the end of Husserl's life more fruitful than either avenue of his earlier thought. But is it the case that Husserl's thought can be considered in terms of disparate periods of his life each of which can be accepted or rejected as independent episodes? His historical interpreters (e.g., Spiegelberg, Ricoeur, de Waelhens), as opposed to those who have used Husserl as one starting point for their own reflection (e.g., Heidegger, Sartre, Merleau-Ponty), do not believe so. They argue that there is a consistency in Husserl's *intentions*, although they recognize, in the words of Paul Ricoeur, that "it is necessary to orient oneself in the work of Husserl as in that of Leibniz" since "it is a labyrinth with several entrances and perhaps with several centers each relative to different perspectives in the whole of the work."[7] In expounding Husserl, we must therefore attempt to appreciate both the intentions of his method and the problems in which the effort to realize those intentions involved him.

Husserl received his Ph. D. in Vienna in 1881 with a thesis

in mathematics on the calculus of variations. It was not until 1886, when he heard Franz Brentano lecture, that his interest turned toward philosophy. Soon afterward he decided on a professional career in philosophy and in 1891 published his first book (never completed), *Philosophie der Arithmetik*, which he dedicated to Brentano and in which he attempted to "derive the fundamental concepts of mathematics from certain psychological acts."[8] This "psychologism," the attempt —widespread in the nineteenth century—to make psychology the foundation for logic, was later rejected by Husserl. And in the first volume of his *Logische Untersuchungen*, entitled *Prolegomena zu einer reinen Logik*, published in 1900, he submitted it to a searching critique,[9] concluding that, since logic depending on empirical generalization was at best only probable and subject to contradiction by the discovery of a single contrary instance, it should be abandoned in favor of a logic the truth of whose propositions was immediately certain and not dependent on empirical evidence. The "pure logic" with which Husserl proposes to replace psychologism is based on the laws comprising the various sciences. The laws of each science, whether theoretical or practical, are a priori. And the laws themselves may therefore be the subject of reflection quite apart from any empirical referent. Pure logic would ultimately consist in a theory of the conditions of the possibility of science in general.[10] An aspect of Husserl's analysis which assumes great importance in his later philosophy is what Herbert Spiegelberg calls the "two-level structure" of pure logic.[11] The first level refers to the truths or meanings of the laws in question, the second to the things to which the meanings refer. Even in *Philosophie der Arithmetik* Husserl had recognized the two-level structure of mathematical propositions. Now, having rejected the notion that mathematical laws could be derived from psychological states, he was beginning to seek a foundation for philosophy itself which would be free from psychologism and at the same time guarantee to philosophical statements the certainty attributable to mathematical propositions.

The first four studies of the second volume of the *Logische Untersuchungen* involve an analysis of language based on the principle of a pure logic. The final two studies formally introduce the notion of the intentionality of consciousness which Husserl had actually employed in the earlier analyses of both volumes. Husserl credits Franz Brentano with having first elaborated the idea. Brentano did develop the concept of intentional objects of "psychical" acts as something totally different from "physical" objects. His purpose in doing so was to find an adequate basis for distinguishing psychology from the physical sciences. What Husserl adopted from Brentano was the idea of the directedness of consciousness toward an object.[12] But in Brentano's view the objects intended were immanent in the act of consciousness itself; they were "in" consciousness. Husserl rejected this idea and distinguished between the intentional act of consciousness and its intentional object (the noetic-noematic structure of consciousness in *Ideen* I). In these early logical studies Husserl centered his attention on a description of the objects as they present themselves to consciousness. His interest was in "the things themselves," though he meant by this objects *of consciousness*, not objects in the external world. Empirical experience, while not irrelevant to the appearance of these objects of consciousness, cannot be the basis on which we grasp them. They are available only through *intellectual intuition* in which their *essences* are seen. This attempt to grasp the essences of objects as they present themselves to consciousness left unresolved some important methodological problems such as, for example, the foundation for the validity of the intuitions and the adequacy of evidence uncovered by the intuition of essences. As Husserl turned his attention to these methodological problems his phenomenology became less object-centered and more subject-centered, inasmuch as it was in the Ego that eventually he discovered the foundation for grasping with certainty the objects of consciousness.

But the solution did not reveal itself immediately. Between the appearance of the *Logische Untersuchungen* and his five lectures on the *Idee der Phänomenologie* in 1906-7, Husserl experienced what Paul Ricoeur refers to as a "true crisis of skepticism." [13] A hiatus seemed to deepen between the consciousness and its objects. If the objects were not "in" consciousness, how could a relationship be established between consciousness and its objects? The breakthrough came for Husserl first in his lectures and unpublished manuscripts between 1906 and 1911 and then in the *Ideen* I of 1913. Here for the first time he introduced the phenomenological reduction based on the *epoché* or suspension of the "natural attitude," as the means by which to "return" to consciousness as the *region* of absolutely certain knowledge. But the phenomenological reduction brought with it also a transcendental "egology" as the *foundation* for the certainty of knowledge of objects given to consciousness. [14] In the *Logische Untersuchungen* Husserl had denied the existence of an Ego behind the acts and objects of consciousness. Now, however, he affirmed its necessity, and he altered the fifth and sixth studies of the second volume of the *Logische Untersuchungen* to conform to his new understanding. This transcendental "egology" received its climactic formulation in the *Cartesian Meditations* [15] where Husserl describes a world *wholly constituted by consciousness*. The problem of the relation of consciousness to nature is thus resolved; for the Ego becomes the foundation of nature itself, and what does not appear to the Ego simply is not. In other words, being is identified with what appears to consciousness. Husserl's transcendental phenomenology is therefore idealistic in the sense that the world is constituted by the Ego. However, it is not a metaphysical idealism in the traditional sense, inasmuch as it remains neutral regarding the status of the external world. The latter remains unimportant. What is important is that the being of the phenomena be the same as their appearing. The constitution of the world by the Ego guarantees that this is and must be the case.

Although the notion of intentionality is maintained throughout Husserl's radicalizing of phenomenology, it shifts meaning as the context changes. Thus in the early logical studies (1900-1) intentionality is a psychological concept and as such refers to the receptivity (passivity) of consciousness.[16] In the *Ideen* I it is active as well as receptive.[17] In the *Cartesian Meditations* it is wholly active, both "productive" and "creative."[18] The development of the idea of intentionality is thus intimately related to the development of a transcendental "egology." The intentionality of consciousness, at first a grasping of objects presenting themselves to consciousness, becomes finally the constitution of those objects. And just as the "egological" constitution of consciousness guarantees that the being of objects is their appearing, so the intentionality of consciousness guarantees that consciousness intuits the essences of objects presented to it.

The affirmation of a transcendental "egology" appeared to aggravate the problem of an intersubjective world. Husserl apparently believed that he had overcome solipsism in the *Cartesian Meditations* (though his interpreters are unanimous in contending that he did not). Nevertheless, after 1930 Husserl was led by his awareness of the tragic situation developing in Europe to reexamine his entire philosophical program. The events which troubled him later became evident to everyone. In 1928 Heidegger succeeded to Husserl's chair of philosophy when Husserl retired; the National Socialists came to power in 1933 and for a time Heidegger supported them; Husserl for his part was forced into silence because of his "non-Aryan" ancestry. It was the idea of rationality itself that Husserl believed had been lost in Europe, making the triumph of such irrationalism possible. Thus Husserl, who had never before been concerned with the question of the origin of knowledge but only with the question of its certainty, now sensed the need to refer his ideal of reason to historical verification. By recounting the history of European rationalism, he hoped to show where it had gone astray and to recommend transcendental phenomenology as the only means by which Europe could recover its proper roots and restore its balance. He initiated this task in lectures written between 1935 and 1937, generally referred to as the *Krisis* lectures.[19] His sense of being on a new and fruitful path but one which he could not himself follow to the end, is well captured in the pathos of this comment made to a friend during his last and fatal illness:

Just at the moment when I was so totally penetrated with the feeling of being responsible for a task, at the moment when, in the lectures of Vienna and Prague, then in my article ["The Crisis of the European Sciences and Transcendental Philosophy"], I was for the first time exteriorized with a spontaneity so complete, and when I had succeeded in making a feeble beginning, at this moment my work was interrupted and my task was left unfulfilled. Precisely now that I have arrived at the beginning and that all is ended for me, *I know that it is necessary to begin everything over again from the beginning.*[20]

The significance of the *Krisis* lectures was first brought to the attention of French philosophers by Merleau-Ponty, who studied the unpublished manuscripts in the Husserl Archives at Louvain in 1939.[21] They are of central importance in relating what Husserl believed he was doing to what Merleau-Ponty believed Husserl was doing. In order to understand both points of view adequately, we must set forth the central points of Husserl's analysis.

In the first of the three parts of the central *Krisis* documents [22] Husserl defines the crisis of Western man and sets forth the twofold task of tracing that crisis historically and suggesting how transcendental phenomenology is the only answer to it. The crisis is based on the perhaps unwilling betrayal of the idea which constitutes Western civilization. That idea, Husserl believes, is the vision of a universal knowledge based on reason. The ideal here is not a final complete system of knowledge, for the fundamental experience of Western man has been precisely that of wonder before the infinite tasks opened to reason through the rationalization of experience. Rather, what the ideal refers to is a reason which provides an adequate *foundation* for the rationalization of experience, so that a methodological framework will be established on the basis of which knowledge will be genuinely cumulative, making it possible for men in successive generations to contribute to the same tasks and move toward the same goal with certainty in relation both to the knowledge they accumulate and to the method by which they accumulate it.

This ideal of reason which stands at the very heart of Western civilization and only Western civilization [23] was born in Greece in the seventh and sixth centuries B.C.[24] Plato and Aristotle, by beginning with "wonder," which Husserl interprets as the suspension (*epoché*) of all practical interests and the adoption of the attitude of a detached observer, instituted a new attitude.[25] Prior to this philosophical and theoretical attitude the people of Greece, just like those in every other culture, lived in a "pretheoretical world" (*Umwelt* = *Lebenswelt*). The *Lebenswelt* is the environing world, the prereflective world accepted simply as given. It has its values and meanings, but these are all finite or relative; they are practically oriented toward dealing with the environing world. As the environing world changes historically and culturally, values and meanings are also likely to change. But they do not thereby become universal. The *Lebenswelt* remains a local, finite, enclosed world. When the theoretical attitude is adopted, however, as it was in ancient Greece, the *Lebenswelt* is relegated to the status of appearance, while knowledge of reality or being is seen to belong only to things not subject to change, ideal entities (or essences) true for all men at all times. Opinion (*doxa*), which is a limited knowledge available in the *Lebenswelt*, is now transcended by a true knowledge (*epis-*

témé) which discloses infinite horizons (in the sense already suggested). However, the philosophers of ancient Greece never forgot that *epistémé* was an idealization of the *Lebenswelt*.

Had this ideal been faithfully followed in Western history, a theoretical knowledge tied to its roots in the practical world of human existence would have resulted. Theoretical knowledge would then have *contributed* to man's understanding of himself in his practical world.[26] And that, Husserl points out, was precisely what was intended when the Renaissance assumed the ideal of classical antiquity.[27] But this ideal instead of being realized, underwent an internal decomposition. In the second part of the *Krisis* lectures Husserl traces the history of this failure from Galileo to Hume and Kant.[28] His intention is not to treat the philosophers discussed in their own terms, but in terms of what he believes to be the true ideal of philosophy.[29] Hence, his history of philosophy will be at the same time a philosophy of history.[30]

Husserl begins his analysis with a consideration of Euclidean geometry[31] which went infinitely beyond the relative knowledge available in the *Lebenswelt* by abstracting its object from nature and by elaborating a set of axioms on the basis of which conclusions could be reached deductively. Through this idealization of the *Lebenswelt* the limitations of perceptual knowledge were overcome and a universal knowledge (*epistémé*) was attained. This was the first great revolution in Western history and the one on which the *telos* of Western civilization is based. Galileo, who inherited this science with its ideal of a universally valid knowledge, inaugurated the second great revolution in Western thinking, one which ended by perverting the ideal as it had been understood in the beginning.[32] His perversion was due to the fact that as time passed the realization that geometry was based on an idealization of nature *produced by the human mind* was forgotten, and it came to be regarded as something true *in itself*, having no relation at all to the men who created it. In other words, the thinking mind and the object thought about were divorced from one another. Galileo completed this revolutionary change by mathematizing all of nature, relegating the *Lebenswelt* so completely to the status of subjective appearance that the relation of knowledge of nature understood mathematically to men who live in the *Lebenswelt* became a problem. In short, the world was so objectified that subjectivity was completely lost. Galileo set the stage for the attempt, first made by Spinoza, to construct an ontology on the basis of geometry.

Descartes carried Galileo's analysis one fateful step further.[33] He recognized that, if nature were universally mathematized, the psychical must be separated from physical reality, since the construction of a mathematical nature was accomplished in the first place by abstraction of objects from consciousness. Descartes attempted to restore subjectivity to a naturalistically objectivized universe. The significance of the first two *Meditations* is precisely that they reintroduce the transcendental dimension as the *foundation* of a mathematically naturalized universe. Husserl interprets Cartesian doubt as the suspension (*epoché*) of the natural world in order to find its foundation. This Descartes found in the *ego cogito*, which for Husserl means the *ego-cogito-cogitata*. Not only does the "I" think, it thinks *something*. The naturalistic world is suspended, but the world as it is given to consciousness becomes at the same time a theme for reflection. Consciousness is revealed as intentional consciousness.[34] However, Descartes did not remain faithful to his discovery, but instead, following Galileo, regarded the "I" as a psychological reality which remains when mathematical nature is subtracted from it. Descartes' *epoché* was not radical enough: he suspended the physical world but not the psychical soul. The result was that the soul was placed in the body as a reality distinct from it, but just as abstract. Had Descartes placed both soul and body in suspension and regarded both as constituted by the Ego, then he would have transcended objectivism and subjectivism and placed Western history on the path of elucidating its essential idea. Instead, the history of philosophy since Descartes is marked on the one hand by a rationalism (Spinoza, Malebranche, Leibniz, Wolff) which remains objectivist by reducing either mind to matter or matter to mind; and on the other by an empiricism (Locke, Berkeley, Hume) which is subjectivist insofar as it places the soul in the world, making it subject to the probability attendant upon all objects of perception, and thus ending finally in skepticism. In both cases the net result is a science whose foundations remain obscure and an ambiguity in descriptions of the relation of man to nature.

Hume is the philosopher who recognized the bankruptcy of both approaches. He showed that our scientific knowledge of the world, so far as its foundation is concerned, presents us with a giant enigma. And he also revealed that subjectivism which remains mundane is without foundation.[35] In dissolving both sides of this illegitimate dualism, Hume was actually close to the true solution, namely, a transcendental philosophy, though he did not adopt this solution.[36] However, by stating the problem in such a way that, aside from a genuinely transcendental philosophy, the only alternative was the skepticism which Hume in fact chose, he was closer to a solution than Kant.[37] For although Kant, in answering Hume, attempted to restore subjectivity, he did so in order to consolidate the objective world rather than to reveal how the operation of subjectivity gives meaning and being to the world. One can see this in Kant's bifurcation of the world into phenomenal and noumenal. For subjectivity cannot become the foundation for knowledge unless it has contact not only with phenomena (understood as appearances of reality) but also with being itself.

The point of recounting this history has been to reveal the sickness of the modern European mind and simultaneously to put forward transcendental phenomenology as the catharsis of this sick mind.[38] The idea of rationalism, understood as the infinite task of the progressive rationalization of experience based on a method capable both of accounting for all phenomena and relating them to one another and of producing a certain knowledge, is a valid ideal and one that can be realized. Only when it is conceived in terms of a physicalistic objectivism or a psychical subjectivism does rationalism as an ideal become perverted and subject to doubt. In order to get behind these perversions it is necessary to restore our experience of the world as a *Lebenswelt* prior to its scientific idealization. Only in making *this* world the subject of our reflection can we reconstruct a rationalized (idealized) world which will be free from the perversions of scientific reductionism. It is to this task that Husserl turns his attention in *Krisis* III.[39]

The *Lebenswelt* is, as has already been pointed out, the experienced world. It is the general context or horizon for all experience. In this sense it is the pregiven world. "Pregiven" here should not be taken to mean that the *Lebenswelt* is the world of nature and natural objects alone. For it encompasses as well the cultural accomplishments of men, including the sciences, and therefore refers as much to intersubjective as to natural existence. Viewed in this perspective, science is a cultural accomplishment *within* the *Lebenswelt*. It does not point to some reality behind the *Lebenswelt* but is based rather on the abstraction of certain features within it. Hence the *Lebenswelt* is not to be regarded merely as a point of departure in the drive toward another sphere of being. The *Lebenswelt* is the only sphere and it is all-inclusive. Science, therefore, emerges as a partial theme within the more universal *Lebenswelt*.[40] The question to be raised is whether or not the *Lebenswelt* itself can become the theme of reflection. The insistence in the Vienna lecture on the relativity of the *Lebenswelt* would seem to preclude that possibility. Nevertheless, Husserl asserts that by bracketing out the "objective" sciences, we can get back to the *Lebenswelt* and can discover invariant structures within it.[41] These structures turn out to be the same as the essential structures of the idealized sciences. For example, the *Lebenswelt* is extended in time and space, though it is a lived time and a lived space, not the time and space of mathematical entities. Furthermore, in the *Lebenswelt* we encounter bodies, though they are not the same as the bodies encountered in physics. And, finally, in the *Lebenswelt* there is a regularity of behavior which reveals the principle of causality there, though it is not the causality of the laws of nature developed in science. The fact that the same structures are present in the *Lebenswelt* which appear in an idealized form in the sciences proves that the *Lebenswelt* is the foundation for all idealization.[42]

At this point Husserl's analysis could move in either one of two directions. He could focus his attention on an "ontology of the *Lebenswelt*," a possibility which he himself suggests,[43] or he could attempt through the *epoché* and the phenomenological reduction to make the *Lebenswelt* the basis for a formulation of transcendental phenomenology which would render the *Lebenswelt*, through that philosophical method, the universal foundation for all particular sciences. It is the latter path that he chooses. For our purposes, it is unnecessary to follow his analyses further. Rather, we should raise the question of whether or not Husserl's expressed belief at the end of his life that he was on the threshold of an important new beginning for transcendental phenomenology would not have proved an abortive dream had he lived long enough to see all the implications of his new point of departure. Paul Ricoeur has, I believe, stated most clearly the dilemma in which Husserl's new program involved him. It is that the *Lebenswelt*, inasmuch as it is the ante-predicative world, that is, the world prior to the phenomenological reduction, can never be subjected to a complete reduction; every truth finally meets in the world.[44] Some interpreters conclude that this was only the next logical step of phenomenology and that French existential

phenomenology has therefore been faithful to Husserl's intentions.[45] One even wonders whether or not Heidegger influenced Husserl's *Lebenswelt* philosophy, since the latter
appeared well after *Being and Time*.[46]

The widespread belief that Husserl's *Lebenswelt* philosophy involved insuperable difficulties for a transcendental
phenomenology suggests that, if one is concerned with truths
which "meet in the world," another interpretation of that
method will be called for. It is the dominant theme of Merleau-Ponty's philosophy that all truths do meet in the world,
and his is therefore an existentialist reinterpretation of Husserl's transcendental phenomenology. He was, in fact, the first
philosopher to define phenomenological description, reduction, essential intuition, intentionality, and the ideal of rationality from the standpoint of an existential phenomenology. A
comparison of his interpretation of phenomenology with Husserl's interpretation makes apparent the transformations involved.

Phenomenological *description* for Merleau-Ponty, as for the
early Husserl, is object-centered.[47] Its concern is the apprehension of the (prereflective) world which forms itself around
us, does not depend on us, but constitutes the field or background of all our perceptions. However, this description depends, not on an "egology" as the later Husserl believed, but
rather on immersion in the world. Husserl's phenomenology
was a philosophy of consciousness in which truth dwells in the
inner man;[48] Merleau-Ponty's phenomenology is a philosophy
of the body-subject in which "there is no inner man." Rather
"man is in the world, and only in the world does he know
himself." (*PP* v, tr. xi)

The phenomenological *reduction* led Husserl to a transcendental idealism which Merleau-Ponty says, with most other
critics, ends in solipsism. Merleau-Ponty's starting point, which
avoids this outcome, is our immersion in the world. He identifies this view with Husserl's *Lebenswelt* philosophy and be-

lieves that a return to the *Lebenswelt* involves a recognition of "the impossibility of a complete reduction," [49] a recognition implicit in Husserl's repeated but always inadequate efforts to formulate the idea of reduction satisfactorily. Immersion in the world means that we can never be *wholly* removed from it as transcendent spectators. To make the attempt means a refusal to recognize the meaning the world *already* has as well as that given to it by others.

The meaning of the *eidetic reduction* for Merleau-Ponty is precisely that it leads us back to this world which is already there and in which we are involved. Therefore, to look for the "essence" of the world is to look not for a pure idea but rather for a fact that is present before us prior to any thematization. (*PP* x, tr. xv) The eidetic reduction is thus "the determination to bring the world to light as it is before any falling back on ourselves has occurred, it is the ambition to make reflection emulate the unreflective life of consciousness." (*PP* xi, tr. xvi) We can discover essences only provisionally, in our experience. This does not mean that we can doubt existence itself. For even to be able to doubt presupposes a contact with reality which is always present. It does mean, however, that there can never be an absolute knowledge regarding the essences grasped. Merleau-Ponty asserts that Husserl implicitly accepted this view in his later years.[50]

Merleau-Ponty rejects the view of *intentionality* according to which it is the constituting power of the Ego. For him the intentional world is the world already there. Our task is not to constitute it but to describe its meaning. Intentionality will therefore involve a consideration of the history of things, their present meaning, and their changing relation to other things. The ultimate aim of intentionality is to incorporate every artifact and event in the world into a pattern of human meaning. For everything has meaning in the sense that no matter how chaotic or irrational something may be it is always taken up into human life and transformed into a rational meaning.

(*PP* xiii-xiv, tr. xviii-xix) Merleau-Ponty's view of intentionality thus tends toward an open-ended philosophy of history. As such, it has affinities with Husserl's recognition of a "genesis of meaning" in his *Krisis* lectures. Merleau-Ponty believes that Husserl had accepted this notion as early as 1929, when his second book on logic was published. (*PP* xiv, tr. xix)

Finally, Merleau-Ponty transforms Husserl's understanding of *rationality* by equating world and rationality. Insofar as we are immersed in the world rationality is present as the meaning which the world assumes before us. This meaning is not absolute (once for all), nor is it pregiven. It evolves, changes, but always in the context of the world which is the locus of all meaning.[51] Therefore, "the world and reason are not problematical. We may say, if we wish, that they are mysterious, but their mystery defines them: there can be no question of dispelling it by some 'solution', it is on the hither side of all solutions." [52] The difference between this formulation and what one may find in Husserl's *Krisis* lectures is, to use Herbert Spiegelberg's phrase, that, while Husserl's late philosophy was world-*based*, Merleau-Ponty's philosophy is world-*centered*.[53] For Merleau-Ponty the ideal of rationality means the ideal of progressively clarifying the meaning of the world. For Husserl, however, as we have seen, it never ceased to mean providing a foundation for the meaning of the world.

It is interesting that the preface to *Phenomenology of Perception* can be read independently of the body of that book. There is no attempt to apply the phenomenological method as it is outlined to the descriptions of experience which abound there. We have seen in chapter 2, in fact, that Merleau-Ponty seems to be more directly related to Marcel, Sartre, and Heidegger for the form his ideas assume than he is to Husserl. We must therefore look beyond Husserl for the roots of Merleau-Ponty's method, and I shall postpone until chapter 7 a consideration of the significance of his relationship to Husserl, since important events intervened to alter that relationship.

Initiation of a Phenomenological Philosophy in France: Gabriel Marcel

Husserl did not influence French philosophy before an indigenous descriptive philosophy developed on French soil. In his first published writing, Merleau-Ponty acknowledges a new attempt in French philosophy by Jean Wahl and Gabriel Marcel to get beyond the rationalist position that the world can be treated wholly as an object of thought, or the variant of this notion put forward by Leon Brunschvicg that what cannot be an object cannot even be thought about. Instead of creating a world as a system of thought, they attempt "a *recognition*, a description of existence in all its forms." [54] One can trace Marcel's reactions against rationalism in reflections recorded in his philosophical diary between 1914 and 1933. In them he characterizes rationalism as an "abstract" philosophy, that is, one which separates the object thought about from the thinking person or, in Merleau-Ponty's phrase, one which regards the thinking person as a spectator surveying the world and which inevitably leads to a mechanistic interpretation of the world. Sometimes Marcel speaks as if he is against systematic philosophy as such, because of its tendency to oversimply, reduce, and hence pervert reality. Actually, however, although the complexity he has always recognized in the data of human existence has made it extremely difficult for him to systematize his own reflections, he is not against systematic philosophy itself, but only against the claim put forward by rationalists that they can, by proceeding in this way, exhaust reality.[55] Over against the ideal of abstract thought so conceived, Marcel puts forward his "concrete" philosophy or "metaphysics of spontaneity," [56] which is an attempt to think the subject and the object together, to transcend the dilemmas posed by a pure empiricism or a pure idealism.[57] A concrete philosophy will not end with a synthesis of the subject based on transforming it into an object; nor conversely with a synthesis of the object regarded as belonging to a thinking subject. Indeed, the notion of "synthesis" must be done away with entirely, since it implies some kind of final resolution. Marcel does not mean to affirm, in saying this, that all forms of existential unity are impossible, but only that they are provisional. What we need, he says at one point in his diary, is an "irrational unity," [58] by which he means, not that reality is unintelligible or incomprehensible, but rather that it is inexhaustible and that no given attempt at thinking the unity of reality will succeed. Life is always more than can be thought, because the verification of thought depends on a freedom of the subject which always transcends verification.[59] Or, to put this another way, the freedom of man is such that it can never be wholly objectified.

Marcel soon transposes his notion of freedom as the indeterminate into that of mystery. Mystery, as opposed to problem, cannot be wholly contained in any explanation of reality; it resists reduction to the categories of thought. This does not mean that it is unknown or absent—which would render thought about it altogether impossible—but rather that it cannot be given by the thinking subject himself. It is an *unfolding* of reality—both internal and external—*as we live*, a clarification of our relationships to others and to things *in time.* This concept of mystery, introduced in relation to human freedom in an attempt to develop an alternative to empiricism and idealism, is similar to the idea of "ambiguity" which plays such an important role in *Phenomenology of Perception.* The principal difference is that, while for Merleau-Ponty ambiguity remains a totally immanent notion, Marcel develops his idea of mystery primarily in terms of man's relationship to God. Indeed, like St. Augustine and Kierkegaard before him, Marcel believes that the mystery of freedom posits the God-relationship, for man is so far different from every object in the world that he can understand his unique individuality only in relation to the Thou who can never become an object.[60] Man's relationship to God is the most personal, the most *human* relationship possible. Hence, a concrete analysis of what it means to be related to God can perhaps best clarify other relationships of involvement in the world. It is for this reason that Marcel concentrates his analyses on traditional theological notions such as faith, grace, hope, fidelity, and commitment. Merleau-Ponty does not, like Marcel, attempt to base human freedom on man's God-relationship. Significantly perhaps, he does not even comment on Marcel's conversion to Catholicism and his articles on faith when he reviews *Etre et avoir*, though these comprise a large part of that book.

The thrust of Marcel's "concrete" philosophy is in the direction of a *personal* world. The upshot of Marcel's analyses of the body is, as we have seen, that the body is our means of access to a personal world. When we objectify our bodies as objects, we lose our individuality and the world takes on the character of an impersonal abstraction in which all things are related to one another as objects but in which there is no inter-*subject*ive relationship, and hence no involvement and commitment. Whatever other value such a world may have, it certainly cannot have a *social* value. Intersubjectivity depends on a genuine subjectivity or individuality. This notion of a personal world is in some respects similar to Merleau-Ponty's idea of "mutual presence." For both Merleau-Ponty and Marcel, as opposed especially to Sartre but also in some respects to Heidegger, my individuality is *enhanced* rather than diminished by the recognition of the individuality of others. Authentic individuality includes an authentic social existence. However, Marcel's world is much more securely anchored in the personal than Merleau-Ponty's world. For in Marcel's world it is God, "the absolute 'thou' who can never become a 'him',"[61] who guarantees a personal universe. Our relationship to God, since it cannot be objectified but depends on a faith that is real only insofar as it is an act of commitment expressed through worship, fidelity, and testimony, is a paradigm for our existential relationships to others. Our relationship to God, because it is a relationship "of being to being," [62] constitutes the possibility of relationships to other persons in the world involving the same qualities as our relationship to God. But for Merleau-Ponty, as we shall see, the establishment of authentic "mutual presence" depends in his early postwar philosophy on the creation of a political order and in his later philosophy on the creation of a cultural order, in which authentic intersubjectivity is possible. In a sense it is true to say that Merleau-Ponty retains but immanentizes several important aspects of Marcel's view of the world.[63]

Merleau-Ponty's silence regarding his relationship to Marcel is not, I think, due to the theological interests of one which are absent in the other, though of course the possibilities of misunderstanding Merleau-Ponty's intentions might have been appreciably increased had he attempted to relate himself to Marcel's philosophical theology. The silence is due rather to Marcel's lack of a method for dealing systematically with our concrete existence. Merleau-Ponty makes this clear in his critique of *Etre et avoir*:

The objection which presents itself to the mind in the presence of such a philosophy is that it lacks *obligatory* force. ... To characterize, to discover criteria which resist doubt, to make an inventory of objects of thought, these favorite operations of philosophers are far from defining the intelligence itself. It is a question in these instances of a certain usage of intelligence, nothing more. Marcel knows this, and his philosophy never sounds "anti-intellectualistic." Nothing conforms to reason more than this disavowal of a certain type of reason. But can the intelligence, once "reequipped", serve only to strike down the obstacles which are opposed to decisive intuition? Marcel says: "... One can proceed here only by appeals, as Karl Jaspers does in his *Philosophy of Existence*; if, as I have had the occasion of verifying, certain consciousnesses respond ... this is because a true path has been opened up. But ... this path can be revealed only by love, it is visible for love alone." The author feels more keenly than anyone else that the place here for philosophy properly so called is narrow. Therefore, if the "I have seen" is a last argument, does this philosophy not authorize as well no matter what pseudo-intuition? How can we distinguish authentic intuition from illusion? This is a question the author sets aside, because we are asking for a criterion for what, not being of the order of "it", could not involve a criterion. Moreover, we *know* very well how to distinguish, for example, true lyricism from frenzy. ... We are therefore invited to clarify this immediate distinction between what is above reason and what is below it. If every intuition is sufficient, if there is no path, no dialectic which leads from inadequate knowledge to more adequate knowledge, how can each being enclosed in his imperfect intuitions feel the need of going further, of passing to more reality? Do not the existences of which we have knowledge have a certain structure, do they not present themselves to us in partial aspects which are felt as such, from sides each of which invites us to go further? Marcel undoubtedly believes this, since, in part of his work he maintains the possibility of a dialectic and speaks of a "hyper-phenomenological" method. We do not have to do here with a fulfilled philosophy. It is presented to us as a thesis. ... Nothing would be more rash or more unjust than to oppose "refutations" to suggestions.[64]

It was thus an adequate phenomenological method that Merleau-Ponty found lacking in Marcel. For this we must look to Sartrian existentialism in France, which was more immediately related to the phenomenological method developed by Heidegger in Germany.

Heidegger and the Phenomenological Method

Heidegger's relationship to phenomenology is almost entirely the history of his relationship to Husserl.[65] For several years the two men worked closely together. At Husserl's suggestion, Heidegger was appointed to Husserl's chair of philosophy at Freiburg in 1928 when Husserl retired. Heidegger became a coeditor of Husserl's phenomenological yearbook. But each man was an independent thinker, and their attempts at collaboration ended in a personal estrangement. Heidegger let the yearbook die and, after 1931, even dropped the term phenomenology from his course lectures.

Their estrangement first became evident in 1927 when Husserl requested Heidegger's collaboration on the "Phenomenology" article he was writing for the *Encyclopaedia Britannica*. Heidegger's independent draft, which did not appear in any form in the final article, characterized the task of philosophy as the quest of being.[66] What he really refused in Husserl's draft was the latter's transcendental idealism. The divergence in viewpoint which this refusal represented is highlighted in *Being and Time* (paragraph 7), written during the period of the attempted collaboration on the *Britannica* article. Since Heidegger soon afterwards abandoned phenomenology, this paragraph constitutes his only discussion of phenomenological method, though he indicated that it was only a "preliminary" discussion.

According to Heidegger, phenomenology can be defined in terms of its two component terms, "phenomenon" and "logos." The "phenomenon" must be distinguished from an "appearance," either as something which reveals itself as something other than what it is or as something which will never become manifest (the Kantian understanding). Appearance in either sense *presupposes* the phenomenon as something which *shows itself* (i.e., announces itself, not something else), and as something which shows itself *from itself* (i.e., represents itself, not something else). This means that phenomenology is object-centered. "Logos" means revealing, bringing the phenomenon out from hiding and making it manifest. Logos constitutes the possibility of truth and error: error consists in letting something lie hidden, truth in revealing something. Hence, showing itself from itself (phenomenon) by revealing (logos) is phenomenology. But what is the phenomenon to which phenomenology points? The Being of entities. Hence phenomenology is our *way of access to ontology*. Phenomenology and ontology together constitute the whole of philosophy. The task of a phenomenological ontology is *interpretation*, that is, uncovering hidden entities so that Being becomes manifest. Thus phenomenology is a *hermeneutic method* whose task is to interpret the manifestation of Being, as well as to assist in bringing about that manifestation.

Merleau-Ponty is closest to Heidegger in the latter's definition of phenomenon and logos. Both regard the phenomenon as an original datum of experience which does not depend on us but rather confronts us. It is in this sense that both affirm the object-centeredness of phenomenology. Moreover, the phenomenon is understood by each thinker as both present and hidden. However, hiddenness does not mean "error" for Merleau-Ponty as for Heidegger, but rather constitutes an essential part of the presence of a thing. This difference is rooted in what each thinker defines as the "object" of phenomenology. For Merleau-Ponty the objects of phenomenology are entities *in-the-world*; and it is essential to every finite perspective that presence be also a partial absence, for without flux existence ceases. But for Heidegger the object of phenomenology is Being, and insofar as Being remains hidden it is unknown. Further, insofar as Being is unknown we do not understand ourselves and live in error. For Heidegger man and the world are significant only insofar as they reveal Being; for Merleau-Ponty man is not the means to another end but the end itself—existential analytics *is* philosophy.[67]

German Phenomenology Comes to France: Jean-Paul Sartre

Sartre began his phenomenological researches earlier than Merleau-Ponty, reading Husserl, Scheler, Heidegger, and Jaspers during a year's residence at the French Institute in Berlin in 1933.[68] He remained in Germany a second year and during one semester attended a course offered by Heidegger after the latter had become Rector of the University of Freiburg.[69] After he returned to France he introduced Merleau-Ponty to Husserl's *Ideen* I which he considered "must" reading.[70] Shortly after that, in 1936, he published his first phenomenological study and continued to develop his understanding of phenomenology through other studies between 1937 and 1940. Several of these are important in their bearing on Merleau-Ponty.

In his first study, *The Transcendence of the Ego* (1936), Sartre rejected the Husserlian notion of the transcendental Ego. If the "I" constitutes objects, Sartre argued, then it is not itself an object, but stands outside consciousness. Not only does this result in solipsism but it also renders consciousness ultimately unintelligible. In order to avoid these consequences Sartre includes the Ego in the phenomenological reduction, so that the Ego, like every other object, transcends consciousness (i.e., stands outside consciousness) and is thus an object of consciousness like every other object. Consciousness itself, in this view, becomes a stream, a spontaneity, a "nothing" in the sense that nothing is "in" consciousness but rather everything is outside consciousness as an object *of* consciousness. Consciousness and the world therefore emerge together inasmuch as consciousness is defined in relation to objects outside itself at which it aims. Consciousness does not constitute the world in the Husserlian sense, but finds a world *already* constituted and aims at this constituted world. Here we have the point of passage from transcendental to existential phenomenology: reflecting consciousness does not aim at a consciousness reflected upon, it aims at the world. In connection with this point Sartre affirms that the original relationship between consciousness and world is an impersonal or prereflective relationship. For example, as soon as I say "I hate Peter," there is an "I" conscious of hating. But the primordial relationship is that of "hating" in which consciousness and hate are one. So regarded, Sartre's existential phenomenology is direct-

ly related to that of Merleau-Ponty. For both men, phenomenological description is *object*-centered and the objects with
which it is concerned are in an already constituted world (i.e.,
a prereflective world), not in a "region" belonging to consciousness alone.

If there is no "self" in the sense of a transcendental Ego,
then the question arises of how a self emerges from this impersonal stream of consciousness. Sartre's answer is that the
self is the result of its experiences in the world. With respect
to its "essence," the self is "nothing." It becomes something as
it exists. This is what Sartre means when he says that "existence comes before essence." [71] In works subsequent to this
early treatise Sartre's primary concern is the self which emerges
in the world, or rather the world as it exists for this self which
has been constituted. This led him, as it had led Husserl, to
the problem of the foundation of the relationship between self
and world. That is, Sartre moved away from an object-centered and toward a subject-centered philosophy. The ultimate
outcome was an idealism in which the world depends on the
self for its meaning.[72] Merleau-Ponty was doubtless influenced by Sartre's early object-centered approach to phenomenology [73] and found in him a kindred spirit. But he always
regarded *Being and Nothingness* with a more critical eye, and
after his break with Sartre he subjected it to a searching
critique.[74]

In a second study, published about the same time as the
first, Sartre criticizes the views of modern philosophers on the
relation between imagination and perception.[75] All of them
erred, he believes, in identifying imagination with perception in one way or another. Either images were weak perceptions (Descartes, Spinoza), or both depended on thought which
synthesized them (Leibniz), or the distinction disappeared altogether (Hume). The result was that images were regarded
as *things*: things radically different from thought as in Descartes, or things identifiable in principle with thought as in

Leibniz, or the only things to which we have access at all as in Hume. Sartre attributes to Husserl a methodological advance insofar as his understanding of the intentionality of consciousness [76] provided a means by which the distinction between imagination and perception could be described and understood. According to Sartre, Husserl's advance remained methodological only, since he did not provide the descriptions of perceptual consciousness and imagining consciousness.[77]

Sartre attempted to supply this deficiency in a second book on the imagination published several years later.[78] His study is divided into two general parts, the first and shorter section (Part I) dealing with a phenomenological description of the *essences* of images which can be known with certainty when we reflect on the images given to consciousness; and the second section (Parts II-IV) dealing with the *nature* of images, which cannot be known with certainty but only with probability. For our purposes it is necessary to consider only the first part of Sartre's analysis.

A phenomenological description of consciousness of images yields four certain characteristics of imaginal consciousness as opposed to perceiving consciousness: first, both imaginal and perceptual consciousness refer to objects, but each is related to these objects (i.e., aims at these objects) in a different way; second, perceptual consciousness sees objects from various perspectives and each perspective can add some new knowledge to views from other perspectives, but imaginal consciousness sees its object completely with the first consciousness of the object—nothing new can be added to the imaginal consciousness of an object once it is intended by consciousness; third, in imaginal consciousness the object is present as an absence, whereas in perceptual consciousness the object is present empirically, concretely; and fourth, imaginal consciousness is spontaneous, that is, the intended object is present so long as the imaginal consciousness actively intends it, while in perceptual consciousness the object is present as an empirical phenomenon so that consciousness aims at an actual object rather than at an imagined object and hence is passive rather than active in its intentionality.[79] The result of this descriptive analysis is clear: imaginal consciousness is *wholly different* from perceptual consciousness. On the basis of this sharp distinction, Sartre analyzes the "image family," that is, the various types of images at which consciousness can aim. The range is indeed wide, beginning with portraits or caricatures which aim at real persons and which consciousness can intend when these objects are presented to it, and concluding with various hallucinatory images which we may see in fire, spots on walls, or rocks in human form—images which are completely unrelated to objects intended by consciousness. So much says Sartre, we can know with certainty about imaginal consciousness. Everything else depends upon the empirical manifestion of images, and to descriptions at this level only a higher or lower degree of probability can be attached.

For Sartre, the radical distinction between perceptual consciousness and imaginal consciousness points to different ways of being-in-the-world. The perceptual consciousness is related to a world of "real" objects, while the imaginal consciousness is related to a world of its own construction. It nevertheless manifests a way of being-in-the-world, namely, as denying the world,[80] and in a negative way reveals that consciousness in relation to the world is *free*. Despite the fact that both perceptual and imaginal consciousness point to the freedom of consciousness in relation to the world it inhabits, this radical separation between them raises a critical problem, namely, whether, if imaginal consciousness does not depend on a prior contact with the "real," we can *know* that we are in the world in the sense that we have contact with "being" and not simply with "appearances." Sartre solved the problem in *Being and Nothingness* by making the only meaningful "world" that is possible dependent upon the self which constitutes it. It appears that the manner in which Sartre stated the relation between imagination and perception accounts in part for his need to move beyond an object-centered to a subject-centered perspective. Merleau-Ponty refused to be drawn in this direction. Regarding *The Psychology of Imagination*, Merleau-Ponty remarked that Sartre could not in practice maintain a rigid distinction between imagination and perception, inasmuch as what he had asserted as certain in the first part of the book he called into question in the second part. (*SHP* 34, tr. 74) The task of philosophy is to remain object-centered, that is, to describe the interpenetration of images and perceptions, appearances and reality, truth and error, on the basis of a world which is already there, not, as Sartre is led to do by his formulation of the problem, to speculate on how it is possible for the world to be there.

Merleau-Ponty's first real critique of *Being and Nothingness* centered around the social philosophy implied in it. (*AD*, chap. 5) But after having made a clean break with Sartre's political views, Merleau-Ponty returned later to the philosophical implications of Sartre's dualism, focusing his attention on the relation between imagination and perception. (*VI* 77-130) We shall consider these in their proper context (chap. 5), where the significance of the critique can more properly be assessed.

Generally speaking, we can conclude from the foregoing comparisons of Merleau-Ponty with Husserl, Marcel, Heidegger, and Sartre, that, more than any of these men, Merleau-Ponty is immersed in-the-world. He refuses to transcend immanent social experience through the transcendental Ego (Husserl), through the God-relationship (Marcel), through Being (Heidegger), or through consciousness (Sartre). Rather, he takes as the theme of his reflection man in the world related to other men in various ways. His is, in short, a *social* philosophy, a philosophy of intersubjectivity. This became evident after the war when he translated his ideas into a political philosophy. To understand this translation and the initial meaning of Merleau-Ponty's philosophy interpreted as a social philosophy, we must look beyond all the thinkers considered thus far to the role of Hegel and Marx in postwar French thought.

Hegelian and Marxian Roots of Merleau-Ponty's Social Philosophy

In an article which assesses the extent to which Hegel can be allied to existentialism (*SNS* 125-39, tr. 63-70) Merleau-Ponty writes:

All the great philosophical ideas of the past century—the philosophies of Marx and Nietzsche, phenomenology, German existentialism, and psychoanalysis—had their beginnings in Hegel; it was he who started the attempt to explore the irrational and integrate it into an expanded reason which remains the task of our century. He is the inventor of that Reason, broader than the understanding, which can respect the variety and singularity of individual consciousnesses, civilizations, ways of thinking, and historical contingency but which nevertheless does not give up the attempt to master them in order to guide them to their own truth. (*SNS* 125-26, tr. 63)

And further along he adds:

There would be no paradox involved in saying that interpreting Hegel means taking a stand on all the philosophical, political, and religious problems of our century. (*SNS* 126, tr. 63-64)

These are extraordinary statements and we must first attempt to see the context in which they take on meaning.

As late as 1930 Hegel exerted very little influence on French philosophy.[81] He had been virtually ignored in favor of neo-Kantianism between 1850 and 1900, and the brief revival of his thought which attempted to dispel widespread misconceptions of his ideas was cut short by World War I, after which there was a reaction in France against everything German. When Alexandre Koyré wrote the article cited above, the study of Hegel was beginning anew in France, and it continued

throughout the 1930s. At the end of World War II the interpretation of Hegel emerged as an important part of French
philosophical thought.

Interpretation proceeded in two opposite directions. The
first type of interpretation was that initiated by Jean Wahl,[82]
who emphasized the decisive influence of Hegel's early religious interests on all his later works. Even in the most abstract works, Wahl contends, we find the theologian behind
the philosopher, the romantic behind the rationalist, and the
unhappy consciousness of the romantic, the mystic, and the
Christian behind the satisfied consciousness of the Berlin
philosopher. The dialectic of the *Phenomenology of Mind*
was born from the desire to unite classical Greek objectivism
and Christian (especially Protestant) subjectivism; hence the
movement of the unhappy consciousness from Stoicism through
Judaism to primitive and medieval Christianity, and finally
to eighteenth-century subjectivism. Thus Wahl contends:

> Far from believing that the philosophy of Hegel is a purely ration-
> al philosophy, we would say that it is an effort to rationalize a
> depth that reason does not attain. ... What was there originally,
> at the bottom of the soul of the author of the *Logic* was a Christian
> vision of the cross and a Boehmean vision of the anger of God.
> What is there at the bottom of the soul of the rationalist is this
> double mystery; and at the bottom of the soul of this optimist [is]
> this double sorrow.[83]

Others also soon began to give attention to Hegel's early theo-
logical interests as a background to his later philosophy.
Alexandre Koyré initiated lecture courses on Hegel's religious
thought at the Ecole pratique des Hautes Etudes in 1931.[84]
And the most prolific writer on Hegel in France, especially
since the end of World War II, devoted his first articles on
Hegel to his early development, stressing with Hegel's major
German interpreters, his religious concerns.[85]

But a second type of interpretation of Hegel appeared four
years after Wahl's book, when Alexandre Kojève, who taught

Koyré's course at the Ecole pratique des Hautes Etudes from 1933 to 1939,[86] put forward a radically naturalistic interpretation of Hegel's *Phenomenology of Mind*. Merleau-Ponty says of these lectures that "they created a deep impression." (*PC* 436) Merleau-Ponty knew Kojève during these years and attended his lectures. [87] Through his naturalistic or atheistic interpretation of Hegel, Kojève reconciled the *Phenomenology of Mind* both with Marxist humanism and with Husserlian phenomenology. This accounts for his influence on the postwar existentialists, and partly for the noncommunist interpretation of Marxist humanism among French intellectuals, as well as for the assimilation of Hegel and Husserl in French phenomenology. We must therefore look at Kojève's interpretation of Hegel.

The central thesis of Kojève's interpretation of the *phenomenology of Mind* is that the Absolute Spirit represents man in the world. All of his other conclusions are based on this central assertion. The first conclusion is that God in the Christian sense, a God both transcendent and immanent, is dead. Hegel replaces this God with a purely immanent God, that is, he makes man into God.[88] Kojève believes that the romantic poets, the philosophers Schelling, Jacobi, and Kant, and the theologian Schleiermacher were all essentially atheists, so that the denial of a transcendent God was not an Hegelian innovation.[89] But he believes that Hegel drew certain consequences from it, primarily the view that being is essentially finite. Thus, insofar as there is any fulfillment in human existence it must be a worldly fulfillment.[90] And any such fulfillment depends in the first instance upon man's acceptance of his finitude.[91] Acceptance of finitude means acceptance of death, or better still, freedom for one's death.[92] Finally, then, freedom for death and Absolute Knowledge are identical.[93] Freedom for death is asserted through *action*, that is, through the denial of what is for the sake of the realization of human possibilities. Ontologically, this denial takes the form of a transcending of nature interpreted as spatial and given, through temporal action:

The profound base of Hegelian anthropology is formed from this idea that Man is not a Being who *is* in an eternal identity with himself in Space, but a Nothingness which *nihilates* as Time in spatial Being through the *negation* of this Being, through the negation or transformation of the given on the basis of an idea or an ideal which *is not* yet, which is still nothingness (project), through the negation which is called *Action (Tat)* by Struggle and Work (*Kampf* and *Arbeit*).[94]

Politically, the denial takes the form of revolution, a refusal to accept the given on the basis of the realization that reform will not alter social structures.[95] Such an interpretation also requires the transformation of Hegel's view of history. And, consistent with his previous descriptions, Kojève contends that for Hegel the end of history is finite, commensurate with human life. He believes that Hegel viewed Napoleon as the culmination of the movement of history,[96] and that he regarded himself as the person who alone was capable of making Napoleon conscious of his historical role,[97] so that Hegel identified himself and in the final analysis his book with universal history.[98]

These are certainly strange conclusions when compared with any other modern interpretion of Hegel's *Phenomenology of Mind*. A critique of Kojève's view of Hegel will not serve our purposes here [99] as much as will an attempt to delineate some of the alliances and implications which underlie his interpretation.

Three alliances are readily apparent. The first is Kojève's identification of Hegel's *Phenomenology of Mind* with Husserl's phenomenology. This follows from Kojève's interpretation of Hegel's view of history as nondialectical (i.e., as culminating in Napoleon and Hegel), so that he interprets the book as descriptive rather than as dialectical. "The Hegelian *method* is not 'dialectical'; it is purely contemplative and descriptive, indeed *phenomenological* in the Husserlian sense of the term." [100] This leads him to conclude that Husserl was wrong to oppose his method to that of Hegel. [101] Here we have the basis for the *rapprochement* between Husserl and Hegel which is part of French phenomenology. [102] The second alliance is that with Heidegger. Kojève's notion of being as finite in essence and of the expression of finite freedom primarily through a freedom for death are directly related to "What is Metaphysics?" and *Being and Time* respectively. [103] The third alliance is that with Marx. The title page of Kojève's published lectures contains a quotation from Marx's early philosophical writings, and it is evident in several respects that Kojève is very Marxian in his interpretation of Hegel, for example, in the view that only the slaves can make history, [104] in the view that religion is an ideology, [105] and in the view already cited that change will require a revolution and cannot be brought about within the present social structures. Though this is impossible to document, much significance must be attributed to Kojève's interpretation of Hegel as a source of the influence of the young Marx among French intellectuals.

A third link between Kojève and French philosophy is evident in the close parallelism between Kojève's identification of nature with the spatially inert and of time with human action as a means of nihilating the given in order to create something new, and the Sartrian dichotomy between the in-itself and the for-itself. [106] Jean Wahl describes this parallelism in some detail. [107] However, it is difficult to say whether or not there was a direct influence of Kojève on Sartre. Sartre never mentions Kojève in *Being and Nothingness*. Even more significant, perhaps, is the fact that in her autobiography Simone de Beauvoir never says that she and Sartre were aware of Kojève's lectures, and indicates that she began to read the *Phenomenology of Mind* for the first time on July 6, 1940. [108] Perhaps we can uncover a more direct influence of Kojève on French existentialism by considering the extent to which Merleau-Ponty's article on Hegel reflects Kojève's interpretation. Certainly Merleau-Ponty's opening statement in that article, quoted at the beginning of this section, reflects an awareness of the alliances Kojève had made between Hegel and Marxism as well as between Hegel and phenomenology. Merleau-Ponty agrees with Kojève in interpreting the *Phenomenology of Mind* as a concrete description of man's being-in-the-world. But he believes that the book remains on this level and that it envisages the level of the absolute mind not in terms of any immanent end as represented, for example, by Napoleon and Hegel, but only in terms of a style of life. (*SNS* 128, tr. 64) What Kojève interprets as the intention of the *Phenomenology of Mind* Merleau-Ponty considers to be the intention only of Hegel's late works. (*SNS* 127-28, tr. 64) Hence for him Hegel's early philosophy is even more radically in-the-world than is the case in Kojève's interpretation. Furthermore, Merleau-Ponty interprets the difference between man and nature in Hegel in much the same way as Kojève. He denies a "human nature" given once for all, as Kojève does in behalf of Hegel, and asserts that man is man only so long as the final stage of his history remains unattained. (*SNS* 130-31, tr. 65-66) Finally, Merleau-Ponty emphasizes freedom for death in Hegel, as Kojève does. But he denies that this is primary. Rather, freedom for death has as its end a freedom for life (*SNS* 134-35, tr. 67-68), and Merleau-Ponty affirms that this is also true for Heidegger (*SNS* 138-39, tr. 69-70). In a later text—the only explicit reference Merleau-Ponty ever makes to Kojève—he says that Kojève's interpretation of the end of history in Hegel as a return to the cyclical life of nature is really an idealization of death which cannot translate the central thought of Hegel. (*AD* 277)

The real importance of Kojève's interpretation of Hegel, insofar as it is significant for Merleau-Ponty's development, is the emphasis he placed on the *Phenomenology of Mind* as a concrete descriptive philosophy of being-in-the-world. It was through the influence of Hegel, and partly also of Kojève's interpretation of Hegel, that Merleau-Ponty's philosophy of the social world received its earliest frame of reference. But in the final analysis Hegel's philosophy was inadequate because in his later years Hegel abandoned his openness to being-in-the-world and replaced it with a dogmatic philosophy of being. (SNS 137-38, tr. 69; 270-71, tr. 133)

Marx, in Merleau-Ponty's view, rescued the *concreteness* of Hegel from the pitfalls of systematic philosophy. (SNS 253-77, tr. 125-36) Marx is to be distinguished from contemporary "orthodox Marxists" in this respect. For the latter believe that man's social relationships are reducible to natural relationships, that they can be described in terms of "social laws" analogous to the "laws of nature" employed in the physical sciences. But aside from the fact that physical laws of nature are not permanent even for the natural order, man can never perceive what the "dialectic of nature in itself" might be, since when he observes nature it is always nature for man that is observed. There is no way to reduce human to natural phenomena. "Orthodox Marxists" also err in regarding the *ideas* of men as purely chimerical. Marx does not say, as do some of his contemporary disciples, that religion, to take one example, has no meaning at all, but rather that it represents an abortive attempt to establish interpersonal relations among men and that, failing to accomplish this, it becomes another manifestation of man's alienation from himself and from others. It is not less but more meaning that needs to be attributed to religion in order that it may become clear what the elimination of alienation as reflected in religion will be.[109] In reality, contemporary "orthodox Marxists" are mechanistic when they think in terms of their own vision (i.e., they regard it as a necessary development) and idealistic when they reflect on the bourgeois civilization they reject. Marx, however, consciously fought against both extremes, contending that every civilization is a "totality" in which the various systems of ac-

cepted ideas are intimately related to the political and economic structures of that civilization. Neither can be taken in
isolation, but both must be understood dialectically, in relation to the other. (See *SNS* 225, tr. 112)

Merleau-Ponty's interpretation of Marx is heavily dependent
upon Marx's early philosophical writings, in particular his
Economic and Philosophical Manuscripts published in 1844.[110]
In that treatise Marx argued that the money economy, which
produces a property class (capitalists, landowners) and a propertyless class (workers, peasants), and in which the property
class exists by virtue of its exploitation of the propertyless
class, results in a total social structure in which men are
alienated from one another. Man is not primarily a natural but
rather a *social* creature; it is only as he transcends his natural
functions (eating, drinking, procreating) through self-conscious activity that he becomes free, that he realizes the social
or "species" nature of his being. In a bourgeois civilization,
however, the self-conscious activities of (propertyless) men are
reduced to natural activities, that is, what should be a means
of expressing a free *human* being becomes instead a means of
subsistence.[111] Marx believed that in describing "alienation"
in terms of labor interpreted as capital he had gone beyond
the abstract description of Hegel for whom alienation was a
product of self-consciousness and beyond Feuerbach for whom
religion was the cause of alienation. Alienation became for
Marx, not an abstract philosophical or theological category,
but a concrete reality through which bourgeois civilization
could be understood.[112] Having discovered the key, Marx also
believed he had discovered the answer to the dilemma. If
alienation is caused by the surplus value extracted from
workers in the form of money, then, through the abolition of
a money economy and of private property which money represents, alienation can be overcome.[113] But if money and
private property are abolished, this will mean that a whole
new social structure—religious, political, economic—will super-

sede the present structure. For Marx, Communism represents this new "totality":

> Communism is the *positive* abolition of *private property*, of *human self-alienation*, and thus the real *appropriation* of *human* nature through and for man. It is, therefore, the return of man himself as a *social*, i.e., really human, being, a complete and conscious return which assimilates all the wealth of previous development. Communism as a fully-developed naturalism is humanism and as a fully-developed humanism is naturalism.[114]

If Communism should replace bourgeois civilization, then alienation would no longer characterize the human situation, for the society would be organized in such a way that it would be excluded. Marx writes:

> From the relation of alienated labor to private property it also follows that the emancipation of society from private property, from servitude, takes the political form of the *emancipation of the workers*; not in the sense that only the latter's emancipation is involved, but because this emancipation includes the emancipation of humanity as a whole.[115]

This, then, is the humanistic Marxian vision. The idea of the inevitable triumph of Communism is not present here as it is in Marx's later writings on political economy.[116] He does assert that *if* there is to be a genuine historical development, Communism is the necessary form that this development must take in the immediate future.[117] However, there is no suggestion that history must progress. Structures of society are as dependent upon the free activity of men as men are dependent upon received structures. "The *social* character is the universal character of the whole movement; *as* society itself produces *man* as *man*, so it is *produced* by him." [118] Therefore, if a new "totality" is to be realized, it must become a human project. Men must not only envision a new order; they must act to bring the new order into being.[119]

It is this humanistic vision that Merleau-Ponty has before him when he asserts that "Marxism is not a philosophy of the subject, but it is just as far from a philosophy of the object: it is a philosophy of history." (*SNS* 264, tr. 130) He understands by "philosophy of history" precisely what the young Marx understood by it, namely, a philosophy which remains concrete by reflecting upon the structures of existence and which, in analyzing those structures, seeks to embody a vision of their totality which can become the basis for a new social order. Merleau-Ponty never abandoned this position, and in this respect his social philosophy always remained "Marxist." As we turn now to the earliest statement of his philosophy of the social world, it will become evident that the young Marx stands in the immediate background and that Merleau-Ponty's philosophy, notwithstanding all the other influences apparent in it, is, in his own mind, a Marxist social philosophy.

The Redefinition of Metaphysics as Social Philosophy

Merleau-Ponty wrote the first programmatic statement of his social philosophy in 1947 (*SNS* 165-96, tr. 83-98), and in it he did not hesitate to say that a genuine social philosophy is a metaphysical philosophy. But metaphysics no longer means a philosophy of first principles; now it refers to a philosophy of being-in-the-world, a *philosophy of finitude*. The significance of this redefinition is threefold. In the first place, metaphysics no longer concerns itself with that which transcends the world (God, Being, consciousness), but only with experience, "this world, other people, human history, truth, culture." (*SNS* 188, tr. 94) Philosophy now cannot retreat to an ivory tower. It must grasp the truth in a contingent event or structure and must therefore remain open in each moment to new experiences which will bear in upon it and require a new synthesis. It is the antithesis of "the system" as a complete synthesis. (*SNS* 191-92, tr 95-96) This requires, in the second place, that the categories with which philosophy works be recast. For philosophy does not deal with a "subject" or with an "object" but with various *relationships* in terms of which these are perceived together. For example, language cannot be reduced either to laws or to a speaking subject but must be grasped in terms of the interaction between these in various cultures; here the lived or existential configuration which language assumes will be the object of philosophy. (SNS 172-76, tr. 86-88) The same is true of other phenomena of intersubjective existence: social relationships (SNS 176-80, tr. 88-90), history (SNS 180-85, tr. 90-92), and religion (SNS 192-93, tr. 96-97). Finally, it is *human* meaning which is the concern of philosophy.[120] Philosophy seeks to describe, to clarify, and perhaps to transform man's intersubjective experience.

The idea that the task of philosophy is to describe how men who have intentions (i.e., who are free) are related to the world (i.e., "totality") which is always already there before them is the fundamental constant in Merleau-Ponty's philosophy. The presupposition underlying such a task is that, despite the multiplicity of perspectives which men have on the world (what Merleau-Ponty will later call the "private world" of each man), there is a discernible human unity. Such a presupposition allied to a descriptive metaphysics can lead in either one of two directions. On the one hand, descriptive metaphysics might attempt to evaluate the concrete meanings that men find in the world with a view to judging between them on the basis of the degree to which a particular meaning of an individual or group is at the same time an expression of a genuinely universal meaning. An evaluatively descriptive metaphysics of this kind is likely to be politically oriented and to assume that the attainment of universal meaning is an immanent human possibility. Here we have the secular counterpart of the idea of the presence of the Kingdom of God. And as in the case of those who, throughout western history, have attempted to establish the Kingdom of God on earth, such a philosophy will take the form of a descriptive program of the way things are in relation to the way they ought to be. It will become a concrete political manifesto. On the other hand, a descriptive metaphysics might attempt to comprehend the various meanings men discover in the world, not in order to evaluate their relative merits, but rather in order to uncover the *basis* on which all these meanings inhere together in the same world. A descriptive metaphysics of this kind will concern itself with the interrelationships between the various ways in which men understand themselves (psychologically, sociologically, etc.) and will take the form of an ontology of the lived world.

Although each of these alternatives depends on the same presupposition and hence presumably aims at the same end, they do not in reality come out at the same point. The first alternative is millennial; it involves the additional presupposition that the multiplicity of history can be reduced to a final unity. The second alternative involves a more radical contingency; human freedom may be led in many (unpredictable) directions, and the task of the philosopher is to describe at a given instant the inherence in one world of all the directions in which men are led. The first alternative ultimately sacrifices multiplicity to unity; the second seeks to found unity on multiplicity.

Merleau-Ponty chose both these alternatives in succession. The first choice involved him in a close relationship to Marx and Marxist politics in France, the second in a close relationship to Husserl, Bergson, and others interpreted as philosophers of culture. I shall trace now the shift from the first to the second alternative in order to make clear not only the development of Merleau-Ponty's thought, but also its significance as a social philosophy.

PART II

The Evolution of
a Social Philosophy: 1945-1955

IV

Merleau-Ponty and Postwar Politics in France: Marxism and Beyond

> For in the last analysis each one of us knows ... that the world as it is, is unacceptable.
>
> *Merleau-Ponty*

> To be silent is not the same as to say why one does not wish to choose.
>
> *Merleau-Ponty*

The Context for a New Social Philosophy: France, 1945-1947

On August 25, 1944, General de Gaulle, representing the Resistance government of France, arrived in Paris, bringing to a close the "New Order" of "Work, Family, and Fatherland" initiated by the Vichy Regime in 1940 under the watchful care of the aged Marshal Pétain. Only a year before, de Gaulle had succeeded in uniting the various Resistance groups around himself. His return to Paris in the wake of an insurrection initiated by the Resistance six days earlier—which forced the Allies to abandon plans to bypass the city, and to liberate it immediately—was a great moment in French history.[1] There was a feeling of unity among all elements of the population, as well as the belief by many that they were about to witness the birth of a new era. Had not de Gaulle himself spoken of "this great revolution" in France's history just before he left North Africa?

Indeed he had. But once in Paris he substituted for "revolu-

tion" the word "renovation." Underneath the surface unanim-
ity of the Resistance groups, the battle lines were being drawn
between those who wanted a "new France" and those who
simply wanted to "return to normal." Merleau-Ponty aligned
himself with the former. "The War and the Occupation alone
have taught us," he wrote in the first issue of *Les Temps
Modernes*, "that values remain nominal and indeed have no
value without an economic and political infrastructure to make
them participate in existence." [2] Values up to now evident
only in men's minds had to be socially organized.

Signs were not lacking, however, that the future of France
belonged to those who wanted to "return to normal." Eco-
nomically the basic fiscal reforms proposed by M. Mendès-
France, which constituted the precondition of a forward national movement, failed to win acceptance. The result, as
Mendès-France had predicted, was the triumph of the black
market over the official market, the starvation of the working
class, the ruination of those in the middle class with fixed
incomes, and a continuing spiral of inflation.[3] Politically the
situation was little better. Elections had been set for October,
1945. Out of the maze of Resistance and political groups, three
major parties emerged and presented themselves to the electorate: the Communists, the Socialists, and the M. R. P. (a
Catholic center party). On August 12, 1945, two months before
the election, the Socialists and Communists met together to
consider the possibility of joint action. The Communists especially were in favor of it. But the Socialists refused. This
sealed the fate of a possible left-wing coalition. In the election itself the Communists received five million votes (26 percent), and the other two major parties four and one half million votes each (24 percent each). Two right-wing parties
received another 21 percent. In other words, the Socialists
and Communists together constituted a majority (albeit a
slight one) and could have governed together. Since the Socialists had repudiated this, but since all three major parties

had accepted, in the main, the C. N. R. Charter,[4] a three-party coalition headed by de Gaulle was established in November, 1945. When de Gaulle resigned his leadership in January, 1946, the Communists once again proposed a two-party coalition of themselves and the Socialists, but again the Socialists refused. The three parties therefore continued their unsteady alliance. Cohesion was possible only because a great many French leaders were united in their desire that France become a link between East and West and remain unaligned in the power struggle that was beginning to take shape between the United States and Russia. The atmosphere remained confused throughout 1946, but events outside France's borders soon began to clear the air.

On December 19-20, 1946, French forces clashed at Haiphong with the Vietnamese in what turned out to be the beginning of a seven-year conflict in that country. Needless to say, such a "colonialist venture" made the position of the Communists in the government equivocal. On March 12, 1947, the U. S. Congress was presented the Truman Doctrine, which not only asked large-scale aid for Greece and Turkey, but also set forth the principle of American support for any people threatened by and resisting communism. This announcement came on the eve of the Marshall-Molotov-Bevin-Bidault Conference in Moscow, which ended in disorder on May 1, widening the rift between East and West. This rift became an irreparable one when, in response to General Marshall's now famous Harvard speech offering American assistance to Europe on the sole condition that the European nations agree on what they wanted, Bidault and Bevin met and called a meeting of all the nations concerned for July 2, 1947. Russia walked out of this meeting, and the world entered the era of "the cold war." By this time the Communist ministers in the French government had resigned. The hardening of East-West relations would have forced them out in any case, but a domestic crisis hastened their departure. On April 30, 20,000 Renault workers went on strike as a protest against the rising cost of living, and against the wage freeze initiated by Léon Blum the previous December and supported by the Communists. Both the Communist ministers and the Communist press came out in favor of the strikes, which meant, of course, that their continued presence in the government was no longer possible. On May 9 they resigned, and Ramadier reorganized his government with a "third force" coalition of Socialists, M. R. P.'s and Radicals.

Instead of adopting a policy and government balanced between East and West, France began to move farther to the right. She was fighting a war abroad and suffering from inflation at home, the latter now being aggravated by a large-scale workers' strike. The only relief in sight was the offer of help by an American government which favored noncommunist regimes. Anticommunist sentiment naturally began to increase. The municipal elections, scheduled for the latter part of 1947, provided the perfect platform for its expression. De Gaulle was the first to take advantage of this situation, organizing the R. P. F. (Rassemblement du Peuple Français) in April, 1947, and attempting, on the basis of a platform of anticommunism, to attract an absolute majority of the electorate. When the R. P. F. announced in August that it would run candidates in every municipal election, the Radical Party joined the Gaullist bandwagon. The coalition government grew alarmed and attempted to counter de Gaulle by adopting a similar campaign of anticommunism. Much was made of Koestler's books, especially *Darkness at Noon*, as well as of Kravchenko's *I Chose Freedom*, in the mounting propaganda war against the Communists.[5] When the election was finally held, the R. P. F. polled 39 percent of the vote; the Communists, against whom the whole campaign had been directed, held their own with 31 percent; the Socialists remained in the running with 19 percent; and the M.R.P. and the Radicals received only 9 percent, being virtually replaced by the R.P.F. The latter gained control of nearly every municipality in France, though this did not affect the National Assembly, which had been elected for five years in 1946. For this reason, as well as the fact that de Gaulle's motley assembly of supporters represented no cohesive political entity in France, the R. P. F. gained little political mileage out of the election. De Gaulle had, however, helped to intensify the anticommunist sentiment of the *petite bourgeoisie* in the latter part of 1947, and he was instrumental in forcing the middle parties back together to form a coalition against extremists at both ends of the spectrum.

The isolation of the Communists from the remainder of the French electorate was completed at the end of 1947. After the resignation of the Communist ministers in May, the Party had taken charge of the striking workers. The strikes had begun as a protest over economic conditions (particularly inflation), but now they took on more of a political character. As a result the government, early in December, crushed the strike with military police. This was followed on December 19 by a split within the working class movement itself. The C. G. T. (Confédération Générale du Travail) remained Communist, while the newly formed C. G. T.-F. O. (Confédération Générale du Travail-Force Ouvrière) aligned itself more closely with the Socialists.

It was in this political situation—the failure of the new order to materialize in France and its aftermath, a wave of anticommunism—that Merleau-Ponty found himself. From November, 1946, through July, 1947, he attempted to counter the anticommunism of the political right with a series of articles in *Les Temps Modernes* dealing with Koestler's *Darkness at Noon*, the Moscow trials on which it had been based, and his critics' replies (which swelled to mammoth proportions in a short time). These studies constituted the major part of *Humanisme et terreur*, published between October and December, 1947.[6]

A Politics of Mediation

Merleau-Ponty's interpretation of the situation we have just recounted turns on an assessment of political forces both outside and inside France. He argued as follows. Outside France two giant powers face one another. One of them, the Western nations, professes the ideals of freedom, justice, and equality for all men, but in practice denies this to certain groups, for example, the peoples in the colonial empire and the Negroes in the United States. The result is the use of good principles to justify bad actions.[7] The Marxist critique rests on this deception at the heart of Western life. However, the practice of Marxism, as exemplified in Russia, is no better. The use of violence in the name of the proletariat has not led to a new humanity as Lenin and Trotsky believed it would, but to the *institution* of violence, a new hierarchical society, and a static regime.[8] Merleau-Ponty drew from this two conclusions. On the one hand, the Marxist critique of Western liberalism remains valid regardless of the shortcomings of any Marxist regime.[9] On the other hand, since both Eastern and Western regimes have failed to live up to the claims of their theories, the French must remain between East and West. "One cannot be anticommunist, one cannot be communist." (*HT* xvii) Inside France itself, the political situation is no less equivocal. For although the Socialists and Communists together constitute more than 50 percent of the electorate, they refuse to join in a coalition which is the only hope of a "third way" in French politics. (*HT* xl ff.) The Socialists, of course, explicitly refuse to cooperate with the Communists. But the Communists themselves have been less than honest on the matter.[10]

This double equivocation led Merleau-Ponty to adopt a three-point political platform which, while attempting to walk "between East and West," was also designed to counter what he regarded as an hysterical form of anticommunism. First, every critique of the U.S.S.R. must be carried out in context and is legitimate only insofar as it is combined with a critique of the democracies. Second, a preventive war against the U.S.S.R. is to be excluded as a possibility inasmuch as the logic of the Communist system does not lead to war (as, for example, that of the Fascist system in Germany did). And finally, it is well to remember that we are not in a state of war with Russia; she has not committed aggression, and until she does, the choice in the West is not between war with Russia and submission to her. (*HT* 196-202)

It is not surprising in the light of both Merleau-Ponty's overriding concern to understand what he spoke about and the political situation in France in 1946-47 that his opponents interpreted his contextual critique as a justification of the Communist system in Russia and failed altogether to see that his primary concern was to offer a "politics of mediation."

The Viability of Proletarian Humanism

Merleau-Ponty's analysis of communism begins with a discussion of Arthur Koestler's *Darkness at Noon*.[11] The thesis of Koestler's novel turns on the distinction he makes elsewhere between the yogi and the commissar.[12] The yogi is the man of spiritual discipline who believes in the absoluteness of inner truth and the ability of the individual to attain it. The means are infinitely important, for the wrong means vitiate the end. The yogi lives in the vertical dimension of feeling and his relation to the world is Man-Universe. The commissar is a revolutionary who believes that the universe is a machine and that a proletarian revolution effecting a reorganization of the system of production and distribution will bring the requirements of the machine and the requirements of history into line with one another. He lives in the horizontal dimension of action and his relation to the world is Man-Society. Koestler believes our history represents an oscillation between this wholly "inner" man and his opposite, the "outer" man, but that we have never succeeded in achieving any real synthesis between the two.[13] Revolution ends in reform or reaction; in either case the revolution loses its momentum before it arrives at its utopian goal. Saintliness leads to nonresistance which ends in murder as, for example, in India where Gandhi advocated nonresistance to the Japanese, thus accepting the death of a few million Indians as the means for maintaining India's moral integrity.

Rubashov in *Darkness at Noon* is the prototype of the commissar who comes to experience life as a yogi but fails to find a synthesis between the two.[14] As a participant in the Revolution, Rubashov believes he is part of an infallible Party which is moving in the direction of History.[15] As an individual, he is therefore unimportant and is perfectly willing to abandon the notion of an "I," [16] as well as his companions in the Party and even his lover, when they come between his attachment to them and his attachment to the Party. But finally Rubashov himself is arrested as an enemy of the Party. He comes to participate in the humanity of men like those he had formerly helped exterminate. He is led through this experience to question the premises on which his actions in the past have been based,[17] and to bring to consciousness the conviction he has long felt, that the masses are no longer behind the Party as they once had been.[18] However, Rubashov never reconciles these two halves of himself. For he does not side with those in jail; indeed, he accepts his past, regarding his confession as a last best service to the Party [19] and suggesting that he would follow the same course of action again even knowing that Number One, who is having him put to death, would be placed in power.[20] In order thus to remain consistent to the end despite his misgivings, Rubashov falls back on the Revolutionary view of History in which he has always believed: "History put me where I stood; ...if I was right, I have nothing to repent of; if wrong, I will pay." [21]

After recounting the central theses of Koestler's novel (*HT*

3-15), Merleau-Ponty argues that it is Koestler, not Marx, who says that history is a clock. Once this thesis is accepted then of course the alternatives of revolt (commissar) or passivity (yogi) are applicable. But if one questions this thesis in the name of Marxism, then Koestler's analysis is non-Marxist and the alternatives he puts forward nonhistorical. We are not caught between either accepting an inevitable movement or revolting against it. Our historical situation is such that we both have an intimation of the direction of things and must act without certainty that our intimations correspond to reality. We are not impotent but neither are we Prometheus. And Marx recognized this. He did not view history as an inevitable movement of events but rather as the milieu in which values are realized; and he viewed his involvement in history as the necessary condition for achieving an intersubjective or inter-human truth. (*HT* 15-26) But if Koestler's analysis of Marx's view of history is deficient, how are the confessions of the Moscow trials to be understood? And behind this lies a more fundamental question: even if Koestler's analysis of Marx is wrong, does not his analysis apply to what Merleau-Ponty had himself referred to as "orthodox Marxism"? And if so, how is one to make a legitimate distinction between Marx and ortho-dox Marxism? In order to answer these questions, Merleau-Ponty focuses his attention on the Moscow trials of 1937-38 which had always disquieted him,[22] and on the official reports of which Koestler's novel was based.[23]

According to Merleau-Ponty, one can understand the Mos-cow trials only by divorcing them from Western notions of jurisprudence. They are not based on past (criminal) facts and objective justice, but on present (political) facts and therefore a subjective justice. For while past acts can be justified in the present, present actions can be justified only in the future.[24] The trials are thus revolutionary trials presented in the guise of ordinary trials. (*HT* 31) Since the future is the criterion of justice, the revolutionary judge is not interested in the motives and intentions of the accused but only in whether or not the results of his activity, viewed in terms of the direction which the revolution actually took, is or is not revolutionary. This means further that guilt and condemnation concern only the historical role of the accused, *not* his personal character. The trial against Bukharin becomes intelligible in this context. On the one hand, he admits his objective guilt (i.e., his political responsibility). On the other, he defends the (subjective) innocence of his intentions.[25]

But how could Bukharin hold both these attitudes together? Merleau-Ponty answers this question by focusing on the historical background out of which Bukharin spoke. During the early years of the Bolshevik regime the pressure of foreign military forces on Russian borders as well as the internal breakdown of the economy brought about the adoption of various policies to meet the situation. All these policies were based on interparty discussion. Some (for example, the early attempt at collectivization) had to be abandoned. Others, as Lenin's NEP, achieved provisional success. But no firm direction was established until Stalin gained complete control in 1928, after which time any viewpoint not in line with official policy was branded "deviationist." Many of the older Party members, however, continued to express their disagreement with Party policy. When, in 1938, Bukharin admits his "objective" guilt, the meaning of this admission can only be that his opposition in 1928, after the Party had adopted a definite policy, was treasonable, since such opposition had the effect of undermining the regime and therefore of selling out the Bolsheviks to their enemies. The truth is that the discussion allowed in 1919 when the Party was attempting to find a policy which would meet the crisis in Russia was disallowed in 1928 after the *Party itself* had initiated a policy. What benefited the Party in 1919 acted to its disadvantage after 1928; hence from the vantage point of 1938 (i.e., the future) Bukharin was a traitor from the beginning: he engaged in actions in 1919 which after 1928 became treasonable; *ergo*, he was a traitor in 1919 also! (*HT* 48-65)

The situation then is not as Koestler paints it, namely, the alternation between the yogi who forgets that his life is realized outside himself and the commissar who is ready to avow anything at all. Psychologically this explanation is untenable. The real situation is that Bukharin capitulated because he saw that history had proven him wrong. And the tragedy of this situation is the fact that *the same man* cannot realize his (subjective) intentions in his political actions. He is not for himself what he is for others. "The division is no longer between man and the world, but between man and himself. This is the whole secret of the confessions at Moscow."[26] From the point of view of the Communist regime, the tragedy is that political "crimes" were treated as violations of the common law, which is only a short step from institutionalizing violence. (*HT* 36-37)

One need not go to the Moscow trials in order to illustrate the predicament of political leaders who make wrong decisions. Merleau-Ponty suggests that the Laval-Pétain trials in France immediately after the war illustrate the same phenomenon. (*HT* 40 ff.) It is conceivable, for example, as Pétain in fact argued at his trial, that both Laval and Pétain were motivated by the desire to save France, not sell her out to Germany. Nevertheless, the objective result of their actions was a betrayal of France. But does their political responsibility—which is unquestionable—constitute also a criminal responsibility? It does not appear so, for they were convicted as criminals only because the Allies rather than Germany won the war. That is, their criminal responsibility rested on an accident of history. And history does not guarantee the triumph of morality. Political responsibility transcends both a morality of intentions and the category of criminal responsibility as that is understood in Western jurisprudence. Regardless of his intentions, every man is responsible for actions which affect others, and his

100 A SOCIAL PHILOSOPHY: 1945-1955

actions involve the risk that he may be wrong—so wrong in fact that he may be convicted as a "criminal." [27]

One wonders, after reading Merleau-Ponty's analysis, what the real difference between him and Koestler is. For even if Koestler's "typology" is regarded as unhistorical, the question remains as to whether or not there can be a "synthesis" between the man of thought and the man of action. Merleau-Ponty answers that there can be insofar as Marxism (in Merleau-Ponty's, not Koestler's, sense) is a viable political alternative. The question between them, then, is the extent to which Marxism is a viable political alternative.

The meaning of violence is as good a starting point as any from which to attempt an answer to this question, for it will enable us to determine whether or not Koestler's idea of the commissar is adequate to describe Marxism. To what extent is violence necessary in social life? Are there limits to the use of violence? Can one distinguish between various types of violence? Will violence ever be transcended in social life? Now Marx, Merleau-Ponty argues, recognized that, politically speaking, the alienation of man from man manifested itself as violence. Merleau-Ponty attributes to him the further conclusion that the removal of alienation will require violence against the "appropriators." [28] However, there are two limitations to the use of violence which allow Marxism to remain humanistic. First, Marxism is honest in its recognition of violence as violence, thus making more likely the creation of a politics which transcends violence. (*HT* 129) Second, violence cannot be indiscriminately employed. It is sanctioned only insofar as it aids the proletariat to achieve political power.[29]

If one looks at the *practice* of Marxism, can one say that this genuinely Marxist prescription has been followed? The answer is obviously no! In Russia all indications are that a new static society is in the making which is no longer open to the proletariat—eliminating the hope of the disappearance of classes—and in which terror is becoming institutionalized. Does this, then, vitiate the distinction between Marxism and communism (or between Marx and orthodox Marxism)? It would seem as though Merleau-Ponty should conclude that it does. But he does not reach this conclusion. Why? Because he clings to the Marxist view of the proletariat as the carrier of a universal humanism and he believes that the proletariat still exists as a universal class even though it does not manifest itself today in a genuinely Marxist politics. (*See HT* 126-27, 134, 168 ff.) In other words, he has not at this point relinquished his hope that a genuinely Marxist politics might emerge in France. But even beyond this hope, he is prepared to affirm the efficacy of his faith in proletarian humanism:

The decline of proletarian humanism is not a crucial experience which annuls the whole of Marxism. It is still valuable as a criticism of the existing world and of other humanisms. By virtue of this at least, *it cannot be surpassed.* Even if it is incapable of giving form to world history it remains strong enough to discredit the other solutions. Considered closely, Marxism is not just any hypothesis which can be replaced tomorrow by some other. It is the simple statement of those conditions without which there would be neither any humanism, in the sense of a reciprocal relation between men, nor any rationality in history. In this sense it is not a philosophy of history; it is the philosophy of history, and to give it up completely would be to strike out historical reason. [After this, all that remain are dreams or adventures.] [30]

How can one maintain this position and criticize Koestler for being "nonhistorical"? Is it not to place oneself above history to declare one's faith in a universal (and transhistorical) class and to say that nothing could happen which could shake one's faith in this class? Is this not to retreat from the concreteness of history at least as much as Koestler is accused of having done? The truth seems to be that Merleau-Ponty was following his own best insights in emphasizing the contingency of history and in making Marx conform to this view of things, but that in the manner in which he accepted the proletariat he was following Marx; however, this double affirmation of contingency and of the proletariat as a carrier of universal meaning involved an equivocation.[31] Merleau-Ponty did not perceive this equivocation because he believed that Marxism, quite apart from communism, was still a viable political alternative in France and perhaps in the world as well. When this alternative was recognized as no longer a historical possibility, his only recourse was to see whether or not the basis of the contradictions within communism could be found in Marx himself. And this is precisely what he did.

The Critics and the Issues

Merleau-Ponty's articles on Koestler, the Moscow trials, and classical Marxism in relation to existing communist governments raised a storm of protest from the political right as well as some disagreement from the political left.[32] Many of his Western-oriented (i.e., conservative) critics were apparently motivated by the fear of a communist take-over in France in 1947.[33] They believed Merleau-Ponty was encouraging such an outcome; hence he was accused of being "pro-Russian," "pro-Soviet", an admirer of the Russian regime, and finally even "pro-Stalin"![34] The charge took various forms. Many read Merleau-Ponty's analysis of the Moscow trials as a justification of them and of the State conducting them.[35] Others pushed this line of reasoning further by contending that Merleau-Ponty confused Russian state capitalism with socialism and was thus led to the conclusion that "whatever is is right." [36] Many of these conclusions indicate a fundamental misreading of Merleau-Ponty's articles. It is evident, for example, that he was not trying to "justify' the state which brought Bukharin and others to trial, but only to understand the confessions made by these men in a way which would be psychologically more convincing than the explanation Koestler had adduced. His critics might have rejoined that his "subjective intention" might have been to "understand" but that the "objective result" of his essays in the revolutionary (or at least unstable) atmosphere of postwar France was to encourage and materially to assist a communist take-over of the government. This may or may not have been true; I doubt that it was. But such criticisms are intelligible only in relation to the atmosphere which produced them. Merleau-Ponty apparently failed to see the connection, remarking that he found "not the least trace of lucidity" in his critics' replies.

There were more doctrinaire replies from both the right and the left. Disputing his analysis of the Laval-Pétain trials, one prominent Marxist writer responded that it was not the concrete comprehension of the immediate historical situation which was important, but rather "the objective content and the real direction of history" which determines guilt and innocence.[37] Laval and Pétain went against the (inevitable) direction of history; therefore they were guilty. One writer on the right devoted an entire book to the question of a "morality of intentions" as opposed to a "morality of responsibility," concluding that a morality of intentions is the surest foundation of politics and that Merleau-Ponty's notion of political responsibility, reducing everything to uncertainty as it does, confuses the body politic.[38] Merleau-Ponty was convinced by the tendency of doctrinaire critics from the right to reduce social responsibility to individual responsibility and by the tendency of those on the left to reduce individual responsibility to social necessity that his own position was alone *historical* and that his analyses represented a middle position between the extreme ideological frameworks characteristic of thinking in both East and West.

One may grant that this was true, though one cannot conclude from this concession that Merleau-Ponty was not ideologically oriented. I have shown that he was, and I believe his best critics sensed this, though it is fair to say that none of them stated the criticism explicitly in this way. It is also fair to say, however, that, even had they done so, it is doubtful that Merleau-Ponty would have found them any more lucid, since he had stated his Marxism in such a way as to place it above criticism and to make any rejoinder to it "propaganda."

The real meaning of these debates in the context of the time is that few people believed a "middle position" actually did represent a viable political alternative in postwar France. For Merleau-Ponty's critics the alternatives were either a return to normal or a complete break with the past—extremes of thought perhaps congenial to French political life! And the critics were right. Merleau-Ponty's position did turn out to be unhistorical. But there is a certain pathos in this. For one certainly cannot say, in the face of the instability and ineptness of the French government during these years and of the equal ineptness of the radical opposition parties, that the alternative which won out was really "viable."

Interlude: France 1948-1955

The failure of the strikes in December, 1947, followed by the split in the working class movement, coincided with the decline of de Gaulle's popularity after the municipal elections of October. The forces for radical change had breathed their last. Neither the extreme left nor the extreme right could muster a majority. Consequently in 1948 France settled down under third force rule. The internal divisions of the French political parties were now based more on factors relating to the international situation. The Marshall Plan had the effect of drawing France closer to the West. Russia responded by organizing the Cominform in October, 1947, and by drawing the nations of Eastern Europe into her orbit of influence in 1948-49. Domestic politics in France tended to reflect this growing polarization of East and West. When the Communist-led C. G. T. organized a second massive strike in October-November, 1948, it was once again crushed by government action, further crippling the political influence of the

Communist Party—even driving it into a peripheral corner of French politics. The government took the offensive early in 1949 by encouraging a libel suit against *Lettres Françaises,* a Communist weekly, which had attacked a book by a defector from Russia, hoping to exploit the trial for propaganda purposes.[39] The Communists responded, in the person of their elder statesman Maurice Thorez, by announcing that French Communists would never take up arms against Russia and by holding a peace rally in April, 1949, for which Picasso painted his famous Dove of Peace.[40]

In the wake of this hardening of positions, the noncommunist left attempted to develop a new alternative through the creation of the R. D. R. (Rassemblement Démocratique Révolutionnaire). Both Sartre and Merleau-Ponty were founding members, though neither assumed a directing role, and both disavowed the enterprise in June, 1949. The group was based on a critique of a Stalinist type of communism, as well as of right-wing anticommunism.[41] It failed both respects. Its anticommunism was exploited by the mounting anticommunist sentiment in France. And its qualified support of communist programs was disavowed by the Communist Party. The middle group which it hoped to attract failed to materialize. Most of its initiators drifted either toward the Communist Party or toward the right.

Both Merleau-Ponty and Sartre were caught between their desire for a third force and the growing alienation of political groups from one another. And when, after a period of silence, each perceived that it was once again possible to speak, they spoke in different ways. The decisive turning point for Merleau-Ponty came in June, 1950, with the outbreak of the Korean War. The official Western reaction was that Russia had ordered the trigger to be pulled, though this cannot be proved. Merleau-Ponty took the view that, even if Russia had not ordered the shooting, she could nevertheless have prevented it, or stopped it very quickly. But she failed to do so. As a result, the United States was rearming. The idea of a third force seemed infinitely remote. More and more the world resembled two huge power-blocs, justifying themselves by discrediting their enemies, waiting to pounce on one another. Merleau-Ponty saw no chance of mediation in such a situation and therefore ceased to write about politics, forcing his silence on *Les Temps Modernes* (of which he was political editor) for two years.[42] The effect of this event emerged only gradually and only in relation to what happened during this same period to Sartre and to the Communist Party.

Sartre accepted Merleau-Ponty's silence in 1950. He was convinced (though he had no evidence until later) that the West had done much to provoke the conflict in Korea. However, in the absence of immediate clarification of his suspicions, silence was the wisest course. Between 1950 and 1952 he came to the conclusion that the West was primarily responsible for that war, but his break with the West came in relation to another event altogether. On May 28, 1952, the Communists ended a long period of silence with a demonstration. The occasion was General Ridgeway's arrival as commander of NATO to replace General Eisenhower. The demonstration turned into a riot which was brutally suppressed by the police. There had been indications several days before that the police were preparing for some kind of showdown with the Communists (as, for example, the arrest of the editor of *L'Humanité*). At the demonstration itself Jacques Duclos (along with Maurice Thorez, the principal leader of the Communist Party and a member of the French parliament) was arrested. The indictment stated that he had been caught "red-handed" at the riots with a loaded pistol, a truncheon, a wireless transmitter, and two carrier pigeons in his car. As it turned out the pistol and truncheon belonged to the driver of the car who was Duclos' bodyguard; the wireless "transmitter" was an ordinary receiving set; and the pigeons were common ones—and dead at that! Moreover, it became known later that

Duclos had been arrested half an hour after the rioting had stopped, not during the rioting. Clearly he had been framed by the police, and although he possessed immunity as a member of parliament (this was voted away later), he was locked up in the Santé Prison and charged with conspiracy. The Communists organized a second demonstration for June 4 to protest Duclos's arrest. Despite the skepticism about the whole affair, particularly the "carrier pigeons," part of the French press (*Figaro*, *France-Soir*, and *Paris-Presse*) proceeded to drum up a tremendous anticommunist scare, perhaps partly because of the second demonstration. About the effect of this episode on his life, Sartre wrote:

I left for Italy; it was spring. The Italian papers informed me of the arrest of Duclos, of the theft of his notebook, [and] the farce of the carrier pigeons. This sordid childishness infuriated me. ... The last connections were broken, my vision was transformed: an anticommunist is a dog; I do not budge from that position, and I shall never budge from it. One will find me very naive and, in fact, I had seen other such incidents without having gotten so excited. But after ten years of meditation, I had reached the point of rupture and needed only a catalyst. In the language of the church, this was a conversion. Merleau had himself been converted—in 1950. We were both conditioned but in an inverse sense. Slowly accumulated, our disgusts were in an instant to discover in one case the horror of Stalinism, in the other that of one's own class. In the name of principles that it had inculcated in me, in the name of its humanism and of its "humanities", in the name of freedom, equality, fraternity, I vowed to the bourgeoisie a hatred which will end only with my death. When I returned to Paris hastily, I had to write or suffocate. I wrote, day and night, the first part of "Les Communistes et la Paix".[43]

The isolation of the Communist Party in France brought about a shift in its attitude toward sympathetic intellectuals. In the years immediately following the war the Communists had been happy to have sympathizers, which is the reason they met Merleau-Ponty's *Humanisme et terreur* with virtual silence, even though what he said was not entirely favorable to them. However, as the Party was isolated from the rest of French political life, it began to demand of its followers (and sympathizers) a whole-hearted allegiance. Merleau-Ponty realized that no third force in French politics would be able to count on the Communists. And inasmuch as Sartre, after 1952, cast his lot with the Party (albeit in his own terms), Merleau-Ponty and Sartre drifted apart. In 1953 Merleau-Ponty ended his eight-year association with *Les Temps Modernes*.

The reason Merleau-Ponty, from this time forward, did not simply abandon political writing is explained by other factors. The death of Stalin had produced a "new look" in Russia; the conclusion of peace in Korea at last made it seem as if war might not be inevitable (in the thinking of the giant powers); and the new atomic stalemate promised at least to ensure a "balance of terror." Within France itself, Mendès-France, a Fourth Republic politician with a real program, began to win support. (See S 434, tr. 349) He failed by thirteen votes in 1953 to win the absolute majority necessary for the formation of a new government. Almost coincidental with his defeat, *L'Express*, a weekly newspaper with the avowed aim of creating a platform for a left-wing noncommunist third force, appeared in Paris. It immediately threw its support to Mendès-France, and when he became premier in June, 1954 (to February, 1955), and again in January, 1956 (to May, 1956), the paper backed his domestic policy of economic reform (which brought about his defeat in 1955) and his foreign policy based on Atlantic unity.[44] In September, 1954, *L'Express* announced that it was inviting specialists in various fields to answer questions from readers. Merleau-Ponty was one of these. *L'Express* thus became a medium through which he once again found a voice in politics. After 1955, however, his articles tapered off. For in April of that year *Les Aventures de la dialectique* was published; in it he settled his accounts with political movements and turned his attention to the broader aspects of social philosophy. A description of the political analyses in that book will disclose Merleau-Ponty's final rejection of Marxism as well as of Sartrian existentialism.

Proletarian Humanism Reconsidered

The question with which Merleau-Ponty had been left after his critique of contemporary communism was whether or not the contradictions one could discover in it were traceable to classical Marxian humanism (which he was still inclined to defend). He attempts to answer that question through a consideration of two Marxists whose lives mirrored the discrepancy by which he was disturbed—Leon Trotsky and Georg Lukacs.

Trotsky's revolutionary career falls into two distinct periods: his participation in the Revolution and his exile from Russia.[45] Merleau-Ponty characterizes his revolutionary period as reflecting the attributes of "classical Marxism": the togetherness of truth and action in the carrying out of the Revolution itself, the proletariat as the means for realizing a new humanity, the limitations of violence to the acts which serve that end. But once the Bolshevik regime was consolidated, Trotsky's "classical Marxism" led him into equivocating positions. The turning point was the death of Lenin which brought on a struggle for power. Trotsky, however, refused to engage in that struggle. At the same time, he refused to acquiesce in actions initiated by the Party which he considered abortive. He therefore chose a third alternative—that of "classical Marxism"—namely, the creation of a *critical* group within the Party which would help it to maintain a revolutionary direction. The result was that Trotsky was removed from effective leadership altogether. He consented to this on the ground that a better future would present more favorable opportunities for rekindling the genuine revolutionary flame, although this was a rationalization which contradicted his genuine Marxism.

What lay behind Trotskys' failure to perceive accurately the situation in which he was involved? It was, Merleau-Ponty believes, the fact that Trotsky transferred a "revolutionary mentality" to the situation of an "established mentality." In the former, truth is something always in the process of being understood; in the latter, truth is something given—present in the revolutionary regime. Trotsky tried to maintain the tension between truth and action through a critical group within the Party; he attempted to maintain the Revolution in a situation in which the Revolution was effectively *finished*.

This equivocation in Trotsky continued after his exile from Russia. On the one hand, he never failed to defend Russia against Western criticisms (S 318-28, tr. 253-60) and, in this regard, would never admit that the Party had betrayed the Revolution. He would only say that it now represented the dictatorship of the proletariat in a "disfigured" form. (AD 113, n. 1) On the other hand, he tried to maintain a critical attitude toward the regime, as in his rejection of the Moscow trials and the "confessions" elicited there. (HT 96)

Thus far Merleau-Ponty's two accounts of Trotsky agree—the one written in 1947 (HT) and the other written in 1955 (AD). But the later account goes further, arguing that if the equivocation noted above is present in Trotsky—who above all others attempted to retain the "revolutionary mentality"—then *it must also be in Marx himself*. Merleau-Ponty argues that if the younger Marx emphasized "alienation" or the *negation* of the existing order by the proletariat, the later Marx emphasized "exploitation" as a scientific principle the analysis of which would yield the *positive outcome* of the negation. In other words, he moved from humanism to "scientific socialism," from the view that the revolution is something to be seized to the view that the revolution is something already present in the nature of things, from the view that men act to the view that things are manipulated. And when this shift takes place a situation develops in which any action is permissible, since any obstacle which gets in the way of the successful manipulation of things may be removed. Moreover, the initiating action of men becomes insignificant, so that the role of the proletariat is no longer that of informing the leaders. A reduction takes place in which the proletariat *is* the revolution, the Party *is* the proletariat, the chiefs *are* the Party.

The equivocation present in Marx and embodied in Trotsky therefore finds its way into the revolutionary regime. The only conclusion we can draw, Merleau-Ponty argues, is that "revolutions are true as movements and false as regimes." (*AD* 279; cf. 281, 293) And, he adds, "This difficulty is not only that of Bolshevism, but that of every Marxist organization, perhaps that of every revolutionary organization." (*AD* 123) He might have added that it is the difficulty of every human institution.

The equivocations discernible in Trotsky are no less evident in Georg Lukacs, one of the most outstanding Marxist thinkers of the past generation. Lukacs began, as Trotsky had, with the belief that there is a dialectical relationship between thought and action, a belief he elaborated in *Geschichte und Klassenbewussztsein*, a book published in 1923 when he was a young man.[46] His line of reasoning is remarkable in that he followed substantially the ideas that are to be found in Marx's early philosophical works, though these treatises of Marx were not discovered and published until nine years after Lukacs' book appeared. In his book Lukacs stated that there is a kinship between men and objects inasmuch as objects, although already in the world and independent of men, are nevertheless shaped and molded by men. Men must interrogate objects in order to understand themselves. Raised to the level of history this means men must interrogate every historical situation. The task of the philosopher is to seize the meaning in the present situation. Now this is the task of the revolution also. What then is the place of the philosopher in the revolutionary movement? It is continually to place the revolution before the present situation, to maintain a *critical* attitude. Since the truth is never possessed but remains always on the doorstep of possession (*AD* 73-74), the truth must be *brought to* the proletariat. This is the task of the theoretician: to keep the revolution rooted in history through his analyses of the past and present.

Lukacs, however, could not maintain this position. In a July 1924, issue of *Pravda*, his book was subjected to a critical judgment which he accepted, so that a subsequent edition was allowed to appear only in a "corrected" form. The same thing happened to Lukacs again after the war. In 1946 he defended the thesis that there is an abiding value in art and literature apart from the fact that they may be products of a bourgeois culture. Hence Shakespeare, Goethe, and Molière might serve as models for socialist writers. In other words, literature at least remains a testimony to the fact that no man can be wholly separated from the true, that there is a human truth which transcends ideology. However, in 1949 Lukacs was forced to withdraw from this position and did so, perhaps because he realized, as Bukharin before him, that his opposition to the orthodox view was damaging to the revolution. (*AD* 92-93; *S* 328-30, tr. 261-62)

Like the old Marx, the old Lukacs denied his youth in rejecting a dialectical philosophy in favor of a naïve realism. The seeds for the justification of the present communist regime which may be found in Marx are also the seeds for the suppression of the dialectical philosophy which he had inaugurated. Thus Merleau-Ponty concludes:

It is difficult to enter into the positive and do something, while safeguarding the ambiguity of the dialectic. The objection confirms our reservations, for it boils down to saying that there is no revolution which contests itself. But it is through this program of continuous critique that the revolution is accredited. In this sense, the equivocation of communist philosophy is, greatly exaggerated, the equivocation of the revolution itself. (*AD* 99)

New Horizons

We have seen that the distinction Merleau-Ponty made in the early postwar years between Marx and communism he abolished later. But his earlier analyses did not imply the conclusions which he saw only later. We must now note the steps through which the change came about.

His questions began where we might expect: with the proletariat as the vehicle of a new (universal) humanity. In 1945 Merleau-Ponty affirmed the existence of the universal consciousness of the proletariat.[47] And in 1947 he reaffirmed this position by distinguishing the proletariat from existing communist systems.[48] However, one year later he acknowledged that the proletariat had forgotten its mission and was unaware of any universal significance its struggle might have.[49] The following year, 1949, he stated that the proletariat had failed to materialize in any universal form, which was only a short step from denying that it could do so. (S 281-82, tr. 222-23) This denial was emphatic in 1955, as we have seen. And in his last statement bearing on politics (1960), he declared that the proletariat as a universal class no longer existed in international politics. (S 19-21, tr. 12-13)

The gradual emergence of this conclusion brought Merleau-Ponty back down to earth, so to speak. He realized that his earlier position of justifying Marxism beyond any of its historical forms had been a supratemporal or nonhistorical type of thinking.[50] I have noted earlier that the equivocation which Merleau-Ponty identified in 1955 as belonging to all forms of Marxism he recognized as present in existing communist states even in 1947. Why, then, did he not conclude earlier that the contradictions within existing communist regimes belong to theoretical Marxism as well? The answer, I think, lies in the change in historical situations. In 1947 he believed that Marxism was a political possibility in France. However, he was wrong, and subsequent events began to make this evident. He soon found himself advocating as a historical option what belonged only to thought. His awareness of this predicament became greater and greater after 1947, and resulted in a rejection of Marxism which reached its final form in 1955.

This reversal of his earlier position led Merleau-Ponty to a reassessment of the political situation both inside and outside France.[51] With respect to revolution he noted that, as was the case in Russia, today the nations obsessed by a revolutionary fever are the most backward or underdeveloped nations. This, he believed, was no accident, since a revolutionary creed gave these peoples the fervor they needed to develop rapidly. However, unlike Russia, the underdeveloped nations today cannot avoid the power struggle between East and West, and revolutionary creeds play into this struggle. Merleau-Ponty believed, however, that an alternative was available. He based this belief on a reassessment of France's political position. If a contagion for revolution exists only in the backward nations and not in the established ones, then there is no reason why an avant-garde in any of the advanced nations should be revolutionary in the communist sense. A genuine revolutionary is one who faces his own situation critically (not one who calls attention to troubles thosuands of miles away, or concentrates only on the troubles of others). It follows that there is no reason why a revolutionary in our time should mean one who believes in overturning all existing institutions.[52] In fact, some type of parliamentary framework is necessary inasmuch as we cannot afford to sacrifice *freedom* any more than we can afford to sacrifice order. (S 397-401, tr. 319-22) A revolutionary outlook is possible today within a parliamentary framework because the question now is not so much one of the mode of appropriation, as it was for Marx, but rather one of social control. We have learned that the dynamics of a society are more decisive than its form.[53]

This reassessment of the notion of revolution, both inside

and outside France, led Merleau-Ponty to draw several conclusions. First, it is possible within the existing framework for France effectively to meet her social problems *if* she will face them squarely. The breakdown of ideology should aid in this process. For example, if the idea of revolution in Russia has been altered from that of seizing the present to that of waiting for the future to work itself out, then the realization of the revolution can be put off indefinitely, and the problem of coexistence is, in principle, solved. A genuine solution to this problem would require disarmament, which should become possible once coexistence is accepted in principle by all the powers concerned. Disarmament would remove a great expenditure from the budget of every Western government and perhaps force each of them to face the social problems which they can mask as long as they can use the excuse that all their resources are needed for armaments. Finally, Merleau-Ponty believed that, in order to keep the former colonial nations out of the East-West struggle as much as possible, France should take the lead in helping its former colonies achieve a modern technological society.[54]

In all the changes in Merleau-Ponty's political thinking there is one constant: the effort to define the place of *France* in the modern world. In a real sense he embodies the struggles—and failures—of his nation.

The shift away from Marxism which I have just described had not only a historical and political significance in Merleau-Ponty's development. It had also—even primarily—a philosophical meaning. For his rejection of Marxism involved also his rejection of Sartrian existentialism, as we shall now see.

V

Merleau-Ponty and Sartrian Existentialism— Political and Philosophical

We are condemned to freedom.
        Jean-Paul Sartre
	We are condemned to meaning.
	        Merleau-Ponty

Hell is other people.
        Jean-Paul Sartre
	History is other people.
	        Merleau-Ponty

Acquaintance and Independent Study: 1927-1940

We have already had occasion to see similar concerns in Sartre and Merleau-Ponty with respect to phenomenological method, the body-subject, and the relation between perception and imagination. There was at the same time, however, a personal relationship between the two which became involved in their philosophical relationship. That story adds a significant chapter to the development of Merleau-Ponty's social philosophy.

Their friendship dated from student days. Sartre attended the Ecole Normale Supérieur from 1924 to 1928. Merleau-Ponty entered the Ecole in 1927. They became known to each other one day when Merleau-Ponty and a friend found the songs of their classmates "too vulgar" for their tastes and hissed at them. The other students became angry and were about to unleash themselves on the two dissenters when Sartre intervened and was able to settle the affair without "loss of face" to anyone. (See *SNS* 83, tr. 41)

When Sartre left the Ecole he served in the army and then began to teach in a *lycée*. Merleau-Ponty followed the same pattern after completing his studies in 1931. Both, as has been mentioned, were dissatisfied with the rationalism of their professors of philosophy and found in phenomenology the hope of a new direction in French philosophy.[1] However, they worked independently until World War II brought them together once again in Paris.

Collaboration: 1941-1952

In 1941 Sartre and Merleau-Ponty joined the same Resistance group, "Socialisme et Liberté," which, however, disbanded after one year for lack of knowing what to do or how to do it. But the occasion was enough to initiate conversations between the two, and these lasted for the duration of the war. Sartre's description of their relationship during this period, which he calls the purest of their friendship, is interesting with respect to the differences it reveals between the two men. Merleau-Ponty was always concerned that their opinions not be represented as without differences, that the multiplicity of perspectives be respected. Sartre, on the other hand, wanted to hammer out a common doctrine on every issue, believing that in all disputes one must either convert the other or be converted by him.[2] Sartre thus confirms what we know also from other texts by the two men, that he was polemical by nature, Merleau-Ponty irenic; that he always attacked an issue head-on, while Merleau-Ponty sought to bring opposing views into dialogue and genuine confrontation with one another.[3] There was a curious reversal of these roles at one point in the life of each—their personal friendship—as we are about to see.

The two men resolved to publish a journal together after the war; *Les Temps Modernes* made its first appearance in October, 1945. Merleau-Ponty was co-editor and in charge of political writing for the journal, but he consistently refused to allow his name to appear on the cover with Sartre's. Sartre professed never to have understood why,[4] though it is probably true that when the break between the two finally came this made it easier and helped to preserve a relatively cordial relationship between them.[5]

"Existentialism" became a rallying point for a pervasively revolutionary attitude among the young in postwar France, and Sartre was its acknowledged leader. Traditionalists deplored his advocacy of "radical freedom" to the young, while Marxists saw in existentialism a diversion from the real revolutionary task ahead. Sartre encouraged this movement in some of his more popular essays by attempting to define it,[6] by attacking the traditionalists (and particularly the writers among them) for their class orientation which he believed went counter to the best interests of the nation,[7] and by reproaching the Marxists for being afraid of freedom and attempting to hide from it in discipline.[8] It was Merleau-Ponty's task to bring Sartre and his critics into dialogue with one another. And though he wrote as a "friend" of Sartre, the differences as well as the agreements between the two men stand out clearly.

In 1943 Merleau-Ponty wrote a review of Sartre's play *The Flies*, describing Sartre's view of freedom—which he accused Sartre's critics of never having understood—as one which charted a middle course between indifference and the fatality of traditions, that is, as involving us in contingency.

Freedom is against nature, it puts back into question the forces in man which tend toward rest, it separates him violently from the world where all things move toward their end: the plant towards the form of the plant. ... All creation is against Orestes.
... innocence and the grace of nature are impossible in man. If he is not free, he will be the slave of the passions and of remorse. It is therefore necessary to will man free. The choice is between this difficult life and the peace of the tombs.[9]

Sartre's emphasis on the hostility of life led his critics to accuse him of concentrating on the horrible.[10] Merleau-Ponty responded that there is today a discordance between the interior and the exterior, and that if they are joined together once again it will not be through harmony or beauty as in Romantic Art but rather through "the violence of the sublime."[11] Neither Marxists nor Christians, he remarked, are willing to call man the "combination of angel and animal" (SNS 87, tr. 43), as Pascal had done. However, Merleau-Ponty concluded, Sartre does not speak *only* of violence. *No Exit*, for example, implies that if "hell is other people," then others are also the instruments of our salvation.[12] And furthermore, in his personal life Sartre has remained open to all kinds of people and has refused noncritical followers. (SNS 83-84, tr. 41) In other words, neither his writings nor his character indicate a preference for the horrible. Sartre's critics, rather than attacking him, should try to describe better than he does the human situation in which we live.

This is precisely what Merleau-Ponty attempts to do, for he believes Sartre's view of freedom in *Being and Nothingness* is too antithetical. The antithesis of my view of myself and the view of others of me, as well as the antithesis of the for-itself and the in-itself, often gives the impression that these are alternatives rather than living relations in communication with one another.[13] The source of the divergence between Sartre and Merleau-Ponty to which this critique points must now be examined.

In *Being and Nothingness* Sartre designates two kinds of being. On the one side there is "being in-itself," that which simply is, identical with itself. On the other side there is "being for-itself," a "hole" in being, or a decompression of the in-itself through which the latter is transcended. It is true to say at once that being in-itself could exist without being for-itself and that no meaning exists apart from that created by the for-itself. Only the for-itself acts, and if there is to be a "world" in any meaningful sense, it can only *be* through the constitution of the for-itself. This means that one cannot speak of a genuine reciprocal influence between the in-itself and the for-itself; it is always the for-itself which acts, and it alone acts.[14] There is an absoluteness of freedom which leads to three consequences. First, time is riveted in the *present*. Not only does consciousness create a world *ex nihilo*, but also *de novo*, since the situation never prescribes what the creation will or can be. Hence freedom loses its temporal thickness.[15] Second, choice is always fixed in *the individual* who creates *his own* world, so that there is no necessary correlation between the world I create and the world the other creates. Indeed, as we have seen before, the fundamental human experience for Sartre is alienation. And this means, finally, that "bad faith" or "inauthentic existence" is unavoidable in social relationships. Man is not a social animal, but a subjective animal who desires to be social—he is a useless passion!

In his early postwar essays on existentialism Sartre emphasizes the fact that one's freedom involves the freedom of others also,[16] an emphasis which stands in sharp contrast to the assertions of absolute freedom in *Being and Nothingness*. The historical reason for this shift may have been a new spirit of hope after the war. But philosophically what one observes is a contradiction between Sartre's phenomenological descriptions and his ontological superstructure.[17] Whereas in his earlier phenomenological descriptions consciousness emerges only in relation to a world already there, in his ontology the for-itself completely constitutes the world. Whether or not Sartre's phenomenology required the ontology he finally imposed upon it is beside the relevant point here, namely, that this dualism has persisted in Sartre without an adequate methodological resolution. It was for this reason that Merleau-Ponty found Sartre's existentialism an inadequate model for a social philosophy.[18]

Verbal Warfare: Ideology and the End of
Ideology—1952-1955

During the years of their collaboration Merleau-Ponty emphasized the points of agreement between himself and Sartre
and stated points of disagreement only in general terms, never
sharply. As late as 1952 Merleau-Ponty dedicated a long article in *Les Temps Modernes*—as it turned out, his last in that
journal—to Sartre.[19] But by this time Merleau-Ponty had turned
away from Marxism, and Sartre had rejected Western liberalism completely. During 1952 and 1953 Sartre's version of
Marxism was for the first time expounded at length as a result
of the "conversion" he experienced in 1952.[20] His articles
became the occasion for a debate with Claude Lefort, another writer for the journal.[21] Merleau-Ponty had the difficult
assignment of editing their articles and was responsible for
the removal of some harsh words from the essays of each.
Discussions which these essays called forth revealed basic
differences in the "style of life," as Sartre put it, between
Sartre and Merleau-Ponty. It is not surprising that the actual
severance of their collaboration resulted from an incident
reflecting their respective attitudes toward Marxism. At the
request of a Marxist, Sartre wrote an article on the contradictions of capitalism. Shortly afterwards, he left Paris on a
previously planned trip. According to the established policy
of the journal, Merleau-Ponty read the article. He attached a
preface to it, suggesting that Sartre should speak also of the
contradiction within socialism and intimating that this might
follow in another article. When Sartre returned he read Merleau-Ponty's preface and, unable to reach him since he in
turn had left Paris, Sartre removed the preface in a "light
state of rage" as he says. The article was published without it.
When Merleau-Ponty saw the published article without his
preface, he immediately telephoned Sartre and resigned. It
was fortunate, Sartre concludes in his account of this incident,

that such an event as this (as idiotic as it was) intervened and terminated an intolerable situation. The journal could not have continued under a joint direction in which the two principal editors no longer saw things the same way.[22]

Three years after their break, Merleau-Ponty attacked at length the position taken by Sartre in his articles. In order to understand the significance of Merleau-Ponty's critique we must first be clear about the nature and extent of Sartre's "adhesion" to Marxism.[23] His first article attempts to state the necessity of such adhesion by considering the relationship in contemporary France between the proletariat and the Communist Party on the one side and the proletariat and the government on the other.

It is impossible, Sartre argues, to separate the Communist Party from the proletariat, because the Party engages in *political* action while the unions, in driving for higher wages, never get to the heart of the matter—exploitation. Without the Party, therefore, the proletariat has no historical mission. In not adhering to the Party the noncommunist left denies the proletariat.[24] The government actively denies the proletariat its rights by concealing its suppression but nevertheless assuring its effectiveness through identifying the Communist Party with Russia, gerrymandering election districts to the disadvantage of the proletariat, and, while claiming communist violence to be illegal, using illegal violence to suppress the communists.[25] In his second article Sartre goes even further, suggesting that the government *provoked* the violence, both to bolster the prestige of an unpopular administration and to repress disapproval of the Atlantic Pact.[26] He also suggests what will become an important theme in the third article, namely, that the government's action is a deliberate and planned effort to break the political will of the proletariat, and that this political repression is integrally related to the economic oppression of the workers.

The police succeeded in breaking up the demonstrations of

May 28 and June 4, 1952, Sartre concludes his initial article, both because the workers were not acting in unison and because they were not thinking in terms of political action. In former generations, workers believed they would live to see the "general strike"; now they no longer believe they will. While formerly they trusted the efficacy of economic action (i.e., strikes of small or independent groups of workers), they see now its ineffectiveness. But instead of grouping themselves for a new kind of action (political action), they despair. Against united political force the only answer is united political force. The workers can transcend their "situation" only through united political action directed by the Communist Party, for only through the Party can sufficient discipline be enforced to insure effectiveness of concerted group action.[27]

Two comments are relevant concerning Sartre's analysis up to this point. In the first place, Sartre treats the Communist Party as an *individual*, analogous to the way in which Marx characterized "classes";[28] the workers united have one will. In the second place, through this collective individual each worker, in Sartre's view, can realize his freedom, because through the Party he can express his refusal to be what he is; he can transcend his "facticity." "Spontaneity" does not characterize the individual (rather "organization" and "discipline" characterize him) but only the Party. Sartre identifies his collective (negative) action with the Marxist notion of "practice."

In his initial reply to Sartre, Lefort attempts to establish three points, all of which seek to demonstrate a radical reductionism in Sartre. First, Lefort argues that in identifying the working class with the Party, Sartre has failed to see that there are many factors affecting class consciousness other than the Party. Moreover, he has removed the effective freedom of the worker, since his only option is to obey the Party. It was precisely these factors which led to bureaucratization in the Stalinist phase of Russian communism; the workers were removed from effective participation in the Party and government and were forced into obedience.[29] Second, the proletariat cannot be wholly defined by alienation. The workers also participate in society, since they are producers. The natural processes are therefore more important in Marxist analyses than Sartre believes they are. The political factors, which are related to the negative role of the workers in capitalist society, cannot be isolated from the economic ones. The worker acts *and* participates. Third, Sartre has reduced all relationships to a dichotomy between stark individuality and organized totality. He has, in other words, attempted to see the situation in terms of the ontology in *Being and Nothingness*. However, one need not choose between these alternatives. The class is a social organism preceding the Party and constituting the context in which the Party operates. This points again to the inseparability of economic and political factors.[30]

Sartre's reply to Lefort is only partly on philosophical grounds. He accuses Lefort of having represented the history of the proletariat as a necessary development with the following characteristics: the bourgeoisie produces the proletariat, the proletariat produces the "Stalinist" apparatus, Stalinism is the death of the proletariat. Lefort could have had only one reason for doing this: to justify his own failure to participate in the class struggle, to take himself out of history. He is a bourgeois and wishes to remain one! [31]

Sartre's second point is more relevant to the issue dividing him from Lefort. Sartre contends that the Party *is* necessary as a corollary to the class because the class is defined in society *not* by its productive role, but *only* by alienation. So "situation" does not produce a revolution: a concentration of workers does not produce class solidarity; there is no cooperation in a situation of exploitation; there is no shifting of classes due to new techniques because the division of labor continues; there is no cumulative experience of the working class —young workers today have no knowledge of the strikes of 1936 (to cite one example). The class is therefore outside history (it belongs to the in-itself). The Party (the for-itself) is its mediator, reintroducing it to history. Sartre goes further here than making the Party an individual. He makes it the transcending consciousness of the class. This transcendence is effected through the "look," i.e., the regard of the Other (the bourgeoisie) which brings forth a corresponding reaction (negation of the Other) by the Party.[32]

Lefort notes this shift from identifying the Party with the class to designating the Party a mediating force, but he contends that, far from changing anything, this only accentuates the dependence of Sartre's analysis on *Being and Nothingness*. His major critique is therefore directed this time toward Sartre's philosophy. Only if one looks at the proletariat as wholly negative, he argues, can one deny its historical unity. Sartre attempts to do this by making consciousness the determinant of everything (thereby failing to take account of social groups), and by reducing the relationship of the proletariat and the bourgeoisie to that of the "look." This, however, will not do, inasmuch as the workers do not see the owners but only intermediaries (i.e., managers).

Lefort does, however, return to political differences toward the end of his reply. One does not solve problems, he points out to Sartre, simply by saying the division of labor is wholly negative (i.e., evil). Marxism has never contended that any means of production is inherently evil. The essential thing is what men do with it. In any case, the clock is not going to move backwards. Moreover, Marxism has always involved criticism from within the Party, and Sartre removes this by making no provision for the disagreement of the proletariat with its leaders. This is the issue which personality disturbs Lefort, for it is the (Stalinist) bureaucracy which has driven him from communism. He sees critique within the Party as the only means of avoiding this. He laments the fact that Sartre has failed to say anything about it, since it is a cause of concern both among communists and among intellectuals of the noncommunist left.[33]

In his final article,[34] written over one year after his first two articles and his response to Lefort, Sartre attempts to justify three major points in his position through a politico-economic analysis of the relations between the bourgeoisie and the proletariat in France during the past one hundred years: first, that history has been created according to the requirements of the bourgeoisie; second, that the proletariat is alienated from the nation; and third, that this alienation constitutes the being of the working class in France today.

History, Sartre argues, is not a series of chances as the anti-communists would have us believe, for if one looks at the history of production in France in the twentieth century one sees a picture of organized oppression.[35] For example, production, which rose from 1913 to 1929, has remained stationary since that time, meaning that only half the population really participates in the consumption of produced goods. At the same time small shop owners have been supported through organized *under*-production (with corresponding high prices for goods) in order to prevent them from falling into the ranks of the proletariat. Small, independent owners and producers make production inefficient (and prices high), but they assure the bourgeoisie of continued support.

In this situation the proletarian workers—unlike the left-wing intellectuals—do not believe they can be integrated into the nation. Their alienation dates from 1848 and 1871—especially the latter year—when their efforts to fight the bourgeoisie ended in violent suppression. Their antagonists reacted by halting production and raising prices. The workers in turn responded with despair; abortions increased among them as they were reduced to a neo-Malthusian state. Their percentage increase over the remainder of the population diminished. The bourgeoisie further assured the slowdown of this increase by instituting a policy with farmers similar to that followed with shop owners and small producers, namely, deliberately keeping farms small through a failure to educate farmers in modern methods, and thus encouraging a tenacious individuality among farmers which worked against their common interests with the proletariat. Furthermore, the absorption of many workers into administrative posts drew them toward support of the bourgeoisie.

The alienation produced among the workers as a result of the machinations of the ruling bourgeoisie has in turn aggravated divisions within the worker movement itself. A plurality of unions, for example, has increased antagonism between less and more advanced workers and completed the process of the total alienation of the working class.[36] The internal dissensions have had the effect also of increasing apathy and passive acceptance of the situation. To transcend this state of affairs, action is necessary—concerted mass action which will force all workers to realize their common interests. Only in such action is there freedom for the proletarian, freedom to *negate* his present facticity—which is the single exercise of freedom open to him.[37]

In relation to Sartre's analysis it must be admitted that the working class in France does feel alienated from the nation. This can be observed by anyone; it is a situation which does not have an exact parallel in any other western European democracy (except perhaps Italy) or in the United States. But whether or not its history even in France can be interpreted *only* in terms of alienation is another question. Even Sartre admits by implication that it cannot, since he describes in his last article a cumulative experience of the proletariat (albeit a negative one) which he had denied earlier. What Sartre is really trying to maintain is the basic Marxist notion that, unless there is a radical transformation of society leading to the dictatorship of the proletariat, there can be no redress for the workers.

Sartre's last article appeared in March, 1954. In April Merleau-Ponty began to write the major parts of *Les Aventures de la dialectique* and by December had completed the book.

It was published in April, 1955. Over one third of the whole is devoted to a critique of Sartre. Merleau-Ponty deals only in a passing manner with the debate between Sartre and Lefort.[38] His concern is Sartre's articles "Les Communistes et la Paix, II-III" and "Réponse à Lefort." He considers in turn four major problems: Sartre's relation to classical Marxism, Sartre's conception of truth, the relation of individual to society (or of self to others) in Sartre, and Sartre's conception of revolution. Discussion of these problems leads Merleau-Ponty to draw three conclusions from Sartre's analyses: first, the pure action of the Party transcends the ambiguities of history, so that "action" is elevated to the status of a principle (AD 139-44); second, action is based on pure will: the will is not motivated by anything outside it but postulates what is necessary in order for it to act (in the same way the Kantian moral subject believes in God and immortality, not because the will is attached to an exterior being but because such a being is necessary for moral action) (AD 145-46); and third, nothing in the class is foreign to the Party, and the two can never be pitted against one another (AD 147-55).

Regarding Sartre's relation to classical Marxism, Merleau-Ponty points out that Sartre places all his emphasis on the idea (of pure action), whereas Marx had always insisted on the importance of the situation, on the *elaboration* of the idea through a given context. Merleau-Ponty appeals to his interpretation of the young Marx here as well as to Lenin. He distinguishes them from Stalinism, not by "bureaucracy" as Lefort had done, but by the Bolshevik belief that communism is inscribed in the nature of things apart from human action (scientific socialism). The Bolsheviks, relying wholly on the facts, reach the same conclusion as Sartre relying wholly on the idea, namely, that from the perspective of the present, whatever succeeds *was* true. Both the Bolsheviks and Sartre forget that consciousness can never be separated from the facts, that both must be elaborated together and in conjunction with one another.[39]

This leads Merleau-Ponty to consider the defects in Sartre's concept of "pure action." He finds two: first, that it makes all action appear necessary; and second, that it fails to recognize that all action is self-transcending (points beyond itself). Philosophically the result is that everything is riveted in the *present*. There is no "temporal thickness," no history; existence is reduced to myth. Truth disappears since it is always what *will be*, never what *is*. Meaning in history thus collapses. The proletariat acts but without hope of gaining any established end.[40] Moreover, there is no way of making historical judgments; Lenin, Stalin, and Malenkov are what they are for you and me and others, but are never anything essentially, so that distinctions between them become impossible. This is not Marxism. (*AD* 178-206)

The disappearance of the temporal field is, Merleau-Ponty believes, attributable to the fact that Sartre bases all human relationships on the "look" so that the *social* world never appears.[41] This means that Sartre is describing *only* the process involved in changing the *inner* man; he never describes the *external* world. In the final analysis his philosophy of "pure action" is one of "pure contemplation." Merleau-Ponty calls this substitution of thought for action Sartre's "ultra-Bolshevism." (*AD* 219-21) It leads Sartre to separate the Party from history (for no integration is possible through existing forms), to emphasize what one never experiences ("pure action"), to alternate between rebellion and indulgence with respect to the Party (i.e., to demand that the Party never be inconsistent, but to approve whatever the Party does), and finally to affirm that anything is preferable to what exists today. In short, if one begins from zero, there will be no criteria for judging between relative degrees of good, which is what we are confronted with. (*AD* 222-48)

These defects vitiate Sartre's view of revolution. He has interpreted revolution as engagement, and he has continued to understand engagement as negativity. This was perhaps valid in 1945 but can no longer be so today.[42] It is wrong to make the only affirmation of the world a negation of it and to set up an imaginary concept which never exists in practice (so that in principle it can never be disproved). Merleau-Ponty traces Sartre's error to his view of freedom which makes it either pure choice or an eternal choice (i.e., an initial choice conditioning all other choices). Merleau-Ponty's rejection of Marxism parallels his rejection of the Sartrian view of engagement inasmuch as it means only the negation of what is.

Sartre never replied to Merleau-Ponty, but he said of Simone de Beauvoir's article in his behalf: "He wrote a book on dialectic and took me apart quite sharply in it. Simone de Beauvoir responded to him not less sharply in *Les Temps Modernes*: this was the first and last time that we quarreled with each other in writing." [43] Apparently, therefore, Sartre regarded Mlle de Beauvoir's reply as his own countercritique. Mlle de Beauvoir labels Merleau-Ponty's analysis "pseudo-Sartrian," by which she means that Merleau-Ponty has attacked and rejected views which he attributes to Sartre but which Sartre does not really hold. She finds this to be the case in his treatment of Sartre's philosophy of subject and object, his philosophy of history, his politics, and his view of revolution.

It is false, Mlle de Beauvoir asserts, to say that Sartre's is a philosophy of the subject. Rather it is a philosophy of consciousness, and the subject or self is an object of consciousness as much as any other object. While consciousness is an immediate presence, the subject is an unfolding which requires mediation.[44] This has several consequences. It means first that the subject is not riveted in the present. Moreover, since the subject stands between consciousness and the world, there is an intersubjectivity. When Merleau-Ponty speaks of a "field of thickness" he is elaborating a Sartrian idea.[45]

In the second place, Sartre does accept a distinction between the real and the probable. History is a mixture, but the

future will clarify the present. His presentation of the necessity according to which the bourgeoisie has created French
history does not mean that he believes in the necessity of all
historical action.[46] The real issue at stake is whether or not
"facticity" can influence the exercise of human freedom. Mlle
de Beauvoir finds such an influence properly accounted for
in Sartre [47] and believes it is further emphasized in the assertion that events have significance beyond what men intend
when they act.[48]

Having restored intersubjectivity to Sartre, Mlle de Beauvoir also finds that action is not discontinuous, arbitrary, or
ex nihilo in Sartre, because he bases his humanism on need
rather than on pure action,[49] he affirms that the French proletariat is an historical reality,[50] and he believes that his view of
the class as an entity made and remade without ceasing is the
same as Marx's view of "practice." [51] And finally, in denying
spontaneity to the masses Sartre is affirming that the leaders
are followed only when they go where the masses want them
to go.[52]

When the interdependence of Party and masses is established, then it becomes false to contend that for Sartre the
revolution is centered on the Party alone. Mlle de Beauvoir
attacks Merleau-Ponty for having abandoned any meaningful
concept of engagement, in particular for standing outside
history by refusing to take a position. Moreover, she believes
that in reasoning that revolutions are true as movements but
false as regimes Merleau-Ponty has abandoned the only meaningful revolutionary position; he has given up the radical
challenge to the foundation of society itself and sided with
those who have something to lose but nothing to gain by revolution, i.e., the bourgeoisie. He has joined Malreaux and
other champions of Western civilization! [53]

The final statement of Mlle de Beauvoir is interesting for
the possible light it throws on the difference between her interpretation of Sartre and that of Merleau-Ponty. She writes:

The attitude of Merleau-Ponty toward communism seems, therefore, to reflect the grudge of a religious soul against a too human
world. This explains in part his irritation towards Sartre whose
path has been the reverse of his own. His *a priori* construction of
pseudo-Satrianism does not remain less surprising for all that. It is
true that Merleau-Ponty has never understood Sartre. Already in
Phenomenology of Perception he denied coldly the whole Sartrian
phenomenology of engaged freedom. In admitting that the reconciliation of Sartre's ontology and phenomenology raises problems
[Footnote: Merleau-Ponty knows perfectly well that Sartre is preparing a work of philosophy which attacks this problem directly.]
one has no right to tear from his hands one "of the two ends of the
chain," and to speak as Merleau-Ponty does . . . .[54]

This passage is instructive when viewed in relation to a review
Mlle de Beauvoir wrote of *Phenomenology of Perception* in
1945. In the latter she describes with enthusiasm Merleau-
Ponty's elucidations of the "interworld" between subject (body)
and object (world). Two sentences from the concluding paragraphs of her review are worth setting over against the statement above:

While Sartre in *Being and Nothingness* underlines at first the opposition of the for-itself and the in-itself, the annihilating power of
the mind in face of being and its absolute freedom, Merleau-Ponty,
on the contrary, sets as his task the description of the concrete
character of the subject which is never, according to him, a pure
for-itself.
One of the chief merits of this book is that it is convincing; another
of its merits is that it does not ask us to do violence to ourselves;
it proposes to us instead that we join the movement of life, which
is belief [*croyance*] in things, in this world, and in our own
presence.[55]

Obviously, Mlle de Beauvoir believed in 1945 that the *intentions* of Sartre and Merleau-Ponty were the same and, furthermore, that Merleau-Ponty provided a necessary supplement
to Sartre's strong contrasts. But in 1955 she concludes that
since Merleau-Ponty diverges so completely from Sartre's
views, it must be the case that he did not understand Sartre

(i.e., was really saying something other than Sartre was saying) in 1945 as well. But the truth of the matter seems to be that Mlle de Beauvoir did not hold Sartre's view of freedom in the early postwar period. In *The Ethics of Ambiguity*, for example, written as a series of articles for *Les Temps Modernes* in 1947, she outlines a phenomenology of freedom in which approximate realizations of freedom are described and arranged in an ascending order of validity. Here the "mixture" of man and the world is the point of departure.[56] Indeed, the word "ambiguity" in the title suggests this. It appears, then, that Mlle de Beauvoir regarded Merleau-Ponty's approach as the more fruitful, but that her allegiance to Sartre outweighed her agreement with Merleau-Ponty when the two came into conflict with one another.

Partial Rapprochement: 1956-1961

After their break, Sartre and Merleau-Ponty did not see each other again for three years (1953-56). According to Sartre, very few people saw Merleau-Ponty during this period because, following the death of his mother in 1953, he remained for the most part secluded.[57] Their friendship was rekindled in 1956 when both attended a conference for writers from Eastern and Western European nations.[58] From this point forward they began to see each other again. Sartre states that all they lacked for a complete *rapprochement* was a common project, and he felt that this would have been found had not Merleau-Ponty's death intervened.[59]

However, this is doubtful. It was fortunate for both men that two original minds could overcome their intellectual differences enough to reestablish a personal friendship. However, their ways of thought were diverging even further, not drawing closer together. A brief exchange between the two in 1958 reveals the contrast. Sartre asked Merleau-Ponty what he was working on and received the reply, after some hesitation, that Merleau-Ponty had been struck by a phrase in Whitehead: "Nature is in shreds." Sartre comments that he did not understand at the time what Merleau-Ponty meant,[60] since for him "nature" referred to physico-chemical processes, a notion with which he was then trying to come to terms in a large book.[61] Merleau-Ponty understood by nature, however, the ensemble of man's relations to other men and to things—the whole sensible world. He wanted to find a basis for a philosophy into which all the sciences of man could be integrated; Sartre wanted to define a Marxist humanism over against the orthodox communist theoreticians and western thinkers. This difference in orientation contains two apparently permanent divergences between Sartre and Merleau-Ponty. First, Merleau-Ponty abandoned the Marxist notion of a universality based on the dictatorship of the proletariat which Sartre did not, although Sartre affirmed this in his own way rather than in the manner of the orthodox communists.[62] The only universality Merleau-Ponty recognized was one which had to be *discovered* through the pursuit of philosophy. Second, Sartre's researches into "nature" seemed to Merleau-Ponty still to be involved in Sartre's dichotomy between in-itself and for-itself. Sartre had never come to terms with the contradiction between his description of an "interworld" and his ontology which in effect denied this interworld. Thus, even near the end of his life, Merleau-Ponty at the same time acknowledged that Sartre had pointed to the interworld which intervenes between being and nothingness [63] and rejected his methodology as leading in an entirely different direction. (see VI 288) What Sartre lacked, and what Merleau-Ponty hoped to develop, was a *methodology* adequate to the task of describing the interworld.

In the preface to *Signs*, the last book Merleau-Ponty published before his death, he characterizes Sartre—just as he does Marx in the same essay—as a "classic," that is, as one who has passed to a secondary level of truth. What Sartre has said of value for social existence has been taken up into the thought of others; but his thought no longer "lives" because it does not describe the situation in which we now exist. Merleau-Ponty interprets an essay by Sartre on one of his schoolmates (Paul Nizan) to illustrate the point.[64] Nizan had been a communist from his youth but bolted the Party when the Russian-German Pact was signed in 1939. Sartre describes him as an example of one whose life was "revolt" and whose attitude is worthy of emulation by the youth of today. In commenting on Sartre's essay Merleau-Ponty asserts that it is not "revolt" which is the proper attitude for the youth of today, but rather *virtue without resignation*. For while history does not tell us what to do, it does tell us that "revolt" is an illusion—in terms of the promise a past generation saw in it—and history never resumes its lost illusions. (S 31-47, tr. 22-35)

The Limitations of Sartrian Existentialism Philosophically Defined

Toward the end of his critique of political ideologies, Merleau-Ponty remarks that the world is not negation but rather a "symbol," an "interworld" between me and others. It testifies to the uniting bond of all things. Somehow politics and culture, anthropology and sociology, psychology and philosophy are all related, intertwined with one another, together disclosing the unity and meaning in the lives of men. (*AD* 264-71) Having freed himself from ideological thinking, Merleau-Ponty turned his attention increasingly to this broader assignment which is not far removed from Husserl's delegation to philosophy of an "infinite task." It is not surprising that from this broader perspective Merleau-Ponty was led once again to the thought of Sartre, this time, however, to its philosophical rather than to its political implications. Unlike his critique in *Les Aventures de la dialectique*, he does not confine himself to saying why Sartre's alternative is illegitimate, but discusses Sartre in relation to his own position which he believes corrects the weaknesses of the Sartrian analysis. Unfortunately, he did not live to complete his task, and the only clearly formulated parts of it, among which is his discussion of Sartre, were published posthumously. Nevertheless, we get a more vivid impression of his philosophical relationship to Sartre in this critique than in the earlier political writings precisely because his own alternative is at least suggested here. Hence, a consideration of his last reflections on Sartre will provide the best possible transition from the old era just described to the final and most suggestive (if not constructive) period of Merleau-Ponty's life.

By the time we begin to seek reasons for determining that there is a world, Merleau-Ponty asserts, we have already stopped seeing the world. Only because we first have a "perceptive faith" in the presence of the world and of things do we believe in the order and connections of our thoughts. Any other point of departure renders the world incomprehensible. This is eminently true in an ontology of being and nothingness, such as Sartre puts forward. The world as being, in this formulation, has no relation to our "thoughts"; the world is foreign to all interiority since it is the absolute antithesis of interiority. All interaction between self and world is abrogated, for there is no point of contact between them. Such a philosophy is beyond both monism and dualism, for what we have are two elements *coextensive* with one another. Each covers the whole of reality from its own point of view. Therefore, a philosophy of negativity ends at the same point as a positivistic philosophy. In both cases, the world is an object for the surveying subject, and the problems of classical philosophy, which always involved the "mixture" or "union" of negative and positive, are abolished.

If we place this view in relation to "perceptive faith," we see that it cannot explain the latter. Take, for example, the perception of a table by two persons. When I perceive the table, the table retains its attachment to being. I do not "appropriate" the table, but at the same time, through my "look" the table is perceived in a context of "lacunae" on the basis of which it becomes a part of my universe. The same thing happens when another person perceives the table. However, his "look" and mine are not commensurate, inasmuch as the "lacunae" are not the same for each of us. Hence, it is a miracle that we communicate with one another. Moreover, the things that others see do not confirm their being, because it is always *my* things that the others see. My case is not assimilable to that of others. This position leads inevitably to a transcendental solipsism, since perception belongs to my inner life. To be sure, others enter to disturb my relation to things, in the sense that they challenge my right to think the world for all. Thus, the "look" of others is a second opening that I have on the world. I do not perceive the other as I perceive a thing, but as something which is not a thing and at the same time not me. Such contact with others makes me aware of my conviction that I am a parasite in the world. In relation to perceptive faith, it is fair to say that this view gives an account of our private worlds without enclosing us completely within them, but no genuine interworld opens up. Each person inhabits his own world in such a way as to be aware that his world is not a total world. (VI 84-86) And therefore, the mixture which characterizes our relationship to the world is denied. For just as "being is" *adds* nothing to "nothingness is," so the "look" of others adds no new dimensions to my universe. It only confirms the fact that I am included in being, but I knew this already. All I learn from the look of others is that there is an outside in general around my universe. (VI 100-1)

The failure of the notion of being and nothingness to account for our experience of the world is revealed by the fact that when the attempt is made to avoid complete separation the result is not a "mixture" but rather a total identification. For when we begin with the intuition of nothingness, the

world is immediately present as complete positivity, a plenitude of being. But inasmuch as this plenitude appears from the
point of view of nothingness, nothingness becomes the interior
of being, i.e., it takes on the characteristic of being itself, and
nothingness rather than being causes there to *be* a world.
Hence, the appeal from being to nothingness is in reality an
appeal from nothingness to being. This reveals that at the
heart of negation there is a snare: if we say that it is, we
destroy the negativity; if we say that it is not, we elevate it to
a sort of positivity and confer a kind of being on it. (VI 96)
Thus, having begun with a complete separation, we end with
a complete identity, and the thickness, depth, and multiplicity
of the perceptual world are lost.

If it is argued that complete identity is in principle impossible since man stands outside being, then we are still left
with the question of how one world is possible. And the only
solution at this point is to posit a kind of Super-being which is
mythical (the In-Itself-For-Itself). Such is the circle of being
and nothingness: either an absolute identity or an absolute
separation, and in both cases a failure to account for our experience of the world. (VI 104-5)

We are therefore driven to the conclusion that, as an attempt to give philosophical expression to our visual experience, the idea of being and nothingness is inadequate. The
true situation cannot be as Sartre describes it. The other

is no more than I am a pure look on pure being, because his views
and mine are in advance inserted in a system of partial perspectives, referred to the same world in which we coexist and where
they are blended. In order that the other be truly other, it does
not suffice and it is not necessary that he be a scourge ... it is
necessary and it suffices that he have the power of decentering me,
of opposing his centrality to mine, and he can do this only because
we are not two nothings installed in two incomparable universes
of In-Itself, but two entrances to the same Being, each [entrance]
being accessible only to one of us, but appearing to the other as
lawfully practicable, because they are both part of the same Being.
(VI 114, emphasis in text)

What in the final analysis merits the name of being "is not the horizon of 'pure' being, but the system of perspectives which are introduced there." These perspectives are "not before me, but at the intersection of my views and those of others." (*VI* 116) Sartre has attempted to express this by saying that the For-Itself is necessarily haunted by an In-Itself-For-Itself which is imaginary. But for me the In-Itself-For-Itself is more than imaginary, since the imaginary is unobservable. What the In-Itself-For-Itself points to is being, and this is genuine in Sartre's intuition. What is not genuine is the refusal to describe our mixture as a participation in being. Sartre has himself done this in other works, indicating what in reality intervenes between being and nothingness.

Our point of departure can be neither that being is a totality, nor that being and nothingness stand in antithesis to one another. Both of these are surveying positions. Our starting point is rather that "there is being, there is a world, there is *something* . . . there is cohesion, there is a meaning." (*VI* 121) Even when perception proves illusory, it is because something is there that can both be illusory and be corrected. Hence, for the antithesis of being and nothingness we must substitute *dialectic*. In dialectic, the relations between things are internal rather than external. (*VI* 124) "Dialectic is the thought of Being-seen, of a Being which is not simple positivity, In-Itself, and not Being-posed with a thought, but *manifestation of Itself*, unfolding, in the act of making itself." (*VI* 125) It refers to a kind of being which is not wholly susceptible to positive designation, that is, to both necessary and incompatible relationships between things. Thus it must envisage "without restriction the plurality of relations and what has been called ambiguity." (*VI* 129) Contrary to the Hegelian version of dialectic, there is in this view no idea of a synthesis. And this denial is not to be taken as skepticism or relativism or the reign of the ineffable. What we are rejecting is the idea that thought can make a system out of life which will be definitive. What we want to find is a dialectic "which will find being before the reflective cleavage, around it, at its horizon, not outside us and not in us, but there where the two movements intersect, there where 'there is' something." (VI 130) It is the meaning this idea of the "intersection of being" assumed for Merleau-Ponty that we must now attempt to analyze.

PART III

Transformations and Continuities: 1950-1961

VI

Toward a Philosophy of Being:
The Intersection of History and Nature

[Philosophy] reserves for itself what remains when the
sciences have said all they can say, when one comes to it
with the question: And we, living men on whom all this
converges, what have we to do with this world and this
history?

Merleau-Ponty

Toward a Dialectical Philosophy of History and Nature

The Structure of Behavior and *Phenomenology of Perception*,
together with Merleau-Ponty's lecture on perception and his
essay on metaphysics in 1947, are concerned with the philosophical elucidation of an "ambiguous" world or "interworld" in
which the proper connections are established between man's
initial contact with a "lived world" and the reflective consti-
tutions of this world characteristic of the various sciences.
However, his postwar political philosophy was a denial of
this perspective insofar as he accepted the privileged role of
the proletariat and the concrete possibility of establishing a
unified political order through its rise to power. Of course,
Merleau-Ponty never believed in the Marxist dogma that the
proletariat *must* rise to power, but only that this was a *desirable possibility* inasmuch as they embodied whatever hope
there was for a "new order." However, as this hope faded[1] he
was forced to recognize that he had come close to holding up

the proletariat as a "final solution" and so abolishing the "multiplicity of perspectives" which had always been an underlying presupposition of his philosophy. Doubtless the influence of Sartre and the position of the Communist Party in the charged atmosphere of postwar France were important factors in leading him away from the original intentions of his philosophy. As soon, however, as he perceived this inconsistency, he rejected both Marxism and Sartrian philosophy, and once having settled his account with them, he returned to the tasks he had outlined between 1938 and 1945 but had largely abandoned between 1945 and 1950.

His return to his original tasks was based, as we saw at the end of the preceding chapter, on a revitalization of dialectical thinking and its correlation with a *philosophy of being*.[2] He characterizes as "ideological" or nondialectical any philosophy which is satisfied with antitheses, as for example, Sartre's philosophy of absolute freedom or a Marxist philosophy of dialectical materialism. Over against these, he wants to affirm a "synthetic" philosophy, the task of which is "to elaborate *one concept of being* such that contraditions [are] neither accepted nor 'passed beyond', [but] given their proper place." (*ACF 1958*, 214, emphasis added) And if contemporary thought has obscured being and dialectic, then one must look to the past to gain a new understanding of their relationship.[3]

According to Merleau-Ponty, dialectical thinking has three essential characteristics. (*ACF 1956*, 175-79) The first is the recognition of contradiction as a principle of dialectical thinking, which means that being must be viewed simultaneously as for-me and for-itself. Being is always at a distance, but is nevertheless grasped only as it is related to me. This implies second that everything has *its own* meaning or truth which I cannot exhaust, but also that it is possible for me to become related to this being which stands over against me.[4] Finally, dialectical thinking is "subjective" in the sense that my relationship to being never can be stated exhaustively or "in a

single proposition." Every synthesis or reconciliation of opposites is provisional; it is therefore essential to dialectical
thinking never to be "possession" but rather always "renewal."
Dialectical thinking thus reflects the unity and multiplicity of
experience. Experiences are multiple, but the unities constructed out of this multiplicity point to a "beyond of being."
Merleau-Ponty refers to this unity as an "absolute," but it is a
"fluid" or historical absolute, immanent in experience. (*ACF
1956*, 175-77; cf. *VI* 203-4) The task of philosophy is always to
think in relation to this "open unity."

When Merleau-Ponty said in 1956 that "a concrete philosophy is not a happy philosophy," [5] he was referring to his
conception of dialectic in terms of which the unity of truth is
historical, relative, finite. Clearly his problem was to justify
his assertions through concrete analyses. A good illustration
of the point of view from which he begins to deal with this
problem, one which both sums up what has already been said
and anticipates what lies ahead, is to be found in an exchange
between Sartre and Merleau-Ponty in Venice early in 1956 (the
first time they had seen each other since their break in 1953),
in the presence of writers from both Western Europe (France,
England, Italy, and Switzerland) and Eastern Europe (Poland,
Russia, and Yugoslavia).[6]

MERLEAU-PONTY: Does the thaw (in Russia) then signify philosophically that henceforth one considers it possible for a non-communist country to attain, not only in physics and astronomy, but also
in the human sciences, truths which could not have been attained
or formulated in communist countries? I ask if this is possible; it is
not a question of justifying *en bloc* American sociology or psychology, of course. But, in principle, does one admit the possibility of
such a cultural development on bases until now considered un-
healthy? If one admits this, we have to make a kind of new universalism. This will no longer be the universalism that was criticized under the name of bourgeois philosophy, that is to say, an
abstract reason which imagines that one can, from principles really
common to all men and independent of situations, state truths and
discover values; . . . [this new universalism involves] the idea that

if one places himself at the level of human life worlds, it is possible, in a non-communist country, for living men to express in all autonomy what they live and to pass beyond the framework of their class or society. A man is more than his class, on the condition that he places himself at the level of what he lives, and not at the level of abstract principles. ... (p. 212)

SARTRE: This manner of posing the question appears to me to constitute a leap. For we must see that a sociology ... belongs to an ideology, has its methods which are not a dialectical method ... and if its truths can be effectively discovered by these methods, a Marxist can never consider them in an isolated state.

MERLEAU-PONTY: I have said specifically that it is not a question of justifying American sociology by this method. The question is whether or not one admits the possibility that a socially inferior regime can attain the truth.

SARTRE: Agreed. Only it is necessary to add this: on the condition that recognition of these truths is made in the Marxist perspective, that the Marxists wish to integrate them into their system. I do not believe that one can ask—whether there is a thaw or not— that men in possession of a cultural ideology such as Marxism accept a truth belonging to another ideological system, without trying to see on what conditions it can be integrated into Marxism. ... We come here to the bottom of the cultural problem: it is that all cultures are also ideologies. This is what one does not note here; and I see in this failure one of the proofs that in the West also there is a need for a thaw. We do not take account of the fact that we live in a period of bourgeois ideology; that our lives, in one manner or another, are conditioned by bourgeois ideology, exactly as the ideas of the Soviets are conditioned by Soviet ideology. ... for me, the true problem is not to seek a universal, in the sense of ideas which would be valuable in one or the other system, but rather to ask for a discussion of ideas in the Marxist perspective, for the communists. ... (p. 216) I am very much of this opinion, as I said recently to a communist, that psychoanalysis can be completely integrated into Marxism; but I would never ask a Marxist to accept psychoanalysis as a solitary discipline. I would ask him to reintegrate it, remarking to him, for example, that after all the individual history of a man badly raised only repeats the history of his family, that is to say, the history of society; and that, consequently, one can very easily ... recover psychoanalysis as a discipline annexed to socio-economic study. But I would never ask him to take psychoanalysis as truth; in saying that one goes too far.

MERLEAU-PONTY: If the Marxist is to integrate it into Marxism, he must begin by taking it seriously. And he cannot do this simply by saying that it is a bourgeois ideology.

SARTRE: It is true that it is a bourgeois ideology; but it will no longer be so if it is freed from the other side. It is bourgeois by its limits and by its negations; [but] it need not be so, if it is taken in its totality.

MERLEAU-PONTY: This is a transubstantiation. It is necessary all the same to begin by recognizing that this bourgeois problem has touched something, and that, as a result, to this extent, the theory of ideologies is in default.

SARTRE: One can always consider that a truth of detail can be found in no matter what ideology; but if one makes it pass into another, it is necessary that it be taken up . . . and integrated. . . ." (p. 217)

There is genuine pathos in this exchange, for what we see here is Merleau-Ponty's reassertion of the viewpoint that had always undergirded his philosophy, restated in confrontation with one who had led him (partially) away from that viewpoint. Having abandoned the idea that "universality" could be achieved on the political level, Merleau-Ponty did not abandon the idea of a human universality itself. He simply abandoned his preoccupation with political philosophy and attempted to place his ideas in a broader perspective. This broader perspective, already asserted in 1947, but undeveloped while political debates raged back and forth, was reaffirmed first in Merleau-Ponty's inaugural lecture at the Collège de France in 1953, and was uninterruptedly pursued from that time until the end of his life. In that lecture he stated:

Meaning lies latent not only in language, in political and religious institutions, but in modes of kinship, in machines, in the landscape, in production, and, in general, in all the modes of human commerce. *An interconnection among all these phenomena is possible*, since they are all symbolisms, and perhaps even the translation of one symbolism into another is possible. (*EP* 76-77, tr. 56; emphasis added)

Thus it is that the very relativity "of nature and history is

already the discovery of a new solidarity." (*ACF 1959*, 232)
We must now turn our attention to Merleau-Ponty's description of this "new solidarity."

The Dimensions of the Relationship between
History and Nature Philosophically Defined

Merleau-Ponty's development of a philosophy of history
moves on three levels, which we may call the philosophical
level, the personal level, and the institutional level. His remarks are not developed systematically, and I shall use this
schema to systematize them.

On the philosophical level the problem is to stand between
two "absolutes," one of which bestows values on history from
the understanding alone (e.g., many Western liberals, Trotsky
during the period of his exile, Sartre's "Marxism in contemplation"), and the second of which sees an immanent logic in
history (e.g., orthodox Marxism, the idea of "progress"). (See
ACF 1954, 180; *AD* 8; *PC* 251) Each of these positions fails to
consult history. In order to overcome this limitation it is necessary in the first place to have concepts which can be applied to
the interpretation of history, but which are intuited from the
particular matter of history being consulted. This means that
there is no universally applicable concept but that concepts are
relevant for particular historical periods and configurations,
and that the concepts are clarified through a dialogue with
the material one is interpreting. Therefore, in the second
place, we do not study "universal history" but only a particular
past and with the purpose of *understanding the present*. Taken
together, these aspects of historical knowing do justice both
to the weight of the past which enters into every decision and
to the future which, though anticipated in our contact with the
past and present, is never known. Our freedom to act is based
on the uncertainty of the future (which involves risk) and on
our calculations with respect to the past (which involves re-

sponsibility for our actions). History is thus a "pure interrogation" of our past, ourselves, and our future.

How does an individual hold his thought and his action
together? Is it possible for a man to realize himself on both
levels at once? We saw in Merleau-Ponty's political writings
how Trotsky, Lukacs, and Sartre—among others—had failed to
do so. A new answer begins to emerge when Merleau-Ponty
generalizes the problem beyond the political sphere and asks,
as he does in his inaugural lecture in 1953, how the philosopher
and the man of action can be the *same* man. He suggests
that the task of the philosopher is to think critically, just as the
task of the man of action is to choose. Few philosophers are
consistently involved in the world, and few men of action
think critically about what they are doing. Therefore, a difference exists between a man of action and a man of thought,
but this difference actually exists in every man as that between his understanding and his choice. Since it is virtually
impossible for one man to be "all things," the man of action
and the man of thought should be open to each other. The
philosopher is peculiarly fitted for the task of criticism by
the very fact that he is "at a distance" from action, for this
enables him to "experience more fully the ties of truth which
bind him to the world and to history." (*EP* 79-85, tr. 59-63)

This does not get to the bottom of the problem, however.
For individuals must not only reconcile their thought with
their action, but they must do so *in relation to institutions*
with which they are involved. Can a man remain true to himself without either succumbing to the requirements of the institutions of which he is a part or divorcing himself from institutional life altogether? Merleau-Ponty believes this is possible only if institutions are "relativized," that is, viewed as
provisionally true, subject to continual interrogation and correction. Hence the criterion for judging an institution is the
extent to which it not only allows, but is capable of inter-
nalizing, self-criticism.

It was through Max Weber, in whose writings he found not only an adequate criticism of the dilemmas Marxism had posed for him but also a philosophy of history which transcended those dilemmas, that Merleau-Ponty attached himself once again to the traditions of Western liberalism. Weber's typology provided the framework for Merleau-Ponty's critique of Marxism. For example, the Marxist revolutionary described by Merleau-Ponty is strikingly similar to Weber's charismatic leader who negates the present order; Merleau-Ponty's description of the "positive revolutionary regime" which betrays its aims parallels Weber's account of the institutionalization or bureaucratization of leadership; and Merleau-Ponty's pessimism with respect to the passage from spontaneity to the routinization of leadership reflects Weber's attitude also. However, it was not Weber's typology so much as his philosophy of history that attracted Merleau-Ponty's attention. This is clear at two points. The first is the fact that Weber's name appears only in the texts of the mid-1950s which are concerned with the philosophy of history[7] and is conspicuously absent in texts during the same period dealing with the sciences of man and the typology of institutions.[8] More important, however, is Merleau-Ponty's attempt to show, in the texts dealing with Weber, how he successfully integrated the philosophical, personal, and institutional dimensions of a philosophy of history in his thought and life.

First, on the philosophical level, Weber, without formulating this as an explicit method (AD 18), practiced an interrogation of the past for the sake of understanding the present and, furthermore, found his concepts *within* the material he was studying (AD 30), thereby genuinely illuminating the facts with ideas and ideas with facts. This is especially evident in *The Protestant Ethic and the Spirit of Capitalism*, which Merleau-Ponty discusses in this connection. (AD 19-25) What interests him most in Weber's analysis is his ability to relate the two "styles of life" (capitalism and Calvinism) as interdependent forces not reducible to one another and not exclusive of other forces also in operation; and furthermore, Weber's ability to take account both of an objective historical context and human action within that context. Neither the material conditions nor the human agents are removed from history, but each has its place. (*AD* 17-18) At the same time Weber affirms historical meaning. He falls neither into the trap of denying meaning (i.e., making contingency a basis for skepticism) nor into that of projecting the meaning he discovers into universal significance for interpreting history. (*AD* 34, 41, 42)

Second, on the personal level, Weber's liberalism is a case study in what Merleau-Ponty means by the philosopher's need to "take a distance" from himself. This is illustrated by the fact that although Weber was not a pacifist he interceded on behalf of some of his pacifist students who had been compromised by pacifist propaganda, as well as by his criticism of Prussian militarism notwithstanding the fact that he was an ardent nationalist. In short, Weber did not accept any "absolutes" which would have closed him off from other men; and he was not involved so passionately in what he held true that he could not, as a thinker, take a dispassionate look at it.

Finally, on the institutional level, Weber recognized the necessity of violence in struggles for political power but refused to accept the finality of violence in political life. Thus, for example, in his lecture "Politics as a Vocation," [9] Weber tried to affirm an "ethic of responsibility" without emphasizing exclusively either the ends of action or the unbridled opportunism accompanying struggles for political power when ends are altogether ignored. What Merleau-Ponty finds most hopeful in Weber is his belief in possibilities other than violence *in spite of* the presence of violence in political life. This he calls an "heroic liberalism" (*AD* 38), a liberalism living in history.

Merleau-Ponty's effort to restore dialectic to history is no more strenuous than his efforts in relation to the problem of nature. He devoted two years (1957, 1958) of his course lectures at the Collège de France to an analysis of the philosophy of nature from Descartes to Husserl. He defined the problem historically as the attempt to overcome the dichotomy between nature as an object external to the observer and nature as an object immanent in the observer (i.e., constructed by him). The first emphasis predominates in Descartes, but the second is present also in his discussion of the conflict between God's will and God's understanding (for God's will does not obey necessary laws). (*ACF* 1957, 204-6) Kant emphasized the second alternative, though there is also in Kant the view that man is the theater rather than the agent of the synthesis between "mind and matter." (*ACF* 1957, 206-9) Schelling identified the "non-knowing" in Kant with a primordial nature on the basis of which we are in living contact with nature prior to reflection. (*ACF* 1957, 209-10) Husserl combined the various elements of this historical development, viewing nature first, in the manner of Descartes, as an external object, but later identifying the body-subject as the point of contact between consciousness and an external world, and understanding its presence in the world as originally "lived." (*ACF* 1957, 212-15) The problem in the tradition has been to remain dialectical. On the one hand, nature cannot be reduced to what it is for a thinking subject. It retains its autonomy vis-à-vis man, or as Schelling put it, "there is in Nature something which imposes itself even on God as a condition independent of his operation." (*ACF* 1957, 203) But on the other hand, nature cannot be wholly separated from man either. The task of reflection is to grasp both the fundamental connections and the disparities between man and nature.[10] To do so will be to reveal that nature "spills over" into historical existence.

Though he does not go beyond this historical analysis in his lectures, it is not difficult to see that Merleau-Ponty is trying to reach a conclusion something like the following:

Modern philosophy has been an attempt, not to reduce the subject to an object or the world as object to a thinking subject, but rather to uncover the relationship between subject and object; the fact that many philosophers, like Descartes and Kant, failed to resolve the problem adequately is incidental to the significant point, namely, that they were attempting to do what we are still trying to do; Schelling had an intuition which should have led him beyond the Kantian impasse, and Husserl has followed up that intuition in a fruitful way. From this line of reasoning we can conclude that Merleau-Ponty views himself as standing within the context of a continuous modern history of the philosophy of nature and that he believes he is developing that history in the direction of its most authentic insights. The fact that, in interpreting Husserl, he relies on the *Lebenswelt* philosophy as he understands it rather than as Husserl understood it is not as important as the fact that Merleau-Ponty's intentions are the *same* as Husserl's in his later years, namely, to understand the relation between knowledge of the natural world and those who possess such knowledge. Merleau-Ponty's awareness that his own later intentions parallel those of the later Husserl accounts for the growing rapport he felt for this philosopher.

This then is Merleau-Ponty's philosophical program: to outline an "ontology of finitude" in which the natural world and historical man are seen in their relations to one another. With the possibility of such a philosophy rests the fate of a genuine humanism.

Note on a Theological Attempt To Bifurcate History and Nature

In a recent book Professor Carl Michalson proposes to show that "nature" and "history" are two structures of reality so different that there can be no conflict between them because they never meet at any point.[11] And he claims to find support for this thesis in the late writings of Husserl, in Sartre, and in Merleau-Ponty.[12] In the light of the preceding analysis, let us examine his right to claim Merleau-Ponty's support.

Professor Michalson defines "history" as that structure of reality which is concerned at every point with the question of the meaning for human existence of what is interrogated. "Nature" is that structure of reality which ignores the question of meaning. Thus stars and sea can be history if they are viewed in relation to their meaning for human existence, while historical events can be nature if the question of meaning is not brought to them. Is this view an accurate translation of Merleau-Ponty's perspective? We may note first that since Merleau-Ponty retains traditional definitions of nature and history, Professor Michalson does not translate the framework in which his discussions are cast. Does he, even so, translate Merleau-Ponty's intentions? To this we may answer that if Professor Michalson simply means that everything is potentially meaningful but that the question of meaning is not asked of every object or event, then perhaps Merleau-Ponty would not have disagreed. Nevertheless, Merleau-Ponty never would have said that reality can be separated into "meaningful" and "meaningless"; this is analogous to saying both that the world is rational and that it is absurd. To bifurcate reality is to prejudge the question of the potential meaningfulness of *all* reality. And this is certainly implied in the statement by Professor Michalson that we must give up all attempts to relate nature and history. How this could be reconciled with any part of Merleau-Ponty's perspective is difficult to see.

Toward the Intersection of History and Nature: The Relation of Science to Philosophy

If philosophers, historians, and politicians are tempted to absolutize what is only a finite point of view, scientists are no less prone to the same temptation. Merleau-Ponty calls the seventeenth century the age of the "great rationalism," the age in which the tendency to absolutize a finite point of view manifested itself in the notion of an infinite Being (God) which provided a foundation for both science and philosophy. It assured the perfect correlation of the human mind with nature and thereby made science and philosophy interlocking disciplines whose task was to dispel the mystery of the universe. (S 188-89, tr. 149-50) Today this unity between science and philosophy no longer exists inasmuch as the idea of infinite Being has been shattered. The crisis in scientific thinking today stems from the fact that the implications of this dissociation have not been recognized from the side of science. Einstein, for example, affirmed the possibility of uncovering "laws of nature"—as did the classical tradition—but he did not try to state what the relation was between the human mind and the laws of nature which it describes as, for example, Descartes did in positing God. He simply called it a "great mystery," an affirmation Merleau-Ponty designates a "cosmic religiosity" on the part of Einstein. His failure to think through its implications led him into contradictions. Take for example the view that time is relative to the standpoint of the observer. As a physicist Einstein developed this theory, but because he believed in the unity of science and philosophy, he also maintained that the philosophical explanation of the relativity of time must correspond to that of physics. However, it is obvious that if the *only* meaningful conception of time is that of Einstein's physical theory of relativity, then the unity of time which we experience as being in the world together is left unaccounted for. Had Einstein recognized the separation between science and philosophy implied in the destruction of infinite Being, he would have been required either to give up his view of their unity or to seek a more adequate conception of time.[13] Einstein's dilemma has been carried over into the generation of scientists who succeeded him. But, unlike him, they have abandoned the classical view of the unity of science and philosophy. At the same time, however, they have continued to search for "laws of nature" to explain a correlation they no longer affirm! Add to this the fact that the general public, which places an extraordinary faith in science and scientists, asks the scientist to illuminate problems transcending the boundaries of science, and the basis for real mystification is no less firm than in other areas of thought and action. The only way to restore a misplaced faith in science is to resume the dialogue between science and philosophy and to seek, if not their unity, at least the points at which they can clarify one another.

In his course lectures at the Collège de France, Merleau-Ponty developed the notion of "institution" as a means of describing the social world in its various forms. (ACF 1955, 157-60) In his inaugural lecture he had already defined an institution as "a symbolic system that the subject takes over and incorporates as a style of functioning, as a global configuration, without having any need to conceive it at all." (EP 75-76, tr. 56) In his course lectures he broadens the idea to include not only the sedimentation of the past but also the renewal of meaning in the present. In this broader context, institutions possess three characteristics. First, they designate a movement from the subject to his world and from the world to the subject; neither can be taken in isolation. Institutions are *relational* concepts. Second, they point both to the unity of human experience and to the multiplicity of perspectives possible within any context. And third, they indicate the necessity of a dialectical understanding of the relationship between past and present, between the given and the novel in experience. We can illustrate these aspects of institution by means of an example.[14] The Oedipus complex designates a connection between one individual and another or between an individual and a society. As an interpretive concept, the Oedipus complex can deepen our awareness of both our individual histories and our collective destiny. However, if, instead of being regarded as an interpretive tool, the Oedipus complex is viewed as a "scientifically objective notion" into which the life history of any individual can be fitted without further ado, then "it is no longer an interpretation of the Oedipus myth but one of its variants." (S 153, tr. 122; see PP 519, tr. 455) Rightly comprehended, the Oedipus complex refers neither to a wholly biological nor to a wholly psychological relationship, but to a life-world which resides between the two. This life-world is individual insofar as the Oedipus complex can assume a multiplicity of meanings; but it is also societal insofar as the Oedipus complex points to an aspect of our collective existence.

What Merleau-Ponty is doing here is showing that *both* science and philosophy begin by *interrogating our life-worlds*. In the book on which he was working at the time of his death, he attempted to state the meaning of this interrogation in the interest of providing an alternative to false rationalism, whether scientific or philosophical. (VI 142-71) Philosophy, he asserts, does not pose questions and bring responses which little by little fill the lacunae of our knowledge. Rather, the questions we ask are internal to our lives, and if they find a response, our lives are most often transformed by it. Philosophy seeks to return to the origin and meaning of the questions and responses, and to the identity of the one who questions. It is in this way that it reaches interrogation. Questions are first of all questions of *fact*, e.g., what time is it? But questions of fact presuppose that there is something. They take for granted the support of being. Hence the question deepens to include the nature of the something that is. And it asks what the relation between being and man is. Philosophy looks at things, therefore, in order to grasp their essence, i.e., their relation to being, their meaning. But this "essence" or meaning is not something which can be determined once for all. It is a historical essence; what I discover as essence today may be changed tomorrow by the introduction of new facts.

This means that essences have to do not so much with knowledge as with life. No essence can be discovered if we think of essence in idealistic terms as given to a pure spectator. When we speak of essences we are trying to express how we open onto the same world as others. Essences have value, therefore, only insofar as they connect my experience with the experiences of others. They can never be regarded as giving us a thing in all its purity, because we never perceive anything in that way. However, this does not mean that we lack contact with essences. It only means that we should redefine the relationship between fact and essence.[15]

When facts and essences are separated from one another, this is done on the basis of the presupposition that being is elsewhere, that we do not have direct contact with being. However, this is a false presupposition since we are immersed in being, enclosed by it.

Things here, there, now, then, are no longer in themselves, in their place, in their time; they exist only at the end of these rays of spatiality and temporality, emitted in the secret of my flesh, and their solidity is not that of a pure object that the mind surveys; it is tested by me from the inside insofar as I am among them and insofar as they communicate through me as feeling things. (VI 153)

This milieu in which we find ourselves and on the basis of which we reject the distinction between fact and essence is the milieu of our life. When we separate our knowledge from our life we are reaching for absolute certitude, but the inevitable result is that the one who asks the questions is eliminated. This is what has been attempted in many of the sciences of man (psychoanalysis, psychology, ethnology, sociology); but where man is in question, no absolute objectivity is possible. (VI 156) Rather must the situation be viewed in terms of man's presence to being which renders the relation between fact and essence comprehensible.[16]

Merleau-Ponty believes that Husserl more than any other philosopher anticipated his own thought in viewing philosophy as interrogation. And in his essays and lectures on the relation of science to philosophy, he often refers to the evolution of Husserl's thought. In an essay written in 1951, for example (S 123-42, tr. 98-113), he points out that in the *Logische Untersuchungen* Husserl declared that the only way to understand a particular (empirical) language was to uncover the essence or "ideal form" of all language. In other words, he maintained that there was an autonomy of thought vis-à-vis empirical data. (S 128-29, tr. 102-3) Later in his life, however —and Merleau-Ponty detects this change as early as 1910 (S 133, tr. 106)—Husserl reversed himself, recognizing that the philosophy of language is no longer opposed to empirical linguistics, but rather is reflection on the speaking subject himself. The task of philosophy is to understand the requirements of speech and the paradox of the subject who speaks and understands. (S 131, tr. 104-5) Despite Merleau-Ponty's admission here that Husserl viewed all this as preparatory to a transcendental subjectivity rather than as the end of philosophy itself (S 138-39, tr. 110), he stresses in a lecture course during the following year that Husserl was *always* mindful of the concrete character of essences, despite the fact that he regarded the knowledge obtained by essences to be absolutely true. (*SHP* 12-14, tr. 53-55; 27-28, tr. 67-68) In both these texts, and later also in a third, Merleau-Ponty cites a letter written by Husserl to Levy-Brühl in 1935 in order to support his contention that Husserl was consciously moving toward this "existential" dimension of his thought near the end of his life.[17] In that letter Husserl admitted the insufficiency of imaginative variation and affirmed the necessity of referral to the facts. Merleau-Ponty criticizes other phenomenologists for not following this direction of Husserl's thought. Scheler is taken to task for analyzing words without reference to empirical facts (*SHP* 35, tr. 75), Sartre (as we have seen) for separating eidetic from empirical science through the attribution of "certainty" to one and "probability" to the other, and finally Heidegger for leaving the sciences of man altogether outside his ontological concerns. (*SHP* 55, tr. 94) It is the reciprocal relationship between science and philosophy which is closest to Husserl's thought, and in this view there is no absolute separation between science and philosophy. In the final analysis, "essence is accessible only in and through the individual situation in which it appears. When pushed to the limit, eidetic psychology becomes existential analytic." (*SHP* 56, tr. 95)

The conclusion we have reached is that philosophy *is* philosophy of science, though we must keep in mind always that "science" here includes both historical man and the natural world. Philosophy is an attempt to think these two things together from the point of view of the various sciences. Let us examine now the extent to which Merleau-Ponty succeeded in thinking the two together in relation to the sciences.

With respect to psychology,[18] the explicit formulation of this methodological approach had the most striking results in relation to Merleau-Ponty's interpretation of the unconscious. For the result required by the affirmation of the *homogeneity* of content in eidetic and empirical psychology is the removal of the absolute distinction between the real and the imaginary. In *The Structure of Behavior* Merleau-Ponty had said that unconscious factors appear on the level of conscious life in explicit formations and can be delineated from conscious elements, so that (for an outside observer at least) both conscious and unconscious elements appear as conscious. (*SC* 191 ff., tr. 176 ff.) Hence, while he did not deny the unconscious, he tended toward the Sartrian view that in nonpathological behavior the unconscious is a species of bad faith. He did not move beyond this position in *Phenomenology of Perception*.[19] Now, however, in affirming that the data of psychology belong to the content of philosophy also, he finds himself required to recognize a latency in both which qualifies the degree of transparency possible in analyzing any experience. In a lecture course some years later, he describes the phenomenon in this way, using the dream as an example:

To dream is not to translate a latent content which is clear to one-self (or to a second thinking subject) into a language which is also clear, but . . . to live the latent content through a manifest content which is not the "adequate" expression of it from the point of view of aroused thought, but which, at the same time, is not the delib-erate disguishing [of the latent content]. . . . (ACF 1955, 163)

Far now from tending toward the denial of the Freudian un-conscious in nonpathological experience, Merleau-Ponty af-firms its permanent significance for phenomenological de-scriptions of experience, inasmuch as it provides a wider latitude for comprehending the diversity of human life-worlds. It is therefore not surprising that in his last reflections on the subject Merleau-Ponty finds that the insights undergirding the Freudian notion of the unconscious are threatened not so much by those who would make the unconscious a "causally determinative concept," but rather by those who would re-move the mystery of the unconscious, deny the latency which forever surrounds it, and end by failing to interrogate it further.[20]

If Merleau-Ponty's changing attitude toward the uncon-scious reveals that the implications of his philosophical meth-od were not evident to him when he first outlined a program for a concrete metaphysical philosophy (SNS 165-96, tr. 83-98), the similar manner in which he always thought in relation to the social sciences reveals that his new emphasis was also continuous with the old.[21] As in this earlier remarks on sociol-ogy, so in an essay written near the end of his life, he criti-cizes the "scientism" of Emile Durkheim, by which he means the tendency to impose on the particular human cultures studied a concept (e.g., Durkheim's notion of the "social") or set of concepts which "explain" the culture in question. In such a procedure the particular "facts" observed, the ways in which men actually experience life, are subordinated to universally valid ideas (analogous to Platonic archetypes). It was a great advance when Marcel Mauss, Durkheim's nephew and collaborator, reasserted the importance of the particular, including in his descriptions, for example, an emphasis on the variations between cultures or even between the ways in which different men in the same culture might experience a particular phenomenon (e.g., magic). However, Mauss, in Merleau-Ponty's opinion, hardly got beyond the statement of this new method. His results still reveal the tendency to "explain" facts by imposing concepts upon them. In order to get beyond this kind of mistake, Merleau-Ponty suggests that it is necessary first to recognize that the concepts, the models which social scientists construct, are not and are not intended to be absolutely true. They are constructed, not in order to "explain" the facts observed, but in order to be tested in relation to various sets of data to see which facts they clarify. Not all social sciences are concerned with particular sets of data. Economics and demography, for example, are little concerned about the individual's experience. But psychology, sociology, anthropology, ethnology must all ultimately refer themselves to lived phenomena, and their findings therefore have a more immediately human significance. (Cf. *SHP* 22, tr. 62-63) Each of these sciences, through the manner in which it clarifies the relation of facts and essences, can illuminate the others. Anthropology, for example, studies the growth of myth in various cultures. By correlating the similarities and transformations of particular myths or mythical ideas, the human intentions behind the development of these myths in each case might be illuminated and, if they are, anthropology could be of great help to psychology. Ethnology, which teaches us to see ourselves as others see us, can provide in part the perspective we need to see particular cultural forms through eyes other than our own—a necessity for understanding them. Merleau-Ponty believes this kind of method is at work in the investigations of Claude Lévi-Strauss. And in an important paragraph near the end of his essay he suggests the possibilities contained in this "infinite task" of articulating fully the interrelationships among the various sciences. At one end of the anthropological scale, he observes, structures are elementary, and men tend to conform to them. In other words, life is static, the freedom of man in relation to nature is minimal, and human life tends to emulate the life of nature. At the other end of the scale are extremely complex structures, which do not describe human life precisely, because men are free in relation to the structures, they dominate the structures and can regard them as relative. Here the bounds of nature are burst and historical existence in its truest form is born. At its most complete, this kind of historical existence means that while men live within various given structures, they also inhabit a universe whose structures they themselves determine.[22] They are both enclosed within a given meaning and free to add to the meaning which they find given to them. It may be that the social sciences can illuminate this interrelationship between the natural (or given) world and historical man. If so, Merleau-Ponty concludes, then "the frontiers between cultures are erased; for the first time, no doubt, a world civilization becomes the order of the day."[23]

In this reformulation of his social philosophy, Merleau-Ponty has defined the "unity" of men as an "infinite task." It is always both present and on the way. It is that on the basis of which life together is possible—a common visible world. But its presence is at the same time an absence since we can never be wholly present to one another—we each inhabit an invisible world of our own making. Thus there is a "unity" of human life without a "synthesis." The multiplicity of perspectives must be respected. Here the genuine insights of Merleau-Ponty's political philosophy, removed from the heat of postwar political controversy and transferred to a broader canvas, find a more authentic philosophical expression.

VII

The Reappropriation of
a Philosophical Tradition

> Between an "objective" history of philosophy (which
> would rob the great philosophers of what they have given
> others to think about) and a meditation disguised as a
> dialogue (in which we would ask the questions and give
> the answers) there must be a middle-ground on which
> the philosopher we are speaking about and the philos-
> opher who is speaking are present together, although it
> is not possible even in principle to decide at any given
> moment just what belongs to each.
>
> *Merleau-Ponty*

From Political Philosophy to Phenomenology

We discovered in Part I, with respect both to *The Structure of
Behavior* and to *Phenomenology of Perception*, that Merleau-
Ponty's method was drawn from a variety of sources among
which he made few distinctions. Even his affinities with the
later Husserl, whom he first discovered in 1939, did not become clearly articulated until well after the appearance of
Phenomenology of Perception. This was due in part to the
political atmosphere of postwar France, in which his social
philosophy found its anchorage more in Marxism and elements loosely described by him as "existentialism" than in
phenomenology. In Part II we traced his break with both
Marxism and Sartrian existentialism, and we have seen in the
preceding chapter that the result of his break was both a
broader perspective in social philosophy and an explicit recognition of himself as a phenomenologist following the
spirit of Husserl's thought. If this is an accurate assessment of
the situation, we should expect to find it reflected in Merleau-

Ponty's interpretation of the relation of phenomenology to the social world. And this indeed is the case.

A series of statements drawn from essays written between 1945 and 1947 and reprinted in *Sense and Non-Sense* reveal that Merleau-Ponty had not yet fully come to terms with the problem of his philosophical method. In one passage written early in 1946 (*SNS* 139, tr. 70), and in another written in 1947 (*HT* 205-6), he attributes to existentialism those tasks which we found him, in the preceding chapter, attributing to phenomenology. In other texts, however, he speaks of "existentialism and phenomenology" as if the two were synonymous. (*SNS* 54, tr. 27-28; 120, tr. 58; but cf. *SNS* 275, tr. 135) In still another he attributes to Marx the initiation of what has been the central feature of phenomenology (*SNS* 265, tr. 131), though in the same article he also identifies Marx with what has come to be known as existentialism. (*SNS* 271, tr. 133) It appears from these texts that either Marxism, existentialism, and phenomenology are in essential respects identical, or that existentialism (perhaps illuminated by Marxism) constitutes social philosophy while phenomenology is an adjunct to it.

A statement made in 1947 indicates that the latter alternative is probably the one intended. After his lecture on perception to the French Society of Philosophy, Merleau-Ponty was asked whether or not perception could really help the scientist who had to go beyond lived experience and formulate facts in terms of cause-effect relationships. He replied: "I do not know whether the phenomenological attitude is of any use to the other sciences, but it certainly is of use to psychology." (*PPCP* 147, tr. 38) This seems to confirm the conclusion we reached in chapter 3, that Merleau-Ponty's social philosophy was primarily indebted to Marxism and existentialism and that phenomenology was not yet a fully integrated part of his method for understanding the social world. In other words, there was in Merleau-Ponty during this period something of a bifurcation between a philosophy of science or a philosophy of philosophy (phenomenology) and a social philosophy (Marxism and existentialism).

Statements made after 1950, however, indicate a marked change. The first is a remark made in answer to a question by Father Jean Daniélou following a lecture. "I have never thought," Merleau-Ponty said, "that phenomenology was only an introduction to philosophy; I believe that it is philosophy." [1] The second statement appeared one year later, in an article intended for a book on contemporary problems in phenomenology. Merleau-Ponty remarked: "In a sense, phenomenology is all or nothing." (S 118, tr. 94) A third statement, concluding a summary of a lecture course at the Collège de France, is more decisive still:

Either phenomenology is only an introduction to true knowledge which remains foreign to the adventures of experience, or it dwells entirely in philosophy, it cannot be concluded by the pre-dialectical formula "Being is", and it must take as its task the meditation on being. It is this development of phenomenology into a metaphysics of history that we have wanted to prepare for in this course. (ACF 1955, 160)

The conclusion is clear enough. The failure of Marxism and existentialism led Merleau-Ponty after 1950 to identify philosophy *wholly* with phenomenology. In the years during which this change was taking place Merleau-Ponty's conception of philosophy deepened to include not only a description of the social world but also an uncovering of its ontological roots. Thus, when he began to identify phenomenology with philosophy, he meant by phenomenology both a descriptive philosophy of the social world and an ontological philosophy on the basis of which the social world becomes intelligible.

If we look now at the development of Merleau-Ponty's interest in Husserl we shall see this thesis substantiated. Before 1950 only two discussions of Husserl appear in Merleau-Ponty, the first in the preface to *Phenomenology of Per-*

ception and the second in an essay in *Sense and Non-Sense* (273-76, tr. 134-36) written in 1947. All the more impressive, therefore, is the list of essays and lectures concerned with Husserl after 1950. Three appeared in 1951: the first a set of lectures considering Husserl's relation to psychology (but which also dealt with the problems of language and history) (*SHP*); the second an analysis of Husserl's relation to sociology and to science in general (S 123-42, tr. 98-113); and the third a lecture on the phenomenology of language. (S 105-22, tr. 84-97)

Between 1952 and 1955, the years during which Merleau-Ponty was reassessing his relationship to Marxism and to Sartre, Husserl is absent from his writings. This is evident in his inaugural lecture (*EP*), in his course summaries (*ACF 1952-55*), and above all in *Les Aventures de la dialectique*, which set him free, so to speak, for new tasks.

But after 1955 Husserl is among the most prominent themes of Merleau-Ponty's reflection. He enters into Merleau-Ponty's discussion of the history of philosophy (S 173-74, tr. 137-38) and of the philosophy of nature—as we saw in the preceding chapter. (*ACF 1957, 1959*) Furthermore, in 1959 Merleau-Ponty wrote an essay for a book commemorating the one hundredth anniversary of Husserl's birth in which he made explicit for the first time the total identification of his view of philosophy with Husserl as he interpreted him. (S 201-28, tr. 159-81) During the following year Merleau-Ponty taught a course at the Collège de France—as it turned out, his last—on some of Husserl's late writings. (*ACF 1960*, 169-73) Finally, the completed sections of the book on which Merleau-Ponty was working at the time of his death emphasize almost exclusively those aspects of Husserl's philosophy which Merleau-Ponty was incorporating into his work,[2] and in the "notes of work" accompanying that text, which were his private thoughts preparatory to what would have been the further elaboration of that book, Husserl is mentioned far more often than any other philosopher, and overwhelmingly in terms of those aspects of his thought that Merleau-Ponty was developing in his own.[3] In other words, Merleau-Ponty began shortly after his break with Marxism and Sartre to integrate phenomenology into the framework of his social philosophy, until at length it became true for him that phenomenology *was* philosophy.

In Merleau-Ponty's progressively intensive preoccupation with Husserlian phenomenology through these years, we can detect profound changes in his attitude toward Husserl, changes which can only be regarded as the reverse side of his rejection of Marxism and Sartrian existentialism. In his discussion of Husserl's ideas in 1945 and 1947 it is quite evident that, while Merleau-Ponty is interested in reinterpreting certain ideas characteristic of Husserl, he expresses no interest at all in reconciling the two directions of Husserl's thought. And this is true to some extent because the consistency of the Husserlian method was not of decisive importance to him so long as he conceived of his own method as indebted primarily to other sources of inspiration. But in all three of the texts between 1950 and 1952 dealing with Husserl, a change is evident. For now, and especially in his Sorbonne lectures (*SHP*), Merleau-Ponty is concerned with the evolution of Husserl's ideas and with the relation between the two directions of his thought. He concludes in all these texts that Husserl moved from a philosophy in which essences and facts are separated from one another to a philosophy in which they are interrelated and that in so doing Husserl opened up the "interworld" which is the proper subject of philosophy. So far, in fact, did Husserl move in this direction, Merleau-Ponty concludes in his course lectures, that he, "who defined philosophy as the suspension of our affirmation of the world, recognized the actual being of the philosopher in the world much more clearly than Heidegger, who devoted himself to the study of being in the world." (*SHP* 55, tr. 94; cf. *ACF 1960*, 172) However, Merleau-Ponty concedes in the earlier two of these three texts that he is pushing Husserl further than Husserl wished to go (*SHP* 32, tr. 72) and that Husserl would never have agreed with his conclusions. (S 138, tr. 110) But in the third text, delivered as a lecture in 1951 but not published until 1952, a second change is implied. Merleau-Ponty writes:

The relation of phenomenological analyses to philosophy proper is not clear. They are often considered *preparatory*, and Husserl himself always distinguished "phenomenological investigations" in the broad sense from the "philosophy" which was supposed to crown them. Yet it is hard to maintain that the philosophical problem remains untouched after the phenomenological exploration of the *Lebenswelt*. The reason why the return to the "life-world" is considered an absolutely indispensable first step in Husserl's last writings is undoubtedly that it is not without consequences for the work of universal constitution which should follow, that in some respect something of the first step remains in the second . . . that it is thus never gone beyond completely, and that phenomenology is already philosophy. . . . From this point on, phenomenology envelops philosophy, which cannot be purely and simply added on to it. (S 115-16, tr. 92-93)

In this text Merleau-Ponty tends toward the conclusion, without stating it explicitly, that insofar as the *Lebenswelt* could never be completely "reduced" the later thought of Husserl required the transformation of his understanding of "constitution" so as to include facts not reducible to mental essences. Here the matter stood until Merleau-Ponty began to concern himself with Husserl again after 1955, when the conclusion toward which he was tending in 1952 becomes explicit. Quoting from the *Krisis* documents in 1956, Merleau-Ponty cites the phrase: "Philosophy as a rigorous science? The dream is all dreamed out." (S 174, tr. 138; see VI 155-56) In other words, he finally reaches the conclusion, not only that Husserl's thought tends in the direction of his own, but that *Husserl himself recognized this fact*. The redirection of Merleau-Ponty's social philosophy thus takes the form of reconciling Husserl with Husserl and with himself, because now he is identifying his own philosophy with Husserl's philosophy and not simply borrowing ideas from Husserl to supplement an inspiration which comes primarily from different sources (i.e., Marxism, existentialism).

This is nowhere more apparent than in the essay Merleau-Ponty wrote in 1959 in commemoration of the one hundredth anniversary of Husserl's birth.[4] He asserts that Husserl was one of the great thinkers in whose works much is suggested for thought which was not followed through in those works and which we have not thought about. Our hommage to Husserl, therefore, should consist in evoking this unthought content buried in Husserl's works.[5] Merleau-Ponty proposes, in doing this, to center his attention on *Ideen* II, a text not published until after Husserl's death. What Merleau-Ponty finds to be unthought in Husserl is interesting for the meaning it allows us to give to Merleau-Ponty's thought at the time of his death. He finds that Husserl, from *Ideen* II on, "does not install us in a closed, transparent milieu," and "does not take us (at least not immediately) from 'objective' to 'subjective'," but rather that he unveils "a third dimension in which this distinction becomes problematic." (*S* 205, tr. 162) This third dimension is what Merleau-Ponty calls the "interworld," the world in which nature and mind are given simultaneously and in a relation that can never be dissolved from either side. What is the nature of this interworld? Merleau-Ponty suggests that we can only formulate Husserl's intentions at this point "at our own risk" (*S* 209, tr. 166), implying that it is the nature of what is unthought to be capable of development in a number of directions. We are thus warned that from this point forward the analysis will be a description of *Merleau-Ponty's* thought, while Husserl is to be regarded as the one who evokes or inspires the direction of this thought. The analysis begins with the body which Husserl suggested in *Ideen* II to be both a subject and an object and thus the point of contact between ourselves and other persons and things in the world. For "if the distinction between subject and object is blurred in my body... it is also blurred in the thing, which is the pole of my body's operations...." (S 211, tr. 167) Once this is recognized, an ontological significance is restored to the sensible world. For while the copresence of two consciousnesses can never be proved, as *Phenomenology of Perception* emphasized, a copresence in the sensible (perceived) world is immediately certain since when another sees, "*I am present at his seeing*, it *is visible* in his eyes' grasp of the scene." My "primary view" is present to his "subordinate view" of the same landscape. (S 214, tr. 169; cf. 91-92, tr. 73; 117, tr. 93) The totality of objects that can be present to us is Nature in its fundamental sense. It is of course true that this totality is more than can present itself to any person. Nevertheless, the "here" and the "self" imply a "there" and "another" as variants. "Each 'here', each nearby thing, each self—lived in absolute presence—bears witness beyond itself to all the other ones which are not for me compossible with it and yet, *somewhere else*, are at this same moment being lived in absolute presence." (S 222, tr. 176) Thus it is that every object and person implies others to which it is related, and there is a circularity of relationship between men and between man and Nature. Husserl did not fail to see the implications of this even for natural science.[6] As Husserl recognized that the natural attitude is not abolished by phenomenology but in fact is reaffirmed by it in the interest of making philosophy relevant to *all* experience, then phenomenology became a problem, for there are things which resist us. A shadow has been cast over the original belief regarding the direction of phenomenology. But, says Merleau-Ponty, "the philosopher must bear his shadow, which is not simply the factual absence of future light." (S 225, tr. 178) And Husserl bore his, since constitution became for him, as his thought matured, "the means of unveiling a back side of things that we have not constituted" (S 227, tr. 180), but to which we are present in ways perhaps theoretically contradictory but nevertheless meaningful inasmuch as what is lived is also (to some degree) understood.[7]

In the final completed chapter of the book on which Merleau-Ponty was working at the time of his death (*VI* 172-204), he succeeded in restating the vision of his earlier philosophy, though this time it is undergirded by a philosophy of being and is elaborated as an expression of Husserlian phenomenology. Indeed, as we analyze what he says we can see his earlier essays on Husserl in the background. When we see things, he begins, the things we see are present in us, but we are also present in them. There is a simultaneous identity (or identification) and distance. In order for a relation to exist between myself and the things I see, it is necessary that "at the same time as felt from the inside, my hand also be accessible from the outside." (*VI* 176) And since through vision, we touch things with our look, "it is necessary that vision be inscribed also in the order of being that it unfolds before us ... that the one who looks not be himself a foreigner to the world at which he looks." (*VI* 177) "The one who sees can possess the visible only if he is possessed by it, only if he *is it.*" (*VI* 177-78) Thus it is true both that we see things at a distance where they are (things are much more than their being-perceived), and that we are stretched out with them through our vision. There is a simultaneous proximity and distance between myself and things. The point of contact is through the body. The body is a being in two dimensions. "From one side it is a thing among things and, from the other, the one who sees and touches them." Furthermore, "we say, because it is evident, that it reunites in itself these two properties, and its double belonging to the order of the 'object' and to the order of the 'subject' unveils to us between the two orders some very unexpected relations. If the body has this double reference, this cannot be by an incomprehensible chance. It teaches us that each calls the other." (*VI* 180-81) Through this interaction in which both subject and object dimensions of reality belong to both body and thing perceived, there is formed a Visibility, a Tangibility, which belongs neither to the body nor to the world. The body sees the world, but it also feels itself seen by things (an experience to which many painters have attested), until one no longer knows who sees and who is seen. This Visibility can be designated "flesh," since there is no name in traditional philosophy by which to designate it. It is a *general thing* and, as such, an "element" [8] of Being. The I who sees and the thing that is seen are taken from the same "element." (VI 184) What we need to show is that "flesh" is a final notion, that it is not composed of independent substances but that it is thinkable in its own terms. If we can show this then we will have no difficulty in seeing how the same relationship of seeing and seen holds true for other bodies than mine. (VI 185) When another person and I see the same landscape there is no problem of an *alter ego*, "because it is not I who see, not *he* who sees, but an anonymous visibility (which) inhabits us both, a vision in general, by virtue of that primordial property which belongs to flesh, being here and now, radiating everywhere and never being individual, being also... universal." (VI 187-88) In this situation we see others seeing, and others see us seeing. Henceforth we are fully visible to ourselves through the eyes of others. The lacunae of our eyes are made up by the eyes of others.

For the first time, the body is no longer coupled with the world; it entwines another body, applying itself carefully to the greatest extent, designating indefatigably with its hands the strange statue which gives in its turn all that it receives, lost outside the world of ends, fascinated by the unique occupation of floating in Being with another life, of making itself the outside of its inside, and the inside of its outside. And then, movement, touch, vision, applying themselves to the other and to themselves, rise toward their source and, in the patient and silent work of desire, begin the paradox of expression. (VI 189)

Reassessment of the History of Philosophy

In *Phenomenology of Perception* Merleau-Ponty leaves the impression that he is not so much concerned to relate himself to a continuous philosophical tradition as he is to dissociate himself from most of the directions philosophy has taken since Descartes. A few modern philosophers—Bergson, Descartes, and Kant—receive a good deal of critical comment. Some others—Hegel, Heidegger, Husserl, Sartre, and Scheler—are often cited to confirm views he is putting forward. Or if, as in the case of Sartre's conception of the body-subject and Heidegger's conception of being-in-the-world, he takes issue with the views of others, he does so without bringing himself directly into relation to the philosopher over against whom he is writing. Between 1945 and 1950 his interests were for the most part centered around political questions and consequently around men like Lenin, Trotsky, and Lukacs, who hardly figure at all in the philosophical tradition.[9] But after 1950, when Merleau-Ponty began to align himself with Husserl's thought and to reject Marxism and Sartrian existentialism, his attitude toward other philosophers reveals a corresponding shift. On the one hand, he is critical, not only of Marxism and Sartrian existentialism, but also of other phenomenologists who deviated from Husserl. And on the other hand, he reappropriates in part the philosophical tradition about which he had been either silent or critical in earlier works.

As examples of his more critical approach to phenomenologists, I might cite Scheler and Heidegger. Merleau-Ponty's earliest published article was a review of the French translation of Scheler's *Ressentiment*.[10] Drawing on works of Scheler other than the one under review, he suggests the effectiveness of Scheler's attempt to show that Nietzsche's analysis of the biological origin of Christian *resssentiment* was reductive; and his description of Scheler's countereffort to establish the structural character of the perceived world (in this case affective states) in terms of a "causality" which will be "no longer physical but essential," is a striking anticipation of his own later work.[11] He notes further that this new approach to philosophy will appear novel to French readers except insofar as they are familiar with the "concrete descriptions" of Jean Wahl and Gabriel Marcel.[12] Strangely enough, however, Merleau-Ponty never returns to a discussion of Scheler's method in relation to his own, even though he continued to read Scheler's books, as is indicated by the fact that three not listed in the bibliography of *The Structure of Behavior* appear in that of *Phenomenology of Perception*. However, all the references to Scheler in *Phenomenology of Perception* —and there are eighteen—are intended to add support to his own views; they imply an essential agreement with respect to method. Between 1945 and 1950, Scheler is not mentioned at all by Merleau-Ponty. After 1950 he is referred to again, but now he is judged critically in relation to Husserl's phenomenology (*SHP* 35, 54-55, tr. 75, 93-94; cf. *VI* 236), and in relation to Merleau-Ponty's own view of the interlacing of all things as opposed to their hierarchical order. (*VI* 324)

With regard to Heidegger, the situation is more ambiguous. In *Phenomenology of Perception* Heidegger appeared, like Sartre, as one from whom Merleau-Ponty had drawn a great deal, and despite the fact that there were significant differences between them even then, the points of agreement were more strongly highlighted. Moreover, though Merleau-Ponty broke openly with Sartre's philosophy, his controversy with Sartre stemmed from a mutual personal involvement in politics as well as in philosophy. Merleau-Ponty never had the same occasion to bring Heidegger into critical focus. Nevertheless, there are indications that he regarded Heidegger's social philosophy in much the same way he came to regard Sartre's. For example, in the second edition of *The Structure of Behavior* he included Alphonse de Waelhens' introductory discussion of his relation to Sartre and Heidegger, a discussion in which de Waelhens concludes that Heidegger's thought is not properly social at all, but rather the thought of a "transcendent spectator" surveying the world. Furthermore, Merleau-Ponty remarked in 1951, as we have already noted, that Husserl was actually more an existential phenomenologist than Heidegger. And although Merleau-Ponty never ceases to allude to Heidegger, often to suggest agreement with him on specific points,[13] only once does he actually situate Heidegger's thought in relation to his own. (*ACF 1959*, 235-37) He suggests in that discussion that Heidegger's concern with Being is similar to his own except that he intends to approach Being through beings (= sensible nature). He accuses Heidegger, in effect (as he had earlier), of bypassing the sensible world. The following year, in the course of his lectures on Husserl, he implies that Heidegger's philosophy, in relation to Husserl's, has moved in an "irrational direction." (*ACF 1960*, 169) Thus, it appears that, while Merleau-Ponty was aware of continuing points of affinity between himself and Heidegger, he recognized at the same time that Heidegger's thought was not directed toward the same end as his own; this accounts for the fact that, while he continues to refer to Heidegger, his references can hardly be regarded as evidence of the life of Heidegger's central notion at the heart of Merleau-Ponty's philosophy.

The obverse side of this critique of other phenomenologists is Merleau-Ponty's reappropriation of the philosophical tradition. This is evident first in his inaugural lecture at the Collège de France where, in discussing Socrates, Merleau-Ponty transfers from its political to its philosophical dimensions the manner in which he had always understood *himself* as an intellectual.[14] Three things, Merleau-Ponty believes, characterize Socrates. First, he is neither rebellious (cf. S 47, tr. 35) nor acquiescent with respect to the laws of the city. On the one hand, he refuses to run away from the city in order to escape punishment, for running away is one form of rebellion. On the other hand, he refuses to accept the charge brought against him or to treat it with respect, for to respect the laws is to acquiesce in them. He remains in Athens not, as he says facetiously, because he is old, has always lived there, and would not be better tolerated anywhere else, but in order to challenge the laws by obeying them, to call his judges into question by identifying himself (in part) with them. It is possession at a distance, an inward relation to the outward, that Socrates reveals. "In the last analysis, the City is in him and they [his judges] are the enemies of the laws. It is they who are being judged, and he who is judging them—an inevitable reversal in the philosopher, since he justifies what is outside by values which come from within." (*EP* 53-54, tr. 38) Second, Socrates is characterized by irony. His criticism of the city is at the same time an expression of his involvement within it. His "judgment" is not a pretension to superior knowledge, but only the recognition "that there is no absolute knowledge, and that it is by this absence that we are open to the truth." (*EP* 55, tr. 39) This means, third, that Socrates cannot exempt himself from the judgments made on him by the community. Since he has no absolute vantage point it is "necessary to give to the tribunal its chance of understanding." For "insofar as we live with others, no judgment we make on them is possible which leaves us out, and which places them at a distance." (*EP* 56-57, tr. 40-41) Thus the philosopher is one who accepts his responsibility within the community and who continually recalls the community to its true function by calling it (himself included) into question. He is the outside of his world, and the world is his inside. He is fully a man, claiming nothing for himself, but interrogating everything while he recognizes the relativity of all that he questions—except the absolute relation which binds him to others.

If we view the philosophers who have lived throughout our tradition as belonging to a "community," then it is possible to see in Merleau-Ponty's characterization of the role of the philosopher in relation to the political community the beginning of a new kind of awareness of the philosophical tradition as well. In the first place, philosophers do not reject out of hand the solutions another philosopher, for example, Descartes, has reached, since an outmoded theoretical framework retains its truth even after it has been replaced by another (S 15, tr. 10) and since, in addition, "those who reject this or that in Descartes do so only in terms of reasons which owe a lot to Descartes." (S 17, tr. 11) At the same time, however, philosophers do not entirely acquiesce in the solutions reached by others since, to pursue the example of Descartes, each thinker singles out what he considers to be essential to Cartesianism, a judgment which "depends on his own way of encountering the problems of philosophy." (SHP 4, tr. 46) In the second place, the history of philosophy can be represented neither as the progressive elaboration of a central theme nor, conversely, as the disparate productions of men working in isolation from one another. What a contemporary thinker does depends on what has gone before, but this past can never be wholly integrated into a contemporary perspective; it always retains its distance as well as its proximity. The history of philosophy is thus the (undefined) unity of a multiplicity of perspectives. (See S 158-60, tr. 126-27) And this implies, finally, that every philosopher is "on the way"; each one, from his own perspective, is working through the problems which have inspired his predecessors. He does not claim that they are still valid or that they have been refuted or that his responses alone are adequate. Rather does he continuously interrogate both his predecessors and himself in order to remain open to the world in which they are present together. (See VI 239, 241)

It was in this spirit that Merleau-Ponty undertook the editorship of a history of philosophy (Les Philosophes célèbres) in 1956. The attitude he had begun to articulate in 1951 is evident in his introductions to the various sections of that volume as well as in the nature of its construction. Moreover, it is only within this context that the significance of many changes discussed in the preceding chapter become evident. For example, his lectures on the history of "dialectic" were his own way of reasserting his relationship to a philosophical tradition which he had interpreted too narrowly in earlier years when he had been so much under the influence of Marx. Similarly, his analysis of the philosophy of nature since Descartes was one way of saying how philosophers try to articulate the same problems and to remain within the framework of a tradition even when they consider that framework inadequate to the problems initiated. Furthermore, although his growing rapport with Husserl, as we have emphasized, was due primarily to the clarification of his philosophical method within his own mind, it was also, to some extent, his "location" of himself within an historical tradition. The same is true of his later reflections on the sciences of man, in which he deals with the historical genesis of a method (e.g., from Durkheim's "scientism" to Lévi-Strauss' "interworld" of fact and essence). And what is true of these preceding analyses we shall find reappearing in Merleau-Ponty's views of language, art, and religion.

This reappropriation of the philosophical tradition is nowhere more evident than in the change in Merleau-Ponty's attitude toward some of his predecessors in French philosophy. We noted at the beginning of this book Merleau-Ponty's critical attitude toward his teachers of philosophy. Included among these was Louis Lavelle, his immediate predecessor in the chair of philosophy at the Collège de France.[15] In his early works he never discussed explicitly the works of his teachers, perhaps, as has been suggested, because he believed their thought moved in a direction different from his own. But in 1953 he no longer believes this to be the case with respect to Lavelle. (*EP* 10-16, tr. 4-9) Even though Lavelle was a philos-

opher of being, Merleau-Ponty remarks, he recognized that
we have no absolute vantage point from which to describe
"pure being" and therefore that we must approach being
through our own existence in the world. No matter how much
Lavelle desired to go beyond the world, he saw that he could
not do so "except by entering into it and that the spirit makes
use of the world, time, speech, and history in a single movement ... animat[ing] them with a meaning which is never
used up." (*EP* 16, tr. 9) Lavelle, of course, never said this, but
his philosophy is intelligible only in the light of this affirmation in Merleau-Ponty's opinion. Here Merleau-Ponty is affirming the sense in which Lavelle speaks to us in his own
terms but also in terms of the questions we bring to his philosophy.

Merleau-Ponty and Bergson

Merleau-Ponty's relation to Bergson, his most illustrious predecessor in the chair of philosophy at the Collège de France,
is the most striking example of his reassessment of the past. In
a lecture delivered in Paris commemorating the one hundredth
anniversary of Bergson's birth, Merleau-Ponty began by remarking that his generation knew only the Bergson whose
philosophy was established and had a large following, the
Bergson "who was already retired from teaching and almost
silent during his long preparation of the *Two Sources*, already
considered an inspiration rather than a threat by Catholicism,
already taught in classes by rationalist professors." (*S* 229, tr.
182) One would surmise from this statement that Bergson was
largely disregarded by Merleau-Ponty's generation, as were
the "rationalist professors." But this is not the case. In his first
book-length study, Sartre devoted a long chapter (chapter 4)
to Bergson's theory of the relation between images and perception. Bergson had defined this relation in *Matter and
Memory* (1896).

In that book Bergson attempts, first, to maintain that "pure perception" and "pure memory" are derived from radically different sources, so that neither can be reduced to the other; and, second, to demonstrate that the distinction between them is an abstraction which *in practice* does not exist, but that matter and memory interpenetrate each other in the act of perception. The first hypothesis, a radical metaphysical dualism, is intended to undercut both realism which transforms everything into an object and idealism which makes objects the function of a thinking subject. The second hypothesis is intended to refute "materialist" doctrines which maintain an independent existence of matter and "spiritualist" doctrines which maintain an independent existence of spirit. Thus Bergson hopes to dissolve classical antitheses while at the same time offering a more adequate explanation of the relation of body and soul. The substance of his reasoning is as follows. "Pure perception" is the coincidence of the perceiving subject with the object (matter) perceived, that is, perception is not in the subject but in the object itself. There is, of course, something more in matter than what is perceived, but this something more is not something different from what is given.[16] Therefore, it is not true (as Descartes maintained) that only the subject is extended; extension belongs to *both* subject and object. Nor is it true that the subject in perception is primarily a "thinking" subject; the subject is first of all a subject-object (a body) which *acts* on other objects. The purpose of the body in perception is to *limit* the intrusion of memories from the past in the interest of a directed present action. Perception intends action; knowledge is a secondary phenomenon, the result of an abstraction from action by the mind. "Pure memory" is consciousness or spirit. It is wholly different from matter, since matter indicates the *presence* of an object, while memory points to its *absence*. But it is also to be distinguished from the mind. The mind is a storehouse of pure memory, but the mind can store only what is *already present* to it. Since pure memory includes the entire past, it is an unlimited phenomenon. Thus, unlike the body which limits in order to act, memory transcends the requirements of perception and points to the *freedom* of the human spirit, its power to encompass limitless possibilities. Now spirit (pure memory) and matter (pure perception) come together in the concrete act of perceiving. On the one side, every act of perception requires a certain duration for its completion; hence the past (memory) enters into the present (perception). Perception is thus always in practice accompanied by memory. Similarly, on the other side, pure memory is retained in the mind as a series of memory-images of the past which are called forth by the body in perception according to the intentions of bodily action. Thus does spirit feed on perceptions (by transforming these into memories) which it borrows from matter in the form of bodily movements; the movements limit freedom of spirit but in turn are transformed through having spirit stamped upon action itself.

Sartre's criticism of Bergson's theory is that it oscillates between the identification of consciousness and things and the complete separation between the two, without ever accounting for their inherence in one another. On the one hand, Bergson identifies the image of the thing itself with the representation (image) of the thing in consciousness (i.e., maintains that what we perceive *is* the thing). The result is either to make consciousness explicable in terms of the (physical) things which individuate it or to render impossible an explanation of how things can remain things in consciousness once they are no longer perceived, since the body, which is required to render images present to consciousness, is no longer acting once things are no longer being perceived. On the other hand, however, Bergson defined consciousness and things as metaphysical opposites, which raises the problem of how a perception differs from an *actualized* memory (the reappearing image of a thing). In attempting to account for the difference between these two, Bergson was led to maintain contradictory theories. The first theory was that a memory, in order to become actualized, had to insert itself into the body, since the body is the seat of motor activity. This theory, however, leads back to an earlier difficulty: that the object perceived determines consciousness. In order to avoid this conclusion Bergson developed an alternative theory according to which memory is not determined by the body at all, but rather is an awareness *sui generis* enabling it to be present as recollection. In this case, the body is passive rather than active, and memory, which according to Bergson's first theory had been passive, is now endowed with active "magical" powers. Hence, Sartre concludes, Bergson's explanations lead either to the complete separation between consciousness and its object or to their identification, but he never succeeds in explaining how the two meet in the act of perception.

Did Merleau-Ponty share Sartre's critical strictures against Bergson? It would appear from his review article of Sartre's book that he did not, for near its conclusion he remarks:

It is possible . . . to find a more profound meaning of "images" in *Matter and Memory* [than Sartre does]. One would think that in presenting the world as an ensemble of "images", Bergson wanted to suggest that the "thing" could neither be resolved into "states of consciousness" nor sought beyond what we see, in a substantial reality.[17]

Hence, two years before the writing of his first book, Merleau-Ponty apparently looked to Bergson's theory of perception as one aiming at that "ambigious" world to which his own thinking was directing him. The form of his early studies also suggests the influence of Bergson. Both men, for example, were concerned to dissolve the classical solutions of realism and idealism regarding the phenomenon of perception and to describe their inherence through an appeal to the data of psychology. But when we look in Merleau-Ponty's first two books for traces of a substantive influence, we are surprised to find only critical references to Bergson reminiscent of Sartre's. For example, in *The Structure of Behavior*, Merleau-Ponty gives Bergson credit for having criticized those psychologists who defined consciousness as possession of an object of thought, thus rendering impossible an adequate account of their interrelationship. But, he adds, Bergon did not follow through with this critique. In fact he became guilty of his own strictures inasmuch as he identified objects so completely with "pure perception" that consciousness became constitutive of the objects before it. (*SC* 230, tr. 213) But this one-to-one correlation between consciousness and its objects does not "explain" our interrelation with the world so much as it dissolves all the problems connected with the description of *how* this interrelation takes place. And it is this description which is lacking in Bergson. (*SC* 178, tr. 164-65) Merleau-Ponty returns to these same points in *Phenomenology of Perception*, where they are not only stated more bluntly,[18] but placed within a different context. For here Merleau-Ponty argues that for Bergson the phenomenal field is an "inner world," and that the "immediate data of consciousness" refer to what is available only to introspection or intuition, a theoretical framework in which it becomes impossible to describe what is *seen* in perception.[19] Like Sartre, Merleau-Ponty contends that Bergson never constructed a methodological bridge between the inner world of intuition and the outer world of objects. But he emphasized, not that Bergson oscillated between two equally untenable solutions, but rather that he opted for the inner world of intuition, remaining an "idealistic positivist" for whom the world is constituted by a reflective consciousness wholly in touch with its objects. Bergson did not return in the truest sense to the things given to consciousness pre-reflectively but lived in a world already conquered by reflection. Merleau-Ponty never relinquished the view that Bergson's was basically a "positivistic" philosophy.[20] The nature and timing of his criticisms suggest that he was probably first led away from Bergson's approach and into a more "existentialist" direction by Sartre's criticism of Bergson as well as by Sartre's more positive contributions to philosophy. Later, when he concluded that Sartre's philosophy was an idealism, this did not lead him back to Bergson's solution. Rather he concluded, in an interesting sentence in his "notes of work" for 1959: "In short: nothingness (or rather non-being) is hollow and not a *hole*. The opening in the sense of a *hole*, this is Sartre, this is Bergson, this is negativism or ultra positivism [Bergson], indiscernible." [21]

Despite his strictures, it is not surprising, given his changing attitude toward the philosophical tradition after 1950, that Merleau-Ponty should have begun to express his appreciation for Bergson's contributions as well as reservations regarding his shortcomings. It is fitting that this appreciation should have been first expressed in Merleau-Ponty's inaugural lecture following his selection as professor of philosophy at the Collège de France, a position formerly held by Bergson. About one third of his lecture, in fact, was devoted to Bergson. He states at the beginning that the Bergson who dissolved rather than resolved classical problems with his theory of intuition and its direct access to things without interposed symbols is the most obvious Bergson. But, he adds, "it is not the only one, nor the most valid." (*EP* 21, tr. 13) "It would perhaps show more attention to his writings," he continues, "if we were to look in them for his view on the living and difficult relations of the spirit with the body and the world...." (*EP* 22, tr. 13) Merleau-Ponty attempts to do this, and he discovers that the coincidence of consciousness with its object which he had criticized in *Phenomenology of Perception* is not what Bergson intended. Rather he meant by coincidence that man "experiences himself as transcended by being." (*EP* 23, tr. 14) Henceforth, coincidence is only a *partial* coincidence and instead of constitution of the world by consciousness, Bergson leads us to the interworld of perception. "What we believed to be coincidence is coexistence." (*EP* 27, tr. 17) When his theory of perception is viewed in this light, then "intuition" can no longer be regarded as congealed in the present. Rather does it call forth a development, referring as it does both to the being which it interrogates and to the meaning which is derived from it (these being no longer coincident). (*EP* 30, tr. 19) Similarly, the "immediate data of consciousness" no longer refer to an inner world in which everything is perfectly reconciled, but to a discordance between known being and being, the latter constituting not an actuality but an ideal limit. (*EP* 33, tr. 22) Merleau-Ponty makes these same points again in his 1959 lecture commemorating Bergson's birth. Here he goes so far as to suggest that Bergson's theory of perception in *Matter and Memory* was the first to describe "the brute being of the perceived world," the "circuit between being and myself which is such that being exists 'for me', the spectator, but which is also such that the spectator exists 'for being'." (*S* 233, tr. 185) He also ascribes an "existentialism" to Bergson, asserting that *Matter and Memory* described the visible and existing world and that this world provided the "mediating image" for intuition (i.e., came between the perfect coincidence of consciousness and its object). (*S* 235, tr. 187)

It is interesting that within one day of this lecture, Merleau-Ponty recorded in his "notes of work" all his earlier reservations about Bergson's philosophy. (*VI* 247-50) He did not really believe that *Bergson himself* had overcome the limitations to which he and Sartre had earlier pointed, but he did believe that he could develop the "unthought" (or perhaps the badly thought) in the margins of Bergson's texts in the direction of his own.

What conclusion then can we draw with respect to the relationship between Bergson and Merleau-Ponty? The evidence points away from the contention that Merleau-Ponty's philosophical method and its first expression, a phenomenology of perception, were shaped by the influence of Bergson.[22] This is not to say that some aspects of Bergson's philosophy—the appeal to the data of psychology, the dissolution of classical antitheses, the primacy of action, the importance of the body in perception, the emphasis on human freedom, the direct contact with things rather than appearances—did not enter imperceptibly into the existential phenomenological frame of reference. But it is to say that Merleau-Ponty and others found the methodology in terms of which Bergson attempted to describe perception inadequate to the tasks they had envisioned for themselves. Hence they read Bergson as they read Descartes—in order to criticize the outcome of his philosophy.[23] They were thus not Bergsonians in the same sense in which they were Husserlians, Hegelians, or Marxians. Fundamentally, Merleau-Ponty's "rehabilitation" of Bergson reveals his own persistent "existentialism," that is, his penchant for transforming every thinker whose ideas he appropriated into an image of himself. It was always true—and we have seen it illustrated time and again in the preceding chapters—that a thinker became important for Merleau-Ponty when he saw himself in that thinker. Merleau-Ponty at length saw himself in Bergson, but he was not led directly by Bergson himself to do so.

A Backward Glance at the Critics

At the end of chapter 2, I outlined the principal criticisms which were leveled against Merleau-Ponty's early philosophy. Let us look now at the extent to which his later philosophy may be said to have responded to them.

The most significant change in Merleau-Ponty's approach was the emphasis on our "opening to being" in his later philosophy, a change which was intended to meet precisely the kinds of criticisms which were brought against *Phenomenology of Perception*, and which in his last work *he* brought against that book. (See VI 222, 237, 253) On the basis of this

new point of departure, Merleau-Ponty might have replied
to Alquié's contention (that his descriptive philosophy lacked
an adequate foundation) that brute being is the foundation of
reason. This would doubtless not have satisfied Alquié, whose
point was that categories of reason should supply the framework for the interpretation of experience. Merleau-Ponty is
asserting, on the contrary, that the "lived world" presents
reason with a structure, and that it is the task of reflection,
not to construct a world from its own categories, but to uncover the categories imbedded in the perceived world. In a
similar manner Merleau-Ponty might have said to Ballard that
the "categories of the natural world" to which he himself referred are not "cognitive" categories in the sense that they are
a priori in relation to experience. Rather are they *derived from*
experience of the world. It is necessary to be careful here not
to imply that, through the progressive uncovering of the being given to reflection in experience, the world may one day
be completely conquered by thought. This will never happen,
for within the horizon of the world there is an inexhaustible
depth of meanings and interrelationships. The task of reflection is to bring the world into focus by continuously relating
itself to the being given in experience. This is an infinite task,
for it is not so much true that brute being is progressively
clarified as that it is always being clarified anew in its
changing historical setting.

To both Ballard and Kaelin, Merleau-Ponty might say now
that if it is true that our contact with things is at the same
time a contact with being, then every *authentic* experience is
an original experience. It may be true, of course, that not every
experience is authentic. Illusion and deception are also involved in experience; but they presuppose a prior contact
with being and are discovered to be false through the being
with which we have contact. Is this really an adequate answer?
Is it enough to say that because our contact with things is a
(partial) coincidence with the being of those things, we are al-

ways in touch with original experience? As in *Phenomenology of Perception* so in his last work *Le Visible et l'invisible*, Merleau-Ponty answers this question only through descriptions of contact with the being of things. Needless to say, this leaves the question of the criterion by which we judge an original experience undetermined. But it could not have been otherwise in Merleau-Ponty's philosophy at any point. For he always maintained that there is no absolute self-evidence. Philosophy is not a source of certainty; it is interrogation.[24] Insofar as he explicitly formulated the idea of the interrogation of being as an infinite task in a manner analogous to Husserl, he precluded once and for all a definitive answer to this criticism. He would not admit, however, that it is an entirely legitimate criticism, for this uncertainty belongs to the nature of philosophy. To say that it does not is not to criticize Merleau-Ponty's philosophy but to begin from an entirely different conception of the nature of philosophy itself.

This point is relevant to the belief of de Waelhens and Strasser that Merleau-Ponty, in *Phenomenology of Perception*, rules out the possibility that there can be "universal" truth. They see him asserting only that truth is historically relative (Strasser) and that it is always what it is for man (de Waelhens). In point of fact, Merleau-Ponty had emphasized, even in *Phenomenology of Perceution*, that truth is *more* than it is for men who perceive it in objects and events, since no perception exhausts what is perceived. At the same time, it is the *existential* world he is describing, and that world is by definition a world of meaning. Hence, it is inaccurate either to view truth as outside man or to view man as the measure of all the truth that exists. In his later years Merleau-Ponty undergirded this theory of truth with a philosophy of being. His understanding of being appears, in the context of his view of truth, to be both absolute and relative at the same time. But does the idea of an "absolute relativity" or of a "relative absolute" communicate anything either rational or meaningful?

This question leads into the contention of Merleau-Ponty's Roman Catholic critics that an "absolute" is necessary to complete his philosophy. Does Merleau-Ponty's later philosophy move in the direction suggested by his Catholic critics? And if not, have they been justified in any case? It does not seem so in the case of Remy Kwant who contended that had Merleau-Ponty given more attention to the question of the universality of experience he would have been required to recognize a human spirit transcending the body-subject. For we have seen that in his later reflection Merleau-Ponty *did* give more attention to the universality of experience, concerning himself, for example, with the interrelationships among the human sciences and with the philosophy of nature. However, this did not lead him beyond a world-centered humanism, for the absolute (being) is an absolute relation to things and others in the world (i.e., to beings), not a relation to God. These remarks apply with equal force to Stephan Strasser since, although Merleau-Ponty would have agreed with him that the affirmation of meaning requires as its corollary the affirmation of dependence on something transcending this meaning, he would not have conceded that brute being—which does transcend all the meanings we find in it—transcends the world. It *is* the world as the totality of possibilities, the "horizon" of all experience.

What of Alphonse de Waelhens' argument that even if God were identified with being he would not introduce certitude but would rather be enmeshed in the world, and that such an identification is necessary if the philosophical enterprise is not to be rendered contradictory? It may perhaps be said that Merleau-Ponty means what de Waelhens means by being in this formulation, but that he would not go on to identify being so understood with God. One can of course raise the question here of whether this may not be a legitimate extension of Merleau-Ponty's thought, whether one could not claim that his philosophy does not contradict (and perhaps even affirms) the idea of a *wholly immanent* God. This may well be the case, but I shall leave further consideration of this point to my discussion of Merleau-Ponty's view of religion.

PART IV

Old and New Perspectives on
Some Philosophical Problems: 1945-1961

VIII

The Role of Artistic Expression in Merleau-Ponty's Social Philosophy

JEAN DANIÉLOU: One of the essential functions of language ... is to maintain what has been said.

MERLEAU-PONTY: No, it is to say it.

J.D: The fact that things have been said once for all in a sacred text appears more essential.

M-P: It is necessary to speak in order to begin: preserve, it is necessary to create.

J.D.: This role of creation exists ... [but] conservation of language is ... more fundamental. You put the accent too exclusively on ... the initiative of present freedom, and not enough on the total historical given.

M-P: A language ... is an effect of tradition, but a tradition is an appeal to renew expression, to begin again the initial creative work.

J.D.: Not uniquely.

M-P: Without this present work, language itself would be able to say nothing.

The Creative Process

We have seen that from his first work to his last, including also the most penetrating aspects of his political philosophy, Merleau-Ponty was concerned with the interworld between an object-nature and a constituting consciousness, a world of meaning or signification for the body-subject who is involved-in-the-world. Artists are preeminently concerned with this interworld and through "expression" seek to bring it to birth. This is doubtless the reason Merleau-Ponty was concerned throughout his life with a philosophy of language and of art. An analysis of the role these played in his philosophical development should illuminate even further the transformations and continuities in his thought documented in the preceding chapters.

We might well begin by asking what is involved in creative

expression. The first thing to be said is that it exists not alone for the artist in moments of inspiration; it exists also for those who participate in what the artist has created. In other words, genuine artistic expression is the joining together of *both* the artist *and* the reader or viewer of his work in an originally expressive gesture; artistic creativity is an intersubjective phenomenon. This is suggested by the nature of the creative process itself in which the artist enters into a "communion" with the world about him. In the experience of painting, for example, the *object itself* speaks; the artist does not simply impose his understanding (or vision) upon it. The object is foreign to him and interrogates him; he does not "control" it but rather seeks to grasp its unity which transcends all partial perspectives. In short, the object tears him away from himself towards the world. In understanding an object he understands himself better inasmuch as he grasps his relationships to a world outside himself.[1] On the other hand, however, it is the *subject* who organizes or synthesizes the object through creative expression. This synthesis of the body-subject points to the fact that the object is not only outside but also *within*. This is what Merleau-Ponty means when he writes in his last published essay that the interrogation of a painting aims at the genesis of things in our body, that the eye is "that which has been moved by some impact of the world which it then restores to the visible through the offices of an agile hand," and that "it gives visible existence to what profane vision believes to be invisible." (*OE* 200, tr. 165, 166) But it is not only the case that the artist is involved-in-the-world and the world in the artist. His synthesis of what he finds around him is also an expression of his *freedom*. We have seen in earlier discussions that this was also the character of expressive speech. It brings to birth what had not been before, and in so doing witnesses to human freedom, the power always to transcend nature (i.e., what is already given, whether naturally or by human construction).

Let us see now what the significance of Merleau-Ponty's philosophy of language and art is in his total philosophy of creative expression.

Language as Creative Expression: Merleau-Ponty and Ferdinand de Saussure

Many descriptive statements regarding the expressive character of speech appeared in *Phenomenology of Perception*.[2] Not until 1951, however, were these further developed.[3] It is interesting to note that Merleau-Ponty's first reflections on a philosophy of culture concurrent with his rejection of Marxism and Sartrian existentialism occur within the context of a philosophy of language. Just to note the texts on language appearing during this period documents the fact well enough. In 1951 Merleau-Ponty considered the problem of language in course lectures, in a public lecture, and in two published articles.[4] His articles on Malraux's interpretation of the history of painting in 1952 were set in the context of a philosophy of language.[5] Both his lecture courses during his first year as professor at the Collège de France (1953) dealt with the philosophy of language.[6] The following year one of two courses was devoted to the problem.[7] Strikingly enough, his essays and lectures for several years after 1954 do not deal directly with the problem of language. Instead, he turned his attention to the interdependence of the sciences of man. We shall see that his philosophy of language was instrumental in assisting him to move in the direction of a broader social philosophy. In *Le Visible et l'invisible*, the philosophy of language had once again moved to the center of his attention. We shall see why momentarily.

The timing and content of Merleau-Ponty's reflections on a philosophy of language suggest that they should be read in relation to three factors. First, Merleau-Ponty found corroboration for his view in H.-J. Pos's article on Husserl to which he refers in virtually every discussion of Husserl's phenomenology of language.[8] The reason may be found in the thesis of the article itself: that Husserl's phenomenology of language directs one to the *speaking subject himself* and not to the objectively scientific point of view in linguistics which consists in a reflective analysis of what a speaking subject has said. Second, Merleau-Ponty learned in the course of his political debates in 1946-47 how difficult it is to communicate with words, how, as Valéry had already said, our words convey intentions to others different from those we actually possessed. These debates undoubtedly account in part for Merleau-Ponty's continued interest in a phenomenology of language. Third, between 1945, when *Phenomenology of Perception* was published, and 1951, when Merleau-Ponty began to write again on the problem of language, he read the course of lectures delivered by Ferdinand de Saussure in Geneva between 1906 and 1911.[9] Saussure was one of the seminal thinkers in the development of a method for the study of linguistics. He wrote a treatise on the Proto-Indo-European vocalic system at the age of twenty, while still a student at Leipzig, which, in the words of his translator, "is still recognized as the most inspired and exhaustive treatment of the Proto-Indo-European vocalism." [10] For ten years Saussure taught in Paris (1881-91), where he was secretary of the Linguistic Society. The last years of his life were spent at the University of Geneva, where he succeeded to the chair of Joseph Wertheimer in 1906. He influenced—and continues to influence—a great many European thinkers. Merleau-Ponty found in Saussure's efforts a point of view analogous to his own within the field of linguistics itself. We have already discussed Merleau-Ponty's *rapprochement* with Husserl, in which the philosophy of language was one link, as well as the political debates following the war and their potential for awakening an interest in a broader social philosophy. In order, however, to assess the significance of the philosophy of language in Merleau-Ponty's development, we must turn to the work of Saussure.

In his *Course in General Linguistics* Saussure defines a linguistic "sign" as a unity embracing a concept (or the signified) and a sound-image (or the signifier). For example, the word "arbor" is a sound-image when uttered, but also suggests the concept "tree." Thought and sound are inseparable from one another and "sign" comprehends both together. That is, a sign does not point beyond itself to a meaning, but rather the meaning is contained in the sign itself.[11] Merleau-Ponty finds in this Saussurian analysis an important corroboration of his description of the body-subject. For just as the body-subject is the point of contact between a constituting consciousness and an objectified world, so the speaking subject is the point of contact between language understood as thought (i.e., concept) and language understood as sensation (i.e., sound-image). For both, meaning transcends the difference between the signified and the signifier. The body provides the locus for the "changing continuity" of language, the "intentional transgression" between thought and sensation. (S 121, tr. 96) This description accounts not only for the way in which a child learns a language, but also for creative expression wherever it is encountered. Never in the latter is there a "surplus" of thought beyond the words spoken. Rather the words fill the thought, the body is wholly absorbed in them, and it is only when the words cease that reflection takes over and deciphers the intellectual content of what was expressed.[12]

The full implications of this analogy become clear only after we take into account a second Saussurian element which appears in Merleau-Ponty: the distinction between "language" (*langue*) and "speech" (*langage, parole*). The former refers to a social deposit which is essential for communication; the latter *includes* this deposit but refers also to an individual act which may contain accessory (or accidental) elements as well. Linguistics deals with "language" because it is homogeneous (while speech is heterogeneous) and is a well-defined object (while speech, involving the accidental, cannot be defined).[13] This does not mean, however, that linguistics ignores speech. The study of language must also embrace a method which allows us to deal, not only with its present accepted form, but also with the accepted form it will take as time passes; for language never stands still; it is always changing within a limited framework. Saussure designates the study of sedimented language as "synchronic linguistics." In this branch of study attention is centered on a comparison of forms in the accepted system, that is, on the "general grammar" or structure of a language.[14] Changes in language, on the other hand, are the subject of "diachronic linguistics," which deals, not with the relations in a given language-state, but with the relations between two (or more) language states which succeed one another in time.[15] In the case of neither branch can the study of language proceed in terms of "laws." For if we take the two defining characteristics of a law—its imperative quality and its generality—we find that synchronic "laws" are general but are not imperative (i.e., may not continue to hold) and that diachronic "laws" are imperative (i.e., force themselves upon language) but are not general.[16] The corollary of this admission is, of course, that neither of the two branches of linguistics is rigidly separable from the other: synchronic linguistics contains its diachronic elements and diachronic changes may become part of a synchronic structure.

Saussure does not press this implication, but Merleau-Ponty does in attributing to Saussure the abandonment of language (*langue*) as an object of linguistic study in favor of the speaking subject. He emphasizes the fact that the synchronic and diachronic elements of language must be taken together. Viewed in horizontal perspective, language is a coherent system, the past of which enters into every present, regardless of how fortuitous the present may be (i.e., the synchronic embraces the diachronic); viewed in vertical perspective, every synchronic system must have lacunae within it if anything new is to appear (i.e., the diachronic embraces the synchronic). This interpenetration of the two aspects of linguistics suggests two tasks which must be performed simultaneously. On the one hand, a means must be found for considering language as an equilibrium in movement; old forms die and new forms are created, but a coherent whole remains during the change. On the other hand, the system of language which always subsists is never completed; latent changes are present within it, but absolutely univocal significations are ruled out.

Let us look at the implications of this analysis for a phenomenology of language. First, if language is an equilibrium in movement centering in the speaking subject, then the speaking subject is the relational term between the signifying (object) and the signified (thought) inasmuch as he combines them in a temporal thickness. As he speaks, the past is brought forward into the present and the future is anticipated in his expressions. Both continuity and change meet in his expression. Furthermore, the universality to which he gives expression in his speech will always be a universality in act, both in the sense that it has reference to one particular language rather than to a "universal language" and in the sense that the unity of speech achieved is a provisional unity. But this means that language is never completed. Even within a given system of language, universality will never be *wholly* realized but will be, so to speak, "in the air" between speaking subjects. (*SHP* 41, tr. 80-81; cf. *ACF 1960*, 171) Merleau-Ponty likens this to an "idea" in Kantian philosophy: the significations of language are poles of acts of expression which congeal discourse but which are not given in it. (*S* 112, tr. 89-90; *ACF 1954*, 177-78)

These aspects of a phenomenology of language lead to the conclusion that there can be no one-to-one correspondence between words and what they signify; rather the creative word belongs to a field, and a change in one involves a change in the other. Thus, words have an oblique or lateral meaning;

their significance cannot be finally fixed but must remain open.[17] And this implies in turn that the meaning of the spoken word appears in the lacunae between what is actually said; in this sense the voice of language is the voice of silence. (S 53, 54, tr. 42, 43) Finally, this structure of languages makes it possible for words to be variously interpreted. Others may understand what I say in a way different from my intentions; the other may understand me, in fact, better than I understand myself. But in any case language establishes both a personal and an interpersonal (or intersubjective) tradition.

It was in part through his reflections on Saussurian linguistics that Merleau-Ponty came to believe that the mixture of essence and existence, which is the starting point of his phenomenology, could be traced in *all* the sciences of man and their unity thus established. As he began his reflections on Saussure, he looked upon linguistics as a point of contact between philosophy and all the other sciences of man, even remarking once that Saussure could have outlined a new philosophy of history had he chosen to do so. (EP 74-75, tr. 54-55) Why Merleau-Ponty did not press this conclusion in relation to the philosophy of language and why it reappeared in his last book will be suggested in the final paragraphs of this chapter. For the moment, however, let us turn to the application of this philosophy of language to working writers.

When a writer attempts to express something which has not been said before, he faces the "problematic" of language or its paradoxes: that language sometimes expresses more, sometimes less, than the writer intends to say; that the intentions do not match the accomplishment of the writer or that the accomplishment is taken as something other than the writer intended; that one can fail to achieve expression by saying something too deliberately, and, conversely, that one often succeeds to the extent that what one says is indirect; that the most intimate secret of the writer which he only suggests in flashes of his writing is communicated to his public more readily than his most conscious thoughts which remain a dead letter; and finally that it is what the man has lived which becomes the substance of what the writer says, and that this fact in itself can cut the writer off from a number of readers. These paradoxes have caused many writers to interrogate, not only their practice, but also the theory of language itself. Merleau-Ponty believes Valéry is a good example of a writer whose creativity was an expression of such interrogation.[18]

Paul Valéry (1871-1945), poet and essayist, experienced a crisis of confidence in language which reduced him to silence in 1892 and became defiance in his notebooks from 1900 to 1910. In them he describes the incomprehensibility of the human body which in sleep is an inert mass but in the service of a painter (for example) does better than the consciousness what the latter would like to do; similarly he finds it incomprehensible that he is a stranger to himself and yet feels affected by the appearance of himself which he reads in others, so that in turn he hides from others an image of themselves, the result being a reciprocal relationship in which he and the other are never absolutely two persons but also never alone. Merleau-Ponty interprets the discovery of these absurdities as a reflection of Valéry's skepticism with regard to language and literature. Language is clear, Valéry wrote, when one passes quickly over words, but the clarity collapses when the language is analyzed; moreover, the writer himself is an imposter in that, though he only says what his language wishes to say, he is taken as profound, while his failings once put into words are no longer recognized as such, and the chance events which entered into the formulation of his ideas pass as the intention of the writer. Valéry finally transcended this nihilism because, Merleau-Ponty says, as impossible as language was, it nevertheless was. Valéry began to appreciate this fact through poetry, a form of language which did not pretend to say anything. But while poetry had little to do with constituted language as such, it was related to the latter in always going beyond it in signification. Poetry, in short, was the combination of language as something signified and signifying. It designated the sedimentation of language by going beyond it to something new. Valéry came to appreciate the variations of language as these were possible in poetry; for meanings could not change if words did not signify something. Hence these variations became the means by which he entered into creative expression rather than a decisive argument for skepticism with respect to language. Furthermore, the justification of language in poetry led Valéry to an appreciation of language in its other forms also. He passed from contempt to acceptance of literature, from refusal of being to the will to live and speak. As a going beyond of the signified to a new meaning which nevertheless remained intelligible and communicable, language designated the possibility of a creative relationship to others. The acceptance of language was also the acceptance of an inherence in a signifying world.

Painting as Creative Expression: Merleau-Ponty and André Malraux

Merleau-Ponty's philosophy of art is set in the context of his philosophy of language. This is clear from his most extended effort at art criticism, an analysis of André Malraux's *The Voices of Silence,* a collection of essays published in one volume for the first time in 1951 and representing the culmination of sixteen years' reflection on art, its history and meaning. Merleau-Ponty's critique of Malraux appeared in 1952 in the last two articles he published in *Les Temps Modernes.*[19] It is preceded by a description of creative expression as this is revealed in Saussure's philosophy of language. (S 49-59, tr. 39-47)

Malraux's major conclusions, of which we must be aware in order to understand Merleau-Ponty's critique, are the following. Art is born in living contact with a culture. It is no longer

viewed in this context, however, inasmuch as art now belongs
to the museums, the development of which is a European
phenomenon of the past one hundred years. Much is lost in
this displacement of art from daily contact with the lives of
men. But one unquestionable gain is our ability to measure
the works of genius in a given period and culture by com-
paring its works of art in relation to its own standards rather
than ours.[20] This measurement has become possible through
modern photography which highlights the *styles* of works of
art—and style is all that remains once art is removed from
daily life [21]—enabling us to compare similarities of style among
works of art separated by continents and centuries, so that the
unity as well as the diversity of human culture may be recognized.[22] But what is characteristic of the style of a great artist?
According to Malraux, a great artist is one who, beginning
with the style of his time (and every artist begins by imita-
tion) creates a new style.[23] This "metamorphosis" of style can
effect either a progress or a regression in the history of art,
and artists are judged by the manner in which they have transformed a given style into a new vision of the world.[24] Malraux finds a fundamental difference between the attitude of
past artists and that of modern artists. The former pursued
their work with some idea of an "absolute" which they attempted to glorify; hence their paintings were *object*-cen-
tered.[25] Today, however, faith in an absolute has disappeared;
the world has been relativized, and art reflects this change
inasmuch as it is now *subject*-centered. Modern art is an expression of the individual consciousness.[26] Nevertheless, as
already noted, there is continuity between various cultures
which may be observed in the comparison across cultural
boundaries of the styles of artistic geniuses. And inasmuch as
artists give expression to this continuity, they reveal more
than any other group the unity of all human culture. Indeed,
since there seems to be a "fate" operative in the world which
tends to nullify all that men do, artists may rightfully be

called "heroes," for they transcend the human condition and reveal a human unity which fate cannot destroy.[27]

Perhaps Malraux's richly detailed analysis attracted the attention of Merleau-Ponty because it appeared precisely at a turning point in his own thinking, and it may have served as a catalyst in suggesting broader perspectives. Malraux's humanism, his emphasis on the cultural unity of man in the midst of a multiplicity of styles of life or visions of the world on the basis of which we are both united to and separated from the past, were always prominent themes in Merleau-Ponty's thought. Now, having begun to turn away from political philosophy, he was seeking a broader basis for his social philosophy and found it embodied to some extent in Malraux's life and work. Merleau-Ponty's criticism of Malraux's formulations of the history and problems of art therefore suggests itself as a plausible starting point for elaborating the constructive aspects of his philosophy of art and the vision of man and society embodied in it.

Merleau-Ponty's critique begins with Malraux's distinction between classical and modern art. He shows that even from Malraux's point of view it cannot be maintained that classical art is object-centered. For Malraux had pointed to the creation of various styles as a transformation of nature, and once this is admitted then nature is already recognized as *more* than an object. Conversely, it is impossible to say of Klee or Cézanne, for example, that their painting represents the annexation of the world by the individual. (S 64, tr. 51) Rather, Merleau-Ponty suggests, it is the attempt to understand nature without the confidence in its essential correspondence to the human mind which was common to earlier times. (S 65, tr. 52) We shall return to this point momentarily.

Merleau-Ponty raises a question, equally fundamental, with respect to Malraux's view of the *unity* of human culture. He points out that Malraux speaks of style as if it were the *end* toward which an artist is moving. This, however, is not the case. What an artist seeks to do is to describe his contact with the world. The way in which this was done in the past may no longer be possible, as was suggested above. But the point is that every artist is in-the-world. He is no "superman" who transcends his empirical experience through the creation of a new style. Maintaining such a view has the effect of "divinizing" the painter. (S 72-73, tr. 58) Merleau-Ponty finds it more natural, more descriptive, to locate the unity of the history of painting in the human body which paints. Malraux's "Mind of the World" is precisely man when he moves, expresses himself. Insofar as there is a "transcendence" involved, it is a human transcendence, designated by human projects. These projects are all based on a common adherence to a perceived world. Works of art, from the paintings on the walls of caves to the most modern drawing, seek to depict this perceived world. There is a multitude of expressions, but the project of expression based on the human body is one and makes the history of expression a single history. This leads Merleau-Ponty to suggest that Malraux is wrong to depict the history of painting as a "cruel history" in which an artist denies his predecessors in creating something new only to be reunited to his antagonists by succeeding generations of artists who see that both he and his rivals were attempting to respond to the same problem. (S 75-76, tr. 60-61) Such a rivalry could exist, Merleau-Ponty concludes, only if painters were united *first* in what they affirmed. If this were not the case their future unity would be impossible to explain. "There is a fraternity of painters in death only because they live the same problem." (S 77, tr. 62)

But if Malraux's view of the history of art is unacceptable, how is one to account for the incontestable difference between classical and modern art? Merleau-Ponty suggests that the real difference between them is the loss of faith in the correspondence between mind and nature which marks our contemporary experience of the world. This loss of faith has consequences for all aspects of modern thought. For philosophy of religion it means that God is no longer some being who hovers over man but that man is the privileged carrier of transcendence. For philosophy of history it means that the present cannot be sacrificed to the future.[28] Now what artists are attempting to do today is to give expression to this "human transcendence," to a world which has meaning *for man*. It is not, as Malraux says, that art is now subject-centered, but rather that it is the conjunction of human freedom with the natural world that the artist seeks to depict. Renaissance artists believed that to understand nature was to understand man also; the correspondence was one-to-one. The problem of the modern world—that nature and human freedom are not so easily commensurate—had not yet arisen. Modern art responds to this new situation in which we live.

In his last published essay Merleau-Ponty goes much further, suggesting that a "model" of nature for our time is adumbrated in the artist's working relationship to nature, inasmuch as he combines understanding and movement. A painter understands *as he paints*, not prior to the movement involved in the work itself (cf. the phenomenon of speech). Nature is not wholly given, but he *makes contact with nature* in his creative expression. He possesses nature *at a distance*; it is something present to (and within) him but also removed from him. Hence he must *interrogate* nature in order to *grasp* its unity. Insofar as he succeeds, through this interrogation, in making available the *unity* of the perceived world heretofore hidden, the artist makes contact with *being*. And since in his work we recognize a contact with being, even though there is no longer a universal conception of being, we must acknowledge that he reveals a "system of equivalences," a logos of lines, lights, and colors, which underlies his concrete expression. A similar manifestation of being is possible in every human endeavor, though Merleau-Ponty suggests that painting has a privileged position in a social philosophy inasmuch as it succeeds more than other expressions in bridging the gap between knowledge and action. (*OE* 195, tr. 161)

Merleau-Ponty had already applied this interpretation of the painter to Cézanne fifteen years earlier. (*SNS* 15-49, tr. 9-25) He rejects the view that Cézanne can be understood either in terms of his own expressions of doubt concerning his ability as an artist or in terms of his relationship to other painters. Rather must one interpret Cézanne in terms of the problem every artist must resolve, namely, that of describing nature effectively in its object-character as it is perceived by the subject, not as the subject "constructs" the object either through a geometrical representation (i.e., and "intellectual" apprehension which, similar to a photograph, imparts the feeling of human construction) or through an imaginary representation (i.e., one which centers on "sensation" as in the primacy of the representation of light in impressionism). Merleau-Ponty believes Cézanne succeeded in resolving this problem. For, in the first place, unlike the impressionists who painted objects as instantaneously given, Cézanne attempted to see an object (or a landscape) as a whole *before* putting it on canvas. Thus it took him one hundred sittings to paint a scene from nature and one hundred fifty to paint a portrait.[29] Sometimes he would ponder one brush stroke for hours. It was the *object* he wanted to apprehend. But at the same time he realized that the object is not given in terms of a geometrical form, but that its very givenness is the task of the artist to grasp. This is indicated by the way in which Cézanne used colors. While the impressionists were content with seven basic colors, he used eighteen, including black and white (which the impressionists excluded). However, his intention was not simply to represent colors and light, but rather to delineate the *several* boundaries and contours of an object. In short, he avoided both the loss of the object in its own givenness ("sensationalism") and the imposition of a conceptual object upon the perceived object ("intellectualism"). In grasping the object as something other than himself but at the same time as related to him, Cézanne reveals the way in which "we are our whole exterior" (SNS 39-40, tr. 21), the way in which nature is both in us and outside us; and in doing so he renders us present to the world which, though not our own construction, is nevertheless an intersubjective world.

Art and Commitment

Merleau-Ponty's analysis of literature and painting leads to the conclusion that both speak to us as much by what they leave unsaid as by what they say. Ideas they communicate are not directly stated but are implied, drawn forth from reflection after the painting has been removed from us or the book laid aside. This is the case because they contain, beyond ideas themselves, *matrices of ideas* which can be developed without exhaustion by the reader or the viewer. Each medium, at its best, installs us in a world to which we do not have the key and compels us to reflect on that world as no analytical work does. Furthermore, it is through the same instrument, the body-subject, that both media accomplish this task. One must enter into the words or the tableau, not as a critic, but as one who follows where the artist leads. Only in this way can art become an expression of "the true," that is, a creative experience for the reader or viewer as well as for the creator.

At least two conclusions follow from this analysis. The first, characteristic of Merleau-Ponty's whole philosophical perspective and evident in my analysis at many points in this work, is that art participates in the fundamental *contingency* of the human situation. The second, and one I wish to pursue here, is that the artist does not work only for himself. He works also for others and has a responsibility toward his society. This raises the question as to precisely what constitutes the *vocation* of the artist in relation to his society. When asked this question by some readers of *L'Express*, Merleau-Ponty replied that the task of the writer was not to persuade his readers to accept his own "doctrine," but rather to encourage them to adopt a critical attitude toward human life.[30] Indeed, he said later, the vocation of the writer consists precisely in raising critical questions.[31] It must be added, however, that the task of raising critical questions is not synonymous with that of offering the right solution to the problems raised. A writer may know what he rejects better than he knows where he wants society to go. "Perhaps," Merleau-Ponty concludes, "this function of criticism is the engagement of the writer." For "if it is true, as Stendhal thought, that all power lies, then we must take all writers seriously who, putting their prejudices aside and remaining open to the future, know what they do not want better than they know what they want." (*ACF 1953*, 154-55) These conclusions imply that writing involves a certain "style of life" within a society which applies to writers of all kinds, and indeed Merleau-Ponty believes it does:

In a broad sense, all literature is engaged when it says something, since it always speaks of our relations—poetic or profane—with the world and with men. At the same time, as it intends to change these relations only by virtue of expression and by means of the truth, it is in conflict with propaganda and the profane techniques of action; it is, if one wishes, disengaged [*dégagée*]. In the narrow and sectarian sense, engaged literature is that which forgets that it is literature, disengaged literature that which says nothing about nothing.[32]

It is the writer's individual freedom and his social responsibility *together* which constitute his "style of life." He can neither abdicate his freedom nor eschew his responsibility, nor can he reduce one to the other without becoming either irrelevant or provincial.[33] The "engagement" of the writer means that he assists in action, while not being reduced either to silence or to lying in behalf of the society.

The "engagement" of the painter differs from that of the

writer. In his last published essay Merleau-Ponty declares that the painter is in a privileged position vis-à-vis the philosopher (or writer of any sort), inasmuch as he can exercise his art independent of the ordinary pressures of society. (*OE* 195-96, tr. 160-62) Thus, for example, Cézanne's remark during the war of 1870 that "life is frightening," while often quoted to his credit, would be considered enough to condemn any philosopher since Nietzsche, for each is expected to take sides, to advise and counsel, to arbitrate issues. Not so the painter. He is the only one privileged enough to be able to look at any situation without having to come to terms with it. Even regimes which criticize painters rarely destroy their paintings but rather store them away until a more propitious moment. Paintings and the painter thus exist in the society but above its battles. As we saw in a previous chapter, Merleau-Ponty tended to deny this distinction in his later years even while affirming it, inasmuch as he viewed the writer also (especially the philosopher) as in some sense above the immediate battles of society. What he never entirely relinquished, however, was the view that art is supremely responsible to society, not as an arm of propaganda, but as a means—even a privileged means—of leading us all to a primordial perception of the world, to a contact with things and others that puts us in touch with an open universe.

The Significance of Merleau-Ponty's Philosophy of Artistic Expression

The philosophy of art always played a significant role in Merleau-Ponty's total philosophy because, as has been made evident, art is related above all to the perceived world with which we are in living contact. It seeks to describe that world through various media, to put us in touch with it, to awaken us to the nature of the world (and ourselves) in the presence of which we live, and to activate our freedom in that world, i.e., to lead us beyond what has been to what can be through human intentions. It is not surprising, in light of the similarity between Merleau-Ponty's philosophical viewpoint and the situation of the creating artist, that a philosophy of art should have assumed such an important place in his philosophical development. We have seen, for example, that it was above all a reflection on the various media of expression through which Merleau-Ponty began to broaden his perspectives beyond political philosophy and to include within his purview the concrete working out of a philosophy of culture. His reflections on language and painting led him subsequently to seek a "system of equivalences" not only in artistic expression but in the sciences of man as well. This task occupied him for the last years of his life. Significantly, however, in his last published article and in the book on which he was working at the time of his death, Merleau-Ponty seemed to grant once again a privileged place to the philosophy of language and of art.[34]

That he should have done so is, I think, in keeping with the nature of his philosophical viewpoint. For it was the "interworld" in which nature and human freedom meet that Merleau-Ponty always intended to clarify. If he turned his attention to the "secondary" accretions of human freedom—what was already accomplished—it was only in order to reveal its roots in a world that was still coming to birth. This is above all the world of the artist who tries to say what has not yet been said or to paint what has not yet been conceived, and in that way to lead others to a primary experience of the world. It may well be, therefore, that Merleau-Ponty's philosophical interests and method were more suited to a philosophy of art than to a philosophy of science (or to establishing the relation between the human sciences), that in a sense his philosophy was antiscientific despite an effort more concerted than that of any other of the existentialists to include the sciences within his philosophical perspective. In sum, it may be that the fragmentary character of his reflections on the sciences of man, his renewed interest in the philosophy of language and art in his last writings, and the privileged place which they assumed near the beginning as well as near the end of his broader social philosophy were inherent in his philosophical method from the beginning.

IX

The Role of Religion in
Merleau-Ponty's Social Philosophy

> For me, philosophy consists in giving another name to
> what has been for a long time crystallized under this
> name of God.
>
> *Merleau-Ponty*

Merleau-Ponty's Rejection of Christianity

Sartre says that Merleau-Ponty had disavowed his Roman
Catholicism by the time he entered the Ecole Normale Supérieur in 1927. "One believes that one believes, but one does
not believe," Sartre quotes Merleau-Ponty as having remarked
to him.[1] Sartre may have had his dates confused, however.
For Colette Audry, also writing after Merleau-Ponty's death,
says, with reference to the incident at the Ecole which first
brought Sartre and Merleau-Ponty into personal contact with
one another,[2] that it was precisely *because* Merleau-Ponty was
a Roman Catholic student who took the requirements of his
faith seriously that the "vulgar" songs of his classmates aroused
his indignation.[3] Merleau-Ponty's remark in 1951 to the effect that he could engage in dialogue with Christians because
he had memories of a religion practiced *even beyond childhood* tends to corroborate Audry's rather than Sartre's version
of the situation.[4]

The first evidence we have from Merleau-Ponty of his attitude toward Christianity, his review article of Scheler's *Res-*

sentiment written in 1935, reflects a state of ambivalence. He asserts that Scheler has shown well the difference between genuine Christianity and its later bourgeois manifestations, and he adds shortly thereafter that "the prometheanism, the religion of civilization" which "impregnates French teaching to an incredible degree," is very far from being essential to the dignity of man.[5] He implies in these statements that there may be a valid Christian alternative to bourgeois religion and to the humanism prevalent among French university professors and students. Furthermore, in dealing with the question of whether or not Scheler does not devalue present existence and bring *ressentiment* back in a more subtle form by accepting a transcendence beyond the givens of human life (an-*other* life) which Nietzsche never would have granted, he asserts that Scheler's phenomenological method [6] has shown that the Nietzschean alternatives of naturalistic immanence or illusory transcendence are false and that, instead, affections such as love must be viewed as ways of being-in-the-world in relation to God and other men. In other words, God, like other persons and things outside us, is to be found in the world.

However, it is precisely here that the questions begin to arise. Where is God to be found in the world and how is one to know what guidance is implied by God's being involved in human existence? Merleau-Ponty points out that even though there is a difference between genuine Christianity and its current practice, Christianity is called into question by the fact that few live its true meaning. Moreover, in France many of the practices as well as the hypocrisy and defensiveness of the Church, "have rendered the approach to Christianity so difficult for some of us." Scheler tends to respond to this difficulty by suggesting that Christianity is a religion based on intention alone and that it has nothing to do with the regulation of behavior. But this is inadequate since the "spiritual person" can never decide anything which does not also affect the "sensible person." As a matter of fact, there are points at which Christianity attempts to regulate the lives of Christians in the world. But no means of assuring the passage of spiritual values into the daily lives of Christians has been found.[7]

This was above all what led Merleau-Ponty away from Christianity, that it had found no way of making its admittedly praiseworthy values realizable in human existence. His rejection of Christianity was not a necessary implication of his philosophical position, as was the case with Sartre. Responding to a question regarding his "atheism" following his lecture in 1951 at the Rencontres Internationales in Geneva, he stated that he employed the term only when provoked, and he added: "I do not pass my time saying that I am an atheist, because this is not an occupation and *it would be to transform into a negation an effort of wholly positive philosophical consciousness.* But in the final analysis if one asks me whether or not I am an atheist, I reply yes."[8] Not only was "atheism" not intrinsic to his philosophical program, but it is also true that he did not regard Christianity as the symbol of a rejected bourgeoisie (as Sartre did), nor was he shocked into reflection by the problem of evil (as Camus was). What troubled him, as his early review article suggests, was first the moral sluggishness of the Church *as an institution.* The Church, he wrote shortly after the war, as if to confirm his earlier apprehensions, is not concerned so much with men as with preserving its own institutional structure. But "God will not fully have come to earth until the Church feels the same obligation toward other men as it does toward its own ministers, toward the houses of Guernica as toward its own temples." (*SNS* 364, tr. 178) That this should have been one reason Merleau-Ponty left the Church is in itself interesting, for his rejection of institutional Christianity came precisely during the period when he was seeking an alliance with Marxism *in some institutional form.* (Indeed, his earliest reservations with respect to Christianity may well have been influenced by a growing attachment to Marxism). And it is also interesting that when he rejected Marxism he did so for many of the same reasons for which he had rejected Christianity, as we can see by a concluding remark in the lecture of 1951 to which we have already referred:

Once again, between Christians and non-Christians, as between Marxists and non-Marxists, conversation is becoming difficult. How could there possibly be any real exchange between the man who knows and the man who does not know? What can a man say if he sees no relationship, not even a dialectical one, between state communism and the withering away of the state, when another man says that he does? If a man sees no relationship between the Gospels and the clergy's role in Spain, when another says they are not irreconcilable? (S 308, tr. 242)

This leads naturally to the question of whether or not, after rejecting Marxism, Merleau-Ponty returned or contemplated a return to Christianity. There is no evidence that he did, though as we shall see, there is much evidence of a greater openness toward religion.[9]

Connected with his rejection of the Church on moral grounds is his rejection of the Christian idea of a transcendent God for the same reason. Belief in such a God, in Merleau-Ponty's opinion, divorced man from existence in the world and alienated him from his fellow human beings. It was beyond all experience and could only be affirmed arbitrarily. Let us see now how he formulated this critique and what its fate was in the changes his social philosophy underwent. In the process I shall not only further corroborate the thesis maintained heretofore, but I shall also make evident the role of religion in Merleau-Ponty's philosophical development and its relevance to his social philosophy.

Interpretation and Reinterpretation of
Christian Religious Consciousness

In an essay written for *Les Temps Modernes* in 1946 (*SNS* 351-70, tr. 172-81), Merleau-Ponty refers to an exchange between Father Jean Daniélou and a Communist intellectual, Pierre Hervé, in which Daniélou had maintained, on the basis of official Roman Catholic texts, that it was possible for the Roman Catholic Church to support freedom and revolution and that, regardless of the fact that for much of its history the Church had been on the side of reaction, its future was nevertheless open; to which Hervé had replied that more texts could be cited to support the position of reaction, that the reactionary nature of the contemporary Church was what he had observed as a youth, and that this situation had driven him from the Church. Merleau-Ponty says that neither man will convince the other, for while Daniélou is right on the level of ideas, Hervé is right on the level of facts. They therefore talk past one another, and the only way to throw any light on the subject is to consider the relationship of Roman Catholic religion to the conservative consciousness and to the revolutionary consciousness, illuminating in this way why the Christian is not for himself what he is for others.

Merleau-Ponty proposes to do this through a twofold "theological typology" of Roman Catholic history. He delineates first the conservative tradition of the "interior God," the God St. Augustine said dwelt in the inner man. To obey this God is to do what one truly wishes since he is more ourselves than we are. He is found in men who do not know him by the name of God. Since faith resides in the inner man it cannot be compelled; it need not even enter the world since, if the perfection of God resides in the inner man, there is literally nothing to do. The corollaries of this perfection are quietism and the unreality of sin. Furthermore, works are an addition to faith which do not augment the sum of the Good. Merleau-

Ponty calls this the "reign of the Father." A second type in the history of Christianity is the alliance of the "internal God" with an "external God" in the Incarnation. God has been among men, he has been seen, and he has left behind him words and memories. The attitude of man is no longer that of reflection but that of interpretation of what God has said and done— an inexhaustible process, since the message is ambiguous. The relation of the inner man to the world is put back into question by the Incarnation. The parables of the Gospels designate not ideas, but relations to others on the basis of the religious life. The same is true of the doctrine of the Incarnation itself and of Original Sin. As ideas they are not clear, but they are valuable (as Pascal said) inasmuch as they reflect the mixture of body and soul, noble and miserable, in man. The world is not vain now, for there is something to do: man is separated from God and must return to him.[10] Man's relationship to God will always remain ambiguous since it is never without separation. As Kierkegaard says, one should not say "I am a Christian," but only "I am becoming a Christian."

The paradox of Christianity, Merleau-Ponty concludes, is that it does not follow either the religion of the Father or that of the Son to its logical conclusion, but adopts an ambivalent attitude in relation to both. With respect to the religion of the Father, for example, Catholicism does not want to give everything over to Christian faith, for it requires in the *Syllabus of Errors* that one affirm the possibility of proving God's existence by reason, but censures those like the modernists who have attempted to transcribe their religious experience of God into intelligible terms. In other words, Catholicism hesitates to say that the God who can be proved is the God who is involved in human existence. This same ambivalence is evident in relation to the Incarnation. The meaning of the Incarnation, as attested by the experience at Pentecost, is that Christ is always with us. However, this lesson was never fully learned, as we can see in the efforts of the Crusaders to locate the empty tomb. What is the reason for this ambivalence? It is, Merleau-Ponty believes, that the religion of the Father was retained even after the Incarnation. If in fact it was true, however, that the Incarnation means the continuous presence of God in human existence, then the religion of the Father should have been *replaced* by that of the Son, and the religion of the Son in turn by that of the Spirit. The doctrine of the Trinity, instead of regarding the Three Persons as coeternal, should have acknowledged that God is known only in terms of the mode of his presence among us.

Historically speaking, Merleau-Ponty's interpretation of the Christian doctrine of God is Sabellian. He holds the view of those Christians of the second and third centuries who contended that there are not three Persons in the Godhead but one God who manifests himself in different modes. This view was rejected because it implied that the Father suffered with the Son; to have accepted such an idea would have compromised the transcendence (i.e., the unchangeability) of God. But that is precisely what Merleau-Ponty wishes to compromise, because in his view it is meaningless to speak about what is completely outside human experience. It is what God is in relation to human existence that matters, and that is all that matters. The point here is that, while in 1935 Merleau-Ponty affirmed that this immersion of God in the world *was* the Christian view of things, in 1946 he said that it *should have been but was not* the Christian view.

Given this interpretation, Merleau-Ponty believes the true relation of the Christian to the political order, at issue in the debate between Hervé and Daniélou, can be clarified. For from this perspective the Church appears ambivalent. The Church looks at the world from its periphery; it does not (historically) become a part of the society of men, but rather crystallizes on the margins of the state. And while the Church affirms the presence of the Spirit everywhere in the world, it claims a special relation to the Spirit. Thus the Church effects *its own* alienation of men from one another. It expresses this alienation when it succeeds in obtaining the support of the secular powers, for it uses these powers to compel acceptance of the true Spirit which resides in the Church. Thus love is turned into cruelty, the Incarnation is reduced once again to suffering and becomes a new form of the unhappy consciousness. When the world looks at the Church it sees a "religion of the Father" which is conservative and a "religion of the Son" which is potentially revolutionary. But inasmuch as the Roman Catholic accepts both at once he is neither quietistic nor revolutionary. He remains "in the margins" of society, not wholeheartedly dedicated to any of its struggles. He may support the status quo (if it protects institutional religion) or he may support the rebellion (if it looks as if it might succeed). But *as a Christian* he will neither defend the status quo completely nor help to bring about a revolution. Thus he disquiets everyone; neither the established powers nor the revolutionaries feel that the Christian is really on their side.

What Merleau-Ponty is saying is that the Christian's relationship to his society is *necessarily equivocal* because the doctrines he accepts prevent him at the outset from effectively immersing himself in the world. If the Christian accepted an internal God and its consequence (indifference to the world), or if he affirmed the Incarnation in such a way as to give up the idea of a transcendent God in the sense discussed, then we would always know where he stood. But to affirm both gods at once, as is characteristic of Christians, is to be in-the-world ambivalently. It is to involve oneself with part of one's being and to survey the world with another part of one's being.

One can see in Merleau-Ponty's interpretation two points at which it is intimately related to his political involvement during this period. First, although he does not say there is no genuine way in which a Christian can be in the world, he does say that there is no way to do so *within the framework of the institutional church*. It is evident that, in reaching this conclusion, Merleau-Ponty had in mind the question troubling him in his political philosophy: Can a person be true to himself as an individual and as a member of institutions (ecclesiastical or political)? He concludes very quickly in the case of religion that this is impossible. Later, as we have seen, he reached virtually the same conclusion regarding Marxism, and was led on the basis of it to reflect once again on the relation of the philosopher to society. And here we come upon a second point. Merleau-Ponty says in his analysis of religion that the Christian is neither a revolutionary nor wholly dedicated to the powers that be. He is "in the margins" of society, possessing it at a distance. But we have seen that, in his inaugural lecture of 1953, Merleau-Ponty described the *philosopher* as one who participates "at a distance" and one of whom no one can be sure. Here the real ambivalence of Merleau-Ponty's analysis of Christianity becomes evident. For he implies that if the Christian accepted either the religion of the Father or the religion of the Son in its "pure" form, then his political choices would no longer be unambiguous. In one case he would be a conservative (or reactionary), in the other a revolutionary. But this assumption underlying Merleau-Ponty's remarks is highly questionable. And the transformations of his own position after 1950 certainly forced him to recognize this fact. There is no "pure" Christian choice, just as there is no "pure" choice within any other framework of thought and action. We are all involved in ambiguities, and to demand that we rid ourselves of all "equivocation" is to demand precisely that we cease to be involved in existence.

So long as Merleau-Ponty was attached to a Marxist position, he did not feel it necessary to examine the role of religion any further, not because, as orthodox Marxists say, Marxism is "atheistic," but rather because his own understanding of what it meant to be involved in the world was denied by the Christian idea of the transcendence of God. This is the meaning to be attached to other remarks regarding religion made by Merleau-Ponty prior to 1950. Following his lecture on the primacy of perception, for example, he was asked by Jean Hyppolite whether man is not "led to pose to himself the question of a 'being of all meaning'... [or] 'absolute being of all meaning';" to which he replied that "you are simply saying... I have no religious philosophy. I think it is proper to man to think God, which is not the same thing as to say that God exists." (*PPCP* 150-51, tr. 40-41) It is clear that what Merleau-Ponty means by "God" here is the unknowable, unchangeable, transcendent being who is not involved in human existence but for whom man is an object. For in his essay on metaphysics written during the same year he says that "metaphysics cannot be reconciled with the manifest content of religion and with the positing of an *absolute thinker of the world*." (*SNS* 192, tr. 96, emphasis added) A God, he adds, who would be for himself rather than for us, is inconceivable to me, since I have no experience of such a being. I can say that I am both transcendent and immanent (i.e., that I am a contradictory being capable of truth even though finite) because I have experienced this contradiction. But such a "transcendence in immanence" could not be posited of "God" because there is no experience through which I could verify the coexistence of these attributes in God. Merleau-Ponty does not say, though he implies, that the only way for Christianity to rejoin human experience is to abandon the idea of transcendence. For, he concludes:

The originality of Christianity as the religion of the death of God is its rejection of the God of the philosophers and its heralding of a God who takes on the human condition. The role of religion in culture is not that of a dogma or even of a belief, a cry. But what else could it be and still be effective? The Christian teaching that the Fall is fortunate, that a world without fault would be less good, and, finally, that the creation, which made being fall from its original perfection and sufficiency, is nevertheless more valuable or was all to the good *makes Christianity the most resolute negation of the conceived infinite.* (SNS 193, tr. 96-97, emphasis added)

Thus, in his discussions prior to 1950, Merleau-Ponty concludes that within Christianity itself there are two irreconcilably contradictory ideas, one of a God wholly removed from human history, another of a God wholly involved in human history. But Christianity itself has chosen neither one nor the other without reservations.

However, after 1950 there is a change in his viewpoint. In his lecture in Geneva in 1951, for example, he says that it is a misstatement of the problem of history to cast the discussion of it in terms of the dichotomy between "vertical transcendence" and "horizontal transcendence." For, he states, "the finest encyclicals in the world are powerless against the fact that for at least twenty centuries Europe and a good part of the world have renounced so-called vertical transcendence." Furthermore, he adds, in Christianity the relationship between God and man is based on the recognition of a mystery and this is due to the fact that "the Christian God wants nothing to do with a vertical relation of subordination." On the contrary, Christianity recognizes that God is impotent until he becomes man, so that "transcendence no longer hangs over man: he becomes, strangely, its privileged bearer." [11] In this passage Merleau-Ponty implies that his interpretation of Christianity is the one which *Christianity itself* has by and large accepted, and likewise that within Christianity there is no need for a transcendent God to whom man would be "subordinated." Thus, he is already moving in the direction of altering his understanding of the meaning of the ambivalence in the Christian interpretation of existence.

Once it is concluded that Christianity is essentially concerned with man's relation to God in-the-world, then it is possible to say that theology is not wholly unrelated to philosophy since, although philosophy does not deal with man's relation to *God* in-the-world, both philosophy and theology are speaking of the human world and of relationships within it. It is not surprising that, having arrived at this conclusion, Merleau-Ponty's later discussions of religion should have centered on the relation between philosophy and theology. In his inaugural lecture (*EP* 57-65, tr. 41-47), his remarks move only by implication beyond a negative attitude toward theology as a "science of man." For he sees in the analyses of modern philosophy by two prominent Roman Catholic thinkers, Father Henri de Lubac and Jacques Maritain,[12] the attempt to prove that philosophy, when it does not affirm the existence of God, is atheistic. In point of fact, de Lubac is concerned only with particular thinkers who *do* attempt to replace God with something else (Comte, Marx, Nietzsche). He does not say that *all* modern thought is guilty of this. Maritain comes much closer, I believe, to affirming that all of modern thought, insofar as it departs from the Roman Catholic view of man's relation to man and to God is, whether intentionally or not, a "decadent humanism" and a cause of the continuing dissolution of Western civilization. Merleau-Ponty grants that both men are right to criticize those who replace one explicative principle by another for in doing so they only reveal that their philosophies are inverted theologies.[13] But he questions whether or not philosophy is reduced either to affirming the existence of a God who can be proved by reason or to replacing this God with another explanation, equally dependent on reason. Actually, he says, "philosophy works itself out in another order, and... eludes both Promethean humanism and the rival affirmations of theology." (*EP* 60, tr. 43) Its domain is that of the contingent interworld where neither man nor God is an explicative principle, indeed, where there is no explicative principle. The philosopher does not affirm or deny the existence of God; rather he treats religion as one of the important expressions of human consciousness and seeks to understand it as such. To call philosophy atheistic is to betray the fact that one has opted for an "explicative theology," which is tantamount to cutting off all discussion between philosophy and theology. Is there a legitimate relation between them? Merleau-Ponty suggests that there is, and that it is found in Maritain's contention that the continuous criticism of idols is essential to Christianity. "Here indeed," Merleau-Ponty says, "we are close to the essence of Christianity." (*EP* 65, tr. 47) However, it is impossible to reconcile this notion with that of a rational concept of God as necessary being. So long as the latter is retained, philosophy and theology cannot come into contact with one another. But if it is placed in abeyance, and if theology will concern itself with the criticism of false idols, then it makes contact with philosophy, for this is precisely the task of philosophy. This, however, raises a problem for theology, for if one chooses this alternative, then it henceforth becomes impossible to say exactly *where* God resides, to say that he is "possessed" by a church. Merleau-Ponty leaves the discussion hanging at this point. His remarks raise the question of whether he has not presented the theologian with an alternative impossible to accept without abandoning his institutional allegiance as well—which would be tantamount to abandoning theology, since all theology takes on meaning only within a church.

In his last extended discussion of religion (*S* 176-85, tr. 140-46), Merleau-Ponty returns to this question, and suggests that the theologian can concern himself with a description of being-in-the-world without abandoning the church as an institution. His remarks are based on a discussion of the idea of a Christian philosophy among some prominent French thinkers in 1931.[14] The thesis presented to the group by Etienne Gilson was that the expression "Christian philosophy" is by no means clear, and that it can be rendered intelligible only by a historical analysis of Western philosophies which would have as its aim to determine whether or not in philosophies since the

rise of Christianity ideas have been given to philosophy which
were not present in Greek philosophy and whose presence
could not be explained apart from the existence of Christianity.
In the discussion under review, Gilson did not attempt to answer the question, but only to state the conditions necessary
for its resolution.[15] Emile Bréhier responded to Gilson that in
the sense in which there can be a "Christian philosophy" it is
of no interest to the philosopher as philosopher, and in the
sense in which it would be of interest to the philosopher there
is no Christian philosophy. By a philosophy which would
really be Christian he means one which would be based on
the truths of revelation as these have been defined by some
accepted authority. But although genuine, such a philosophy
would hold no interest for the philosopher who did not accept the particular "dogmas" in question. By a pseudo-Chris-
tian philosophy he means one which would be based on ideas
allegedly introduced into philosophy by Christian faith. Here
is where he joins issue with Gilson, for he maintains that none
of the ideas utilized by philosophy can be proved to have
been of Christian origin. The idea of the *Logos*, for example,
was not introduced into Western thought by Christianity but
had a history of several hundred years prior to the emergence
of Christianity. Similarly, the idea of creation is to be found
in Plato's *Timaeus* and cannot be proved to have come from
Christianity.[16] Jacques Maritain affirmed his agreement with
Gilson in the debate with Bréhier, and attempted to add to the
discussion by clarifying the issue from a theoretical rather
than from a historical point of view. He distinguished between
the essence (nature) of philosophy and the state of philosophy.
Essentially, philosophy has to do with *reason* and a philosopher
need not depend on the Christian faith in order to remain
faithful to this essence. However, the particular state of philosophy has been influenced by Christianity, insofar as ideas
such as creation, nature, God as being itself, and sin have
been introduced into philosophical reflection. Revelation thus

adds something to philosophy since prior to revelation these notions were totally ignored by philosophers. Maritain concludes that in determining whether or not a philosophy is Christian, one must consider not only the essence of philosophy, but also its particular state (i.e., whether or not it takes into account what Christianity has bequeathed to it). When viewed in this perspective, he believes, philosophy and theology can benefit one another mutually. Philosophy remains free in itself but is nevertheless taught by theology, just as it is used by theology for the explication of theological truths.[17] Brunschvicg remarked that for him the problem was whether or not there could be a *specifically* Christian philosophy, not whether Christianity had influenced philosophy, a fact he readily admitted. In his opinion, Thomism is not a specifically Christian philosophy because of its dependence on Aristotle. He believes, in fact, that there are only two legitimate cases of a specifically Christian philosophy: that of Pascal who sees reason and revelation in contradiction, since reason cannot answer the questions it raises; and that of Malebranche, who sees philosophy as the promulgator of questions it cannot answer and who finds the answers to these questions in theology.[18] Maurice Blondel, in a letter appended to the discussion, agreed to some extent with Brunschvicg, since he believed the question was whether philosophical doctrines should aim at completeness or whether they should admit their incompleteness. Only the latter viewpoint, he contended, is compatible with a Christian philosophy.[19]

What interests Merleau-Ponty about this discussion is the way in which the various views expressed supplement and complete one another. Gilson and Maritain, for example, in concluding that there is no "pure essence" of a Christian philosophy, were not unrelated to Bréhier who maintained that since Christianity dealt with supernatural revelation and philosophy with reason, there could be no Christian philosophy. Similarly, Brunschvicg, in maintaining that the only legitimate

Christian philosophy would be one which finds theological answers to questions raised but incapable of being answered by philosophy, was not far from Blondel, who believed that genuine philosophy was the recognition of the impossibility of answering its own questions. The point is that the question of a Christian philosophy can be settled neither on the level of essences alone nor on the level of facts alone. Whenever this is attempted insoluble difficulties arise. For example, when Bréhier tries to maintain that no ideas can be proved to be of Christian origin, his only recourse is to be reductive, that is, to leave out of account all those ideas which have certainly been added as a result of the influence of Christian history on the philosophical tradition. To recognize the significance of Christianity does not, of course, resolve the question at the level at which the Christian resolves it, since it is one thing to recognize something as historically important and quite another to accept it oneself. (S 179, tr. 142; cf. EP 62, tr. 45) Nevertheless, philosophy understood as interrogation is closer to the practice of a religion which recognizes this interplay of fact and essence than it is to an explicative rationalism. For there is in philosophy and in theology understood as interrogation the same internal conflict between what is understood and what is lived. And a comparison of this conflict as it affects each of them would disclose the genuine relationship between the two. (S 180, tr. 142-43) what Merleau-Ponty had interpreted earlier to be the "bad faith" of Christianity is now taken to be its authentic character. And he could reach this conclusion because he had already changed his view of the relation of the philosopher to society, recognizing that a man always remains ambivalent in the world inasmuch as he must bring what he believes into relationship with his actions, a task which is never assured of being resolved without contradictions manifesting themselves on the level of existence.

The relationship thus established between philosophy and theology will never be that of the identity of faith and reason,

nor their complete separation. It will be the relationship of
"warring brothers." Theology has its own themes for philos-
ophizing: the discordancy between what is visible to all men
in man's relation to God and what is visible only to the Christian, the discordancy, for example, "between the eternal and
the incarnate Word," or "between the God we see as soon as
we open our eyes and the God of the Sacraments and the
Church, who must be gained and merited through supernatural life." (S 183, tr. 145) Now it is no longer the case that
the Christian, in order to be authentic, should opt for either
the religion of the Father or the religion of the Son. Rather, he
should take as his theme of reflection the conflict between the
two, the eternal conflict between God as he has revealed himself to a chosen few and God as he is capable of being seen by
all men in the world where all men exist together. A theology
so understood would find a perpetual companion in a philosophy which has its own questions and partial affirmations. And
only a theology, Merleau-Ponty concludes, which accepts
mediation (i.e., which makes the existing human world the
"necessary detour" on its road to God) can be related to philosophical reflection. (S 184, tr. 146)

There is one final very interesting parallel between Merleau-
Ponty's changing interpretation of Christianity and his own
philosophical development. The discussions immediately following the war centered on the question of whether or not one
could be true to himself and true to an institution at the same
time. But once Merleau-Ponty had cast off his Marxism and
ceased to seek his allegiances within ecclesiastically or politically defined structures, he changed the context of the discussion,
defining the philosopher in relation to the "cultural world"
instead of in relation to the more narrow institutional structures within that world. And when he did this, he changed the
context of his discussion of religion as well. Now he began to
discuss the theologian, not as a member of the Church, but as
a member of the *world*. And he implies, though he never

states, that so long as the theologian is true to the world (i.e., so long as he takes the "theological interworld" as the subject of his reflections) he can remain a part of the institutional Church, since that is the source of the contradictions on which he is reflecting. This is not unrelated to Merleau-Ponty's conclusion that "revolt" from the institutional structures which encompass us is not in our time the order of the day. Rather, our task is "virtue without resignation," that is, working where we are to make the world more acceptable, mindful that whatever structures we might adopt after rejecting those we now live within will be involved in the same ambivalences. Far, then, from being the case that the Christian must be "unequivocal," he must fix his attention on his necessary equivocations and in this way express his human relationship to all other men who, wherever they are, and whatever their tasks may be, are involved in similar contradictions.

The Significance of Religion in Merleau-Ponty's Social Philosophy

The thesis expounded throughout this book has been abundantly illustrated, I believe, by an analysis of Merleau-Ponty's changing attitude toward religion. Regarding religion in the early postwar years as based upon an equivocation capable of being removed only if the transcendence of God were renounced, he came later to accept equivocation as necessary to an authentically human expression of religion insofar as it is immersed in the world. Thus, while in 1947 he had no philosophy of religion, the same cannot be said of him in 1956. To be sure, he never committed himself to a religious faith, but he no longer believed that a philosophy of religion had no place in his reflections. As in other cases, however, Merleau-Ponty could only accommodate religion insofar as he could reinterpret it as agreeing with his own philosophical program. And he was only able to do this after 1950 when he himself began to accept all the implications of that program.

The one religious thinker whose influence seems stamped on everything Merleau-Ponty had to say about religion is Pascal. His distinction between the God of the philosophers and the God of Abraham, Isaac, and Jacob (and his general distrust of "speculation" in religion); his view of the heights and depths of which human nature is capable; his interpretation of the meaning of original sin and the Incarnation; his insistence on the important connection between religious belief and the religious life: all seem to reflect the view of Christianity accepted by Merleau-Ponty while he was still a Christian, and they carry over into his interpretations of Christianity after his rejection of the Church. This influence, I believe, accounts for a certain consistency in Merleau-Ponty's attitude toward religion, even in the midst of his changing interpretations of it. He never relinquished the idea that religion, in order to be available for human reflection, must be "immanent," that is, in-the-world. What God is in himself is not a subject for human reflection, except insofar as it is a measure of the discordancies in existence between the Christian and his fellow human beings. In other words, Merleau-Ponty always insisted on the incompatibility between God as the "wholly other" and human experience. The only "absolute" he recognized is our relations to other men. Hence he always believed that the Incarnation was the authentic Christian expression of man's relationship to God, since our own incarnation is the experience through which we see ourselves in others and others in ourselves. At the same time, however, recognizing as he did in his later reflections that insofar as the Incarnation was the revelation of an "exclusive God," it was not a "wholly immanent" notion as he had implied earlier, but involved as well the idea of a transcendent God, he was acknowledging that there is a legitimate understanding of transcendence in Christianity. In light of this he would perhaps have modified his earlier statement (1947)—that there could be no "transcendence in immanence" since this was beyond our experience—inasmuch as he now acknowledged it as a possibility for some, even if not for himself.

This leads to the question of whether or not the idea of being as a "transcendence in immanence," introduced into his philosophy after 1950, might have influenced the change in his attitude toward religion. Nothing can be said with certainty on this point. But there is unquestionably a striking parallel between his later remarks on the Incarnation and his own philosophy of being. Perhaps it is not too much to say that if, in Troeltsch's words, Scheler is the "Catholic Nietzsche" because he proved that Nietzsche's antihumanism was of Christian origin, then Merleau-Ponty is the "humanist Kierkegaard" because for him Kierkegaard's "absolute relationship to God" in existence through the Incarnation is an absolute relationship to the world and to others.

Merleau-Ponty, of course, never identified his conception of being with God,[20] but this must certainly have been what Sartre and others had in mind when they wondered whether or not Merleau-Ponty was abandoning humanism. It does not appear, from his latest remarks on the subject, that he would have abandoned his reservations regarding the affirmation of God. (See VI 109) But that does not resolve the question of whether his philosophical idea of being *could* legitimately be identified with God. It is my own opinion that it could and that the idea put forward by Alphonse de Waelhens in 1950 was substantially the idea accepted by Merleau-Ponty near the end of his life. I say this because the involvement of God in human experience plays a role in the religious consciousness similar to that of "being" in Merleau-Ponty's philosophical commitment to the world, even though it is also true that the religious idea of God embodies *more* than Merleau-Ponty conveys by his idea of being. The most exact parallel to Merleau-Ponty's view is perhaps to be found in Karl Jaspers, who regards God or Being as the unknown limit confronting us in existence. God in this view is regarded impersonally but at the same time as the basis of our commitment to the world.

This is not to say that such a solution would satisfy Merleau-Ponty's Roman Catholic critics. Even very recent critics regard him as purely and simply an "atheist." This, however, is to end all effort to understand him. It is, even more, to cut oneself off from the possibility of discussion with one whose life and thought is above all else an expression of the desire to remain open to everything authentically human.

PART V

Epilogue

X

The Contingency of Existence
and the Endurance of Meaning

A man is judged by neither intention nor fact but by his
success in making values become facts.

Merleau-Ponty

The Life of the Man and Its Embodiment
in a Philosophical Vision

The past is heavy with meaning and none of us can extricate
ourselves from it. But what is the meaning of "meaning"? In
one sense, meaning is local insofar as each of us has his own
past, his own family history set within a local and national
milieu. Not all of the meanings given to any life by this deposit of the past are compatible with one another, though they
all nonetheless are mutually present to one another. Life is in
part the effort to understand which meanings we can live with
and which we must abandon, the task of a lifetime, since the
past is always accumulating and impinging its meaning upon
the present. But in another sense meaning pervades or inhabits the existence of a whole generation, for it refers to the
unique character of the "time" in which men live, and all time
is unique. Merleau-Ponty was convinced that our time, our
generation, has one meaning which characterizes the experience of all who live within it, and that meaning is the acknowledgment of finitude. The emphasis here must fall on

"acknowledgment" since men have always known that they must die and that what they accomplish will most likely fall into oblivion. But while they have known this, they have never *accepted* it, that is, they have always found solutions to the problem of finitude outside themselves in an ultimate principle of Good or Evil (or both) which assured the permanence and significance necessary for the meaningfulness of existence. The breakdown of these "explanations" began with the modern period ushered in by the Renaissance. Men were not immediately aware of the fact, however. Indeed, a radical optimism pervaded philosophy as it did science. And despite the cries of Pascal in the seventeenth century, the warnings of Hume in the eighteenth century, and the prophecies of Kierkegaard and Nietzsche in the nineteenth century, the explanations were still somehow believed to explain. But the twentieth century, which may be said to have begun in 1914, marks the end of an era, or rather the recognition of what was perhaps implicit at the beginning of the era. In any case, the explanations have disappeared, the stability is gone, the eternal order has evaporated except for those who, unable to bear such a situation, retreat to the haven of some ideological reference system. In our time, Merleau-Ponty said immediately after the war, we can no longer believe with the Christian saint that the battle is already won in heaven, or with Hegel that the battle is already won in history. These alternatives are simply not available to the man of today. He is not a saint closer to God nor is he Prometheus in complete control of his own destiny, nor finally is he the devil who destroys a given order. He is simply man, finite man who, in acknowledging that the world is contingent (i.e., that *anything* is possible), acknowledges at the same time the precariousness of his life.

What attitude is one to adopt in the face of a contingent world? Should one, like Heidegger, attempt to discover the ways in which Being manifests itself in a contingent world?

But did not Heidegger's support of National Socialism, and his subsequent abandonment of the search for Being in favor of "waiting upon Being" reveal as well as anything could that this solution is at best an abstraction unable to deal with contingent realities in the midst of which we live? Should one, then, like Sartre, aware of the radical contingency of existence, use it as the basis for an ontology of the alienation of man from himself and from others, and then make the individual consciousness preside over contingency so that ultimately man becomes the measure of contingency even though he is not enabled by this endowment to overcome the alienation to which it points? But is alienation the whole meaning of contingency, and is it the case that the freedom of man is the negation of all that impinges upon him? Perhaps if Heidegger's view of Being and Sartre's view of consciousness are not adequate to deal with the contingency they acknowledge, one must choose either the impersonal God of Jaspers or the personal God of Marcel. But is there any means of verifying the intuitions on which their philosophies are based, even if it is true that some have been illuminated by their thought? And if one is reduced to saying that either the intuition is seen or it is not seen, has one not created a new "cult" of those who know standing over against those who do not, with no bridge between them? It appears that even the philosophies based on the acknowledgment of finitude have failed, at one point or another, to be adequate as descriptions of human finitude in its concrete complexity. In order to remain concrete, a philosophy of *man*-in-the-world is necessary, not a philosophy "explaining" man through Being or God, and not a philosophy in which man is his own "explanation," but rather a philosophy in which explanatory principles are "mixed up" with what cannot be wholly explained. Contingent man is not "explicable", but neither is he wholly an "enigma." He is at all times a mixture of both.

If this is the case, then man can never be defined in terms of some end, whether this end is always to be alienated or ultimately to be united with God in eternal communion. For it is precisely the character of man always to be "on the way," *between* an irremediable hopelessness and a final reconciliation. And it is because this is true that life requires commitment or, better, passion. Life is an adventure; it is the struggle of freedom in the face of many limitations and constant uncertainty. If there is to be any "triumph" in human life, it will not be the triumph of the saint or that of the devil or that of Prometheus; it will be the triumph of man who overcomes the divisions within himself and between himself and other men. Is such a triumph possible? Can we ever say that it is or will be possible? It is, Merleau-Ponty never ceased to believe, always a possibility for men who will measure the dangers and the tasks. Ultimately a humanistic perspective such as this is based upon a *faith* in finite man, the man of "flesh and bone," to use Unamuno's phrase, man who knows that he is limited in his efforts to free himself from the divisions within and without but who, asserting his limited freedom and struggling against those divisions in order to communicate with other men, remains a man on the basis of the struggle itself, never ceasing to trust his own humanity and that of others to break down the barriers. Of course, the barriers are never wholly removed; many men may, in fact, never experience, even for a moment, the "triumph" of which we speak. What could make men persist with the effort to communicate in the midst of repeated failures or only partial successes except a faith in man, a trust that no matter what the barriers are it is possible to communicate with others and through this communication to enhance the quality of human life?

Once it is recognized that human existence is based upon trust, then the assertion that "there is meaning" is seen to apply not only to the past but also to the future. Even the betrayal of the trust that one has in particular historical institutions (e.g., the

Church, the Communist Party), does not destroy trust because this betrayal itself is added to the past as part of the meaning which determines one's life and becomes the context in which freedom is operative in the present. It is for this reason that separation from other men never separates one from what is human. Both the past and the future remain open.

To a remarkable degree, Merleau-Ponty lived out in his own life this trust which undergirds his philosophical vision. For never did he close off his past or force his future into a preestablished mold. Let us recall the opening pages of this book, where it was noted that Merleau-Ponty rejected the rationalism of his teachers of philosophy. What he never rejected, however, was the philosophical project through which he was joined to them in a communicative effort. And when his philosophical perspective was broadened after an initial preoccupation with politics following the war—and indeed, partly on account of the failure of his philosophy to be realized on the political level —he changed his view of what his professors had been doing all along (even if he never ceased to reject what earlier he believed they had been doing). It was thus as if, as he had said in *The Structure of Behavior*, each experience alters not only itself but the whole configuration to which it is relevant. But even more, as he recognized in his predecessors' halting attempts to communicate through philosophy the unity within the diversity of human life, his past accumulated a great weight of meaning, expanding the world in relation to which he thought. And as his past expanded, so also did his future. His philosophical vision tended to become more and more inclusive, open to more and more phenomena as his debt to the past increased. So, for example, when his political philosophy failed to materialize in a concrete form, he did not abandon political philosophy, nor did he abandon the philosophy of contingency on which it had been based. Rather, he began to see the world as inclusive of much more than politics. The history of art and of philosophy, the sciences of man, and religious experience all received a much more profound and sympathetic treatment as the experience of the past in relation to which they were interpreted accumulated. There was nothing inconsistent in the expansion of his vision; it was simply an application of his presuppositions to more and more phenomena. In each case, what he attempted to delineate was the contingent character of the phenomenon in question and the manner in which, despite its contingency, it endured in human experience. Thus in a real sense, the transformations in Merleau-Ponty's philosophy which have been analyzed in the preceding pages represent not the internal contradiction between an ontology and a descriptive philosophy, but a continual interrogation of what the logic of his presuppositions demanded and an increasing propensity to incorporate the whole meaning of his presuppositions into the project of his philosophy.

In the thought of none of the other philosophers to whom the title "existentialist" is generally applied has there been a more remarkable attempt to translate into a philosophical vision the experiences of a life. But in order to determine the *adequacy* of this translation, we must examine more closely some of the implications of Merleau-Ponty's philosophical vision and of its relation to his life. In doing so, we shall find residual problems in both his vision and his life which will reveal the contributions and limitations of each.

The Limitations and Contributions of the Philosophical Vision

From his first book to his last Merleau-Ponty's overriding interest was in primary perception, as is evident in his repeated appeal to illustrations taken from language and art, phenomena through which we are enabled to grasp the world in a primary expression or gesture. In relation to his elucidation of the primary world, his discussions of the secondary world of science —a world based on an abstraction from the primary world—

appear fragmentary and incomplete. It was suggested in an earlier chapter that Merleau-Ponty's method was better suited to "primary" than to "secondary" phenomena. His concern, in fact, with the secondary accretions of culture was to relate them to the primary world on which they were based and thus to recall man to the freedom of creation necessary for the advancement of culture. This is in itself commendable, and it is highly relevant to the attitude of the scientist no less than to the vision of an artist or writer, for example, to the psycho-analyst who wishes to assist his patient to become free from the secondary (acquired) meanings of his life in order to be able to express new meaning in his future; or to the physicist who wishes to say more than has been said about the phenomena to which he devotes his attention. It goes without saying that primary expression requires that one be fully aware of the secondary or acquired world in relation to which he lives. Primary expression does not preclude but requires the incor-poration of secondary expressions.[1]

In one sense, then, primary perception is methodologically adequate in terms of its relevance to experience. In every case, it seeks to apprehend "authentic" ways of being-in-the-world. But are there "authentic" experiences which fall outside the range of what Merleau-Ponty means by "primary perception"? Is it an adequate understanding of man to say that he is defined by the possibility of going beyond what is to what might be but is not yet? Has Merleau-Ponty not defined one type of experience as normative for all others—that of the creative individual, the intellectual who propounds new ideas, the scholar who breaks new ground, or the artist who creates a new style in painting or a literary masterpiece? And although such persons are very important to every time and culture, are they not a minority and must this not be so in the nature of the case? And if this is so, then have not the majority of men been defined as "inauthentic"? The question here is not whether *in fact* most men do live inauthentically (though this is always a tenuous judgment, since no man can know the mind of another); for even Kierkegaard who, more than any of the other existentialists, makes all men equal (as sinners before God and hence equally near to or equally far from "authentic" existence), admits that perhaps few men in any generation ever reach the level of faith. The question is whether or not the human situation has been defined in such a way that the "intellectual" is favored above all others. Can we conclude that the individual who lives in relation to secondary expressions—whether religious, political, or intellectual—and who does not seek to create new forms but rather to live out of those already created is necessarily inauthentic? Perhaps there is an authentic "secondary world," as there certainly are inauthentic ways of "primary expression."

It is plausible to argue that Merleau-Ponty *intended* to say one could live authentically in relation to his "secondary world" quite apart from any thought of going beyond it, even though that suggestion does not appear directly in his writings. When for example, he asserted that the primary expression of an artist should become a primary expression for the person who grasps the artist's vision, he was saying that openness to the artist's vision is an acceptance of the possibility of having one's own vision of the world transformed, a willingness to be "astonished" by the new perspectives which are always possible. Not to be open to the possibility of the novel is to live in a closed universe, one in which what is acquired is treated as natural, normal, acceptable. That is, it is to sink into banality. But to live in an "open universe" is possible for anyone; it does not require the genius of an artist, although it may also be true that without men of exceptional creative ability others would not be led to a recognition of novelty.

Even if it is granted, however, that this is what Merleau-Ponty intended to say, it does not folllow that remaining open to novelty is synonymous with going beyond the given. It may well be that acceptance of the "given world" is compatible with its novel apprehension. For example, in virtually all teaching and scholarship emphasis is on mastering an acquired tradition. Ideally, both the student and the scholar understand the insights which their learning affords them as a "primary" grasping of the tradition, as a source of illumination both for their lives and for their culture. But there is no immediate thought of "going beyond" what is learned. This implies a limitation in Merleau-Ponty's view of what the scientist is doing. In asserting that the modern artist's view of nature would make a good working model of nature for science since we, unlike the men of the seventeenth century, have no "fixed" conception of being, he was suggesting that the scientist is doing only what the artist is doing, namely, grasping the world anew in a primary perception. This, however, is not wholly true, since, while the scientist may be doing that, he is also living within his acquired world and finding meaning within it apart from any idea of "going beyond." In short, the possibility persists of remaining open to the givenness of one's world and of participating in its novelty and richness without "adding" anything to it or "going beyond" it. At the same time, it is equally possible that not every revolutionary attitude is identifiable with openness and authenticity. Indeed, Merleau-Ponty said as much in reproving Sartre for advising the youth of today that "revolt" was their only possible authentic response to the present.

I am suggesting that Merleau-Ponty was talking about a "style of life," a way of being-in-the-world and, further, that there is a wide range of possibilities for authentic response to one's world. In his later writings Merleau-Ponty emphasized the stability and order of the given world, but he did not bring his discussion to bear on the analyses of freedom penned during the postwar years when he was thinking in revolutionary terms. Thus, while his formal doctrine of freedom emphasizes contingency as its essence, his later thought requires a more adequate description than one can find in his writings of how the freedom of "passing beyond" is modified by the freedom of "living within the given."

Here we come upon another difficulty. If it is possible to be related to the "given world" authentically, how are we to assess the normative character of that world? In his exchange with Merleau-Ponty on the problem of language, Father Jean Daniélou suggested that one must devote at least as much attention to what has been acquired as to going beyond it. Father Daniélou appealed to the normative character of the sacred texts within religious traditions. In doing so he was raising in an indirect way the problem of *authority*. So long as he identified freedom with contingency, Merleau-Ponty was not bothered by the past. It was not until he came to regard the traditions bequeathed by the past not only as the context of our freedom but also as a partial *expression of* the freedom we now experience that the problem of differentiating what in the past is to be normative became a philosophical problem. That he never resolved this problem is evident in the ethical philosophy which is partly explicit, partly implicit in his writings. To make it wholly explicit will be to develop the "unthought" in the margins of Merleau-Ponty's texts and to assess further the residual tension in his philosophical vision.

Merleau-Ponty's philosophy implies an "ethic of contingency." In his view there is no problem which can be solved simply by referring the facts of the case to "immutable principles" inasmuch as there are no "immutable principles." Principles are themselves contingent; they exist, as the "facts" exist, but they exist bound up with the facts. Thus, in order to deal with an ethical problem, principles and facts must be derived together from the total situation. As the situation changes, the principles, like the facts, cease to be relevant, and a new configuration must be grasped in its totality. Now what can it mean to say that principles are contingent? Is this not like trying to define a "square circle"? If there are no principles in terms of which men see a situation in the same way, then is there any *social* solution to ethical problems? Without a common referent, will not the result be a series of individual opinions? For Merleau-Ponty, to say that ethical decisions are contingent (i.e., that facts and principles must be discovered together in a total situation) is to say that the *ethical* dimensions of a problem do not come into focus unless the solution of the problem is seen to depend on the decisions of men, and men do not decide an issue when the situation dictates the solution, i.e., when each situation can be resolved by a priori principles. Thus, far from ethics depending on immutable principles, the case is that to make ethics depend on such principles is to divorce oneself from existence, to cut oneself off from other men and to survey the world with a truth brought to it from another region. Men can and do see particular human situations in the same way quite apart from principles which all hold in common, and they do so because all men live in the same world. There is in every human situation a common experience, even in the midst of a "multiplicity of perspectives."

There is a certain advantage to this "contextualist" view of ethics. For ethics ceases to be reflection on the "ought" and becomes instead reflection on the given and on what of the "ought" is possible within the given. That is, ethics, like politics, deals only with concrete problems. Indeed, it resembles politics above all in its concern with specific problems and with the most desirable possible solutions to those problems. In focusing its concern in this way, ethics does not require an a priori understanding of the nature of man. Rather than assume than man is sinful or rational or whatever, the question of what man is is left open and is examined in relation to the "human condition." The multiple possibilities of human behavior, and therefore a more empirical approach to the problems of human life, are integral features of contextual thinking.

But there are unresolved problems in contextualist ethics. In the first place, if one is to find principles in the facts themselves, does one do this simply as a historian or as an ethical philosopher? Merleau-Ponty cites Max Weber, who discovered the interpenetration of Calvinist theological ideas and a capitalist economy, as one who carried out the kind of analysis of principles and facts that he had in mind. And it must be granted that as a historian Weber has clarified our recent past in such a way as to enable us better to understand our present ethical (as well as political and economic) situation. But historical analysis is not synonymous with acting in the present or even with knowing what action is desirable. Merleau-Ponty admitted as much when he remarked that history does not tell us what to do, though it never resumes its lost illusions. He must have been thinking along these same lines when he stated that a writer may know better what is *not* desirable for the social order than he knows what is desirable. But it is not enough always to be illuminated after the fact. What we want is guidance here and now.

This brings us to the fundamental question raised by contextualist ethics: "What is the context?" If one can find in the past a correlation between ethical systems and social facts, can one find such a correlation in the present? Merleau-Ponty tended to believe immediately after the war that there was a "total context" in which one could think. But after rejecting Marxism and along with it his view of the proletariat as a carrier of universal historical meaning, he began to recognize that every context is partial, that there are, rather than one, a great many possible frameworks in terms of which one can correlate the facts. The problem then is to choose a context. In doing so, however, one implicitly accepts certain a priori principles. In other words, "contextualist principles," insofar as they are ethical and not purely historical, are *brought to* the context and not derived solely from it. Merleau-Ponty's ideas that the task of ethics is to make an always unacceptable world less unacceptable, that one way to do this is to support programs offering greater justice for those who are oppressed, and that in serving the cause of the oppressed one serves the best interests of the social order as a whole are examples of a priori principles. Although their affinities with Marxism are evident, Merleau-Ponty insisted on the validity of these ideas throughout his life. It may be argued that these are empirical and not a priori principles. But they could never be established at the moment of their adoption as empirical ethical principles; that they were empirical could only be established later by historical analysis. In other words, the function of principles is to lead one to action. If there is no action, or if the action is ineffective, the principles will not establish themselves as empirical. If they do establish themselves as empirical, then they have done so by virtue of having been employed as ethical principles *before* they were empirically evident as such. Contextualist ethics therefore cannot escape a priori principles. And the contextualist is in the precarious position of having to show that his principles are in fact empirical by establishing them as such through action.

There is a further problem. Whether a priori principles are proved contextually valid through empirical action which establishes them, or whether they remain contextually questionable by virtue of a failure to become actualized, does not prejudice the question of the *truth* of the principles themselves, but is related only to their historical power or weakness. As a matter of historical fact, such principles have been regarded as true by those who espoused them regardless of their historical fate. This only attests further to their a priori character and to their attachment to certain institutions (a church, a political party) in which they have a self-evident character. It may be the case that some principles, like those espoused by Merleau-Ponty, belong to an entire culture or even to the entire world, apart from particular institutional allegiances. Camus was giving expression to such a possibility when he asserted in

The Plague that one must side with other men and serve them, even though one can give no obligatory reason for doing so. Even if such principles do belong to a culture, however, they are not self-enforcing. That is, one must act in order to make the principles effective. Indeed, it has always been the humanistic Marxist critique of Western liberalism that it has not acted on its good principles. And when one chooses to actualize a principle, then one must choose a means of action, that is, institutional allegiances.

These are all problems suggested by Merleau-Ponty's philosophical vision. Do they represent deficiencies in his methodology or are they only descriptive inadequacies capable of correction within his methodology? This is an interesting question, for Merleau-Ponty asserted that phenomenology as a method could never be passed beyond. However, no two phenomenologists agree completely on what the method is and each of them, as we have seen, is deficient at some point. This leads us to ask whether or not there can be one completely adequate philosophical method. The answer suggested by the analyses in this book is that no one methodology is wholly adequate. But this is a question which remains peripheral to the present discussion, for as I shall now suggest, Merleau-Ponty's failures are integrally related to his life, in which these problems were never resolved. And, as I have attempted to prove throughout this book, his life cannot be separated from his method or from his descriptions.

The Limitations and Contributions of the Life of the Man

In his early postwar political philosophy Merleau-Ponty asserted his faith in the proletariat as a political entity through which the unity of man could be established on the political level. It did not take him long to begin to question this faith, as we saw earlier. But one wonders how he could ever have believed this in the first place. The answer lies partly in the fact that in postwar France all the options of the immediate past were swept aside, and no consensus developed around any one man or party, so that it appeared for a time as if every alternative had an equal chance of acceptance. But that is not the whole answer. For the truth is that Merleau-Ponty could not have accepted the idea of the universality of the proletariat apart from his commitment to Marxism. Now the theory of the proletariat is precisely the point at which Marx, who wanted to free social science from its "ideological taint," developed the most comprehensive ideology to appear in modern times. Of course, as I have emphasized, Merleau-Ponty did not believe in the orthodox Marxist view that the proletariat must inevitably come to power because of the contradictions within capitalism. But there were nevertheless two points at which his faith in the proletariat rested on ideological premises. In the first place, it was ideological to believe that any particular human institution could be the ultimate or universal expression of the hopes and dreams of men everywhere. If ever there was a denial of the "multiplicity of perspectives," this was it. But faith in this institution could not have been so great apart from a second belief, also attributable to Merleau-Ponty's Marxism, that the unity of man could be expressed on the *political* level. This belief was ideological in the extreme because it was a denial of politics itself. Politics is not concerned with such abstractions as the "unity of man" (except insofar as these find their way into much tiresome campaign oratory). Politics has to do with concrete issues, and therefore with concrete goals and programs. To define politics in terms of the "unity of man" is to abolish politics, because it is to reduce the concrete to an abstraction. In relation to my discussion in the preceding section, it is to abolish ethics as well.

Now we have seen that Merleau-Ponty abandoned his Marxism and along with it all traces of an ideological viewpoint. Not only so, but he began to describe the universality of man in terms of the "multiplicity of perspectives" as these are to be found in the various life-worlds through which men express themselves. But despite this transformation, which certainly rendered his philosophy more "adequate" without (as I have emphasized) forcing him into contradictions, there was a sense in which his transformation was inadequate because it never extricated him entirely from the abstraction of which he had been guilty when he placed his faith in the proletariat. For as he backed away, first from the Church, then from Marxism, he did not replace the commitments he shed with commitments to other *concrete institutional structures*.[2] Rather, he retreated into his own reflection, and his analyses of science, art, language, religion, and other institutions must be interpreted in part as efforts to understand from the "outside." The withdrawal from particular commitments within his life-world coincided with the expansion of his philosophical interests. There was thus a sense in which Merleau-Ponty's broadened perspective was at the same time a more "abstract" and less "concrete" perspective, as ironical as this conclusion may appear.

The fundamental problem raised here is what happens to the primacy given to the *present* when one cannot be concretely related to it. Merleau-Ponty's Marxism was consistent with the philosophy of history expressed in *Phenomenology of Perception*, for in that book he had based the philosophy of history on concrete projects in the present world; and in Merleau-Ponty's eyes Marxism was a concrete project aiming at the transformation of the present. But what happens when one is forced to abandon a concrete project and is unable to find another to take its place? Does one's philosophy of history go by the board at the same time? Merleau-Ponty struggled against this conclusion. In his articles on Trotsky and Lukacs he wrote as if each man must realize himself both on the level of thought and on the level of action, criticizing Trotsky for giving too much weight to thought (thus divorcing himself from historical action) and Lukacs for giving too much weight to action (compromising, in the process, the integrity of his thought). In his later remarks on the commitment of writers and artists to culture, however, he recognized that the equivocations he had found in Marxism are in reality equivocations belonging to the human condition in our time, emphasizing as he did that is was extremely difficult to find an acceptable positive course of action, and suggesting that the present is perhaps too tenuous to allow one to visualize anything other than what he does *not* want. But it is not the same thing to "negate" what is and to project oneself concretely into the present. Merleau-Ponty recognized the difference, and he attempted to resolve it by saying that no man could be all things and that the philosopher and the man of action should assist one another. He also pointed to Max Weber, in whose life he saw an attempt to overcome the dilemma. Weber, however, did not envision the problem as Merleau-Ponty did, since Weber did not believe that within the present political order one must initiate a project that aims at making the world less unacceptable. Indeed, he became more and more convinced toward the end of his life that one must live in the politics of the present without much hope of altering its course through ideas and visions of a better future. In a sense Merleau-Ponty reached this conclusion also, but it was an inadequate conclusion in terms of his philosophy of history. If the present is to be meaningful, then it must contain the possibility of a new future. And to intend this new possibility (or these possibilities) is imperative. Otherwise, a humanism of contingent man becomes a "humanism in thought" only, a philosophy of contemplation in the sense in which Merleau-Ponty had characterized Sartre's philosophy as contemplative.

However, the only way to establish the possibility of a new future as a reality is to become committed to institutions whose aim is to bring about something new. But since every institution has necessarily compromised its highest intentions to some degree in the interest of maintaining itself, one who remains within institutions must compromise in part the integrity of his thought (or recognize the difference between what he believes and what the institution to which he gives his allegiance supports). Perhaps Lukacs was right: in order to remain in history one must compromise the integrity of his reflection so that one may remain in contact with the man of action and influence him to some extent. This, then, is the dilemma. In order to render the unacceptability of the world less unacceptable, one must participate in institutions which have compromised their best intentions. If one remains within an institution, one never knows when it has compromised away its potential effectiveness. But if one cannot see in any institution an effective remnant of society's best hopes, then one has no recourse but to abandon institutions. However, to do so is at the same time to abandon a philosophy of history based on the present, since changes come about only through institutional structures.

Merleau-Ponty was up against a perennial dilemma here which seems incapable of solution within any philosophy but appears particularly vexing for his own. No institution will continue for long to be the instrument of making the unacceptability of the world less unacceptable. For this is always a "revolutionary" attitude, and every institution ceases to be revolutionary once it becomes established. The Russian revolution affords a ready example from political history; and many reformations within the Christian Church point to the same phenomenon in religious history. The problem is particularly acute in religious institutions. Two generations ago Adolf Harnack said that the Protestant Reformation did away with dogmatic religious faith—in principle though not in fact. Paul Tillich in our generation has added to Harnack's thesis the contention that the essence of Protestantism is its refusal to absolutize any form of faith, any type of culture, or any political institution.[3] The only "absolute" is that there are no human absolutes; rather everything human is subject to the continual judgment of God. Here we have a theological formulation of what Merleau-Ponty was trying to advocate on a secular level, namely, the idea of a continual reformation based on the recognition that today's revolution in faith is tomorrow's dogma unless the sparks which animated the faith of yesterday are rekindled today and not merely accepted as a tradition to be protected against all challenges. Of course, it may be argued that Protestantism—like present-day communism and Western political liberalism—covers its failure to act with good principles. But the problem is more far-reaching. For this is true of *every* institution. It simply brings us back to the persistent dilemma: either we must commit ourselves beyond our own intentions to the intentions of an institution which we cannot determine but for which we are responsible insofar as we commit ourselves to it; or we must abandon institutions altogether and along with them the possibility of influencing the course of intersubjective existence.

Conclusion

As in the case of other "existentialist" philosophers, there can be no "disciples" of Merleau-Ponty in the strict sense of the word, because his method was his life. To adopt his method is to begin to experience the world in a new way. This, of course, is possible, but if it is done the result will be a new experience and a new philosophy, not a continuation of Merleau-Ponty's life and thought. He belongs to us now, in his own words, as a "classic," one who has given us much to think about that we have not thought about before in the same way. It is not by virtue of his existentialism or his Marxism or his phenomenology that he speaks to us, but rather by virtue of the extent to which, through each of these, he has been able to illuminate the lived human quality of existence. It is thus in and through his uniqueness—one could say his "aloneness"—that he speaks to us and perhaps, in the final analysis, that is the way he wanted it.

Notes

CHAPTER I

1. Although completed in 1938, the book was not published until 1942. A second edition appeared in 1949, which differed from the first edition only by the inclusion of an introductory article by Alphonse de Waelhens. An English translation of this second edition has recently appeared (*The Structure of Behavior*, translated by Alden L. Fisher).

2. "Christianisme et ressentiment," *La Vie Intellectuelle*, VII (1935), 278-306; "Etre et avoir," *La Vie Intellectuelle*, VIII (1936), 98-109; "L'Imagination," *Journal de Psychologie Normale et Pathologique*, XXXIII (1936), 756-61. These articles were reviews of Max Scheler's *Ressentiment*, Gabriel Marcel's *Being and Having*, and Jean-Paul Sartre's *The Imagination*, respectively.

In addition to these articles, Merleau-Ponty assisted Aron Gurwitsch with an article on Gestalt psychology: "Quelques aspects et quelques développements de la psychologie de la Forme," *Journal de Psychologie Normale et Pathologique*, XXXIII (1936), 413-71.

3. *PP* 69, tr. 56. See also "Etre et Avoir," pp. 98-99, 102, *passim*. The suggestion of this gap between the generations is also present in a letter Merleau-Ponty wrote in 1942 to H. L. Van Breda regarding the establishment of a center of Husserlian studies in Paris: ". . . after having consulted my friends Hyppolite and Sartre, I think that we now have here [in Paris] everything necessary for the establishment of a center of Husserlian studies. It would be easy for us, if you wish, to enter into discussion with Le Senne, Lavelle, or any of the professors of the preceding generation. But I would have more confidence in an undertaking managed by men of my own age." H. L. Van Breda, "Maurice Merleau-Ponty et les Archives-Husserl à Louvain," *Revue de Métaphysique et de Morale*, LXVII (1962), 420.

4. Sartre, "Merleau-Ponty vivant," *Les Temps Modernes*, XVII

(1961), 305-6. Sartre's article has recently appeared in English translation: *Situations*, tr. Benita Eisler, pp. 225-326. See also Jean Hyppolite, *Sens et existence dans la philosophie de Maurice Merleau-Ponty*, p. 4.

5. *SC* 1, tr. 3; see also *PP* 489, tr. 428.

6. Herbert Spiegelberg *The Phenomenological Movement*, II, 529.

7. B. B. Wolman, *Contemporary Theories and Systems in Psychology*, p. 62.

8. The neuron theory "teaches that each nerve cell is an individual which carries on its own life as regards nutrition and other metabolic functions. The connection between one nerve cell and another is . . . by means of a synapse or junction point. The synapse is not a fibrous connection, but a point at which the nervous impulse is relayed from one nerve cell to the next." Gardner Murphy, *Historical Introduction to Modern Psychology*, p. 445.

9. John B. Watson, *Behaviorism*, p. 72.

10. *Ibid.*, pp. 51 ff.

11. *Ibid.*, pp. 74 ff.

12. *SC* 45, tr. 43-44. In his last reflections, published after his death, Merleau-Ponty suggests that the results of *all* forms of psychological experimentation, including that of Gestalt psychology, apply only to laboratory conditions and that they cannot be accurately generalized in relation to conditions outside the laboratory. See *VI* 39-42.

13. *SC* 49 ff., tr. 48 ff.; cf. *PP* 58-59, tr. 47. E. G. Boring also states that the leading gestaltists interpreted the notion of form in physicalist terms, though their theory did not require it. *A History of Experimental Psychology*, rev. ed., p. 620.

14. *SC* 76-79, tr. 69-72. Gardner Murphy criticizes the gestaltists for saying *both* that component parts enter the whole, *and* that there are no component parts. *Historical Introduction*, p. 295. It is clear from the dialectic of form that Merleau-Ponty does not deny that there are parts (or localizations). What he does deny is that they can be understood in isolation from one another. Murphy emphasizes (p. 294) that *both* whole responses *and* piecemeal ones occur, i.e., that there is room for more than one psychological system. See also pp. 444-45.

15. The perception of depth and the phenomenon of language will be discussed in the following chapter.

16. *SC* 91-93, tr. 82-84. This idea of "figure" and "ground," utilized in both spatial and chromatic perception, was first in-

troduced into psychology by the phenomenologist Edgar Rubin, in 1915. See Wolman, *Contemporary Theories*, p. 436.

17. We have already had occasion to note that when Merleau-Ponty uses the term "scientific reason" he is referring to a structure of nature which can be formulated in terms of exact laws. Scientific reason is descriptive and reductive. Either the human mind is made to conform to the laws of nature or the laws of nature are viewed as wholly dependent upon the human mind. When he uses the term "enlarged reason" he is referring to human experience which cannot be reduced to exact laws. "Enlarged reason" is descriptive but nonreductive; it points to the inexhaustible complexity of a world in which human freedom is a significant factor.

18. *SC* 114-15, tr. 104-5; see *RE* 31-60, tr. 125-55.

19. *SC* 115-17, tr. 105-7; see *SC* 115-30, tr. 105-20.

20. *SC* 130-35 tr. 120-24.

21. These remarks are based on *SC*, chap. 4 (200-41, tr. 185-224). Much of the chapter is a restatement of the critique of mentalistic and materialistic solutions (204-26, tr. 189-209). The positive conclusions are stated at the beginning and again at the end of the chapter (200-4, tr. 185-89; 228-41, tr. 211-24).

22. Boring, Langfeld, and Weld, *Foundations of Psychology*, p. 11.

23. Boring, *A History of Experimental Psychology*, p. 742.

24. See further, on the distinction between natural and social science, Alfred Schutz, *Collected Papers I*, pp. 5 ff.

25. See, on this, F. W. Matson, *The Broken Image*. Cf. also *SHP* 45, tr. 84-85.

CHAPTER II

1. The book was translated in 1962 by Colin Smith. The translation is literal and accurate. However, it would have been enhanced by the breaking down of long paragraphs into shorter ones (for which the table of contents in the French edition provided the guidelines), by the inclusion of the pagination of the French edition in the margins of the English text (since all secondary works to date refer only to the French edition), and by a more complete index (though no index was included in the French edition).

2. Merleau-Ponty uses the term "world" in two senses which overlap and perhaps complete one another. "World" usually refers

to the context in which experience takes place, whether this context is the simplest figure/ground datum or the most complex civilization. But "world" can also mean the general context or horizon in which any experience whatsoever is possible. (See *PP* 362, tr. 313; 456, tr. 398) These uses of the term remain constant throughout Merleau-Ponty's life, though in his later writings the world as general horizon is equated with our opening to being. (See *VI* 19, 136) On the relation of this to Husserl's view, see *VI* 195, and below, chap. 3, n. 38.

3. "The absolute positing of a single object is the death of consciousness, since it congeals the whole of existence, as a crystal placed in a solution suddenly crystallizes it." (*PP* 86, tr. 71)

4. *PP* 61, tr. 49-50, emphasis added. See also *RE* 12-13, tr. 107-8; 17-18, tr. 112-13; and *SNS* 46-47, tr. 24.

5. "Consciousness is in the first place not a matter of 'I think that' but of 'I can'." (*PP* 160, tr. 137)

6. *PP* 158, tr. 136. See *PP* 119-72, tr. 103-47, especially 119-25, tr. 103-6; 140-44, tr. 120-24; 158-66, tr. 136-42.

7. *PP* 197, tr. 169. See *PP* 180-99, tr. 154-71; and *SNS* 41-48, tr. 21-25.

8. In Heidegger's view this falling into a banality of speech is virtually a necessity.

9. *PP* 203-32, tr. 174-99; see also *PP* 445-51, tr. 388-92; 459-63, tr. 400-4. In a similar vein, Alfred Schutz has written: "In listening to a lecturer . . . we seem to participate immediately in the development of his stream of thought. But—and this point is obviously a decisive one—our attitude in doing so is quite different from that we adopt in turning to our own stream of thought by reflection. We catch the Other's thought in its vivid presence and not *modo praeterito*; that is, we catch it as 'Now' and not as 'Just Now'. The Other's speech and our listening are experienced as a vivid simultaneity." (*Collected Papers*, I, 173)

10. Richard M. Zaner's *The Problem of Embodiment* reached me only after the following analysis had been completed. His is the first detailed study of the problem of the body in contemporary French philosophy. Marcel, Sartre, and Merleau-Ponty are discussed in detail; Bergson is mentioned at the end of the study. The book is disappointing in some respects, since the author treats each thinker in isolation and fails to show the historical lines of development in their views or the influence of one upon the other. Nor does he attempt any substantial comparison of their views in his Epilogue. With regard to his treatment of Merleau-Ponty, his crit-

ical appraisal is based largely on Merleau-Ponty's departures from Husserlian phenomenology, and in some cases simply reflects a different bias rather than the uncovering of difficulties inherent in *Merleau-Ponty's* perspective.

11. Herbert Spiegelberg points out that there were analyses of the body in the earlier German phenomenological movement of which the French philosophers seem to have been unaware. (*The Phenomenological Movement*, II, 507-8)

12. Bergson, *Matter and Memory*, pp. 1-6. (English translation originally published by the Macmillan Co. in 1911. Citations here, however, are to the paperback edition published by Doubleday and Co. in 1959.) Bergson's theory of perception which is developed on the basis of his analysis of the body will be treated below in chap. 7, for reasons which will become evident as we proceed.

13. *Ibid.*, p. 1.

14. *Ibid.*,p. 2.

15. On the nature of this concrete philosophy, see the following chapter.

16. Marcel, *Metaphysical Journal*, pp. 18-22.

17. Sartre is the only one of these thinkers who refers to Schopenhauer's discussion of the body. See *Being and Nothingness*, p. 231.

18. Arthur Schopenhauer, *The World as Will and Idea*, Vol. I, par. 18.

19. "This object [the body] is essentially different from all others," for "it alone of all objects is at once both will and idea, while the rest are ideas, i.e., only phantoms." (*Ibid.*, par. 19)

20. *Ibid.*, par. 20.

21. *Ibid.*, par. 19.

22. See the gradual emergence of this point of view in *Metaphysical Journal*, pp. 18-22, 242-44, 259-60, 273-75, 315-16, 332-39; and in *Being and Having*, pp. 10-14, 82-84, 109.

23. See below, pp. 66-67.

24. Alfred Schutz has written a convincing critique of Sartre's contention that his solution actually overcomes the solipsism he finds in Hegel, Husserl, and Heidegger ("Sartre's Theory of the Alter Ego," *Collected Papers*, I, 180-203).

25. Sartre, *Being and Nothingness*, p. 253.

26. *Ibid.*, p. 285.

27. *Ibid.*, pp. 306-39.

28. *Ibid.*, pp. 339-51.

29. *Ibid.*, pp. 351-59.

30. See further on this, chap. 3, below.

31. *PP* 239, tr. 206; see also *RE* 28, tr. 122.

32. *SNS* 101, tr. 50. See also *PP* 265-66, tr. 229-30.

33. *PP* 281-344, tr. 243-98, especially *PP* 341-42, tr. 295-96. Robert Campbell suggests that the change in Camus's thought between *The Stranger*, which declares the world absurd, and *The Plague*, which recognizes meaning in an intersubjective struggle, may have been influenced by Merleau-Ponty. See "Existentialism in France Since the Liberation," in Marvin Farber, ed., *Philosophic Thought in France and the United States*, p. 146.

34. *PP* 362, tr. 313. In his last book Merleau-Ponty writes, reaffirming this view: "Each perception is mutable and only probable; if one wishes, it is only an *opinion*; but what it is not, what each perception, even if false, verifies, is the belonging of each experience to the same world, its equal power of manifesting the world, insofar as each perception is a *possibility of the same world*." (*VI* 64)

35. *PP* 495, tr. 433; see *PP* 469-95, tr. 410-33. Merleau-Ponty's studies of Montaigne (*S* 257-66, tr. 203-10) and of Machiavelli (*S* 267-83, tr. 211-23) are interpretations of how these men defined their lives and their philosophies in terms of mutual presence to others.

Alfred Schutz puts forward the same solution to the question of how intersubjectivity is possible. We are present to ourselves only in terms of what we *have* done, he suggests, but we are present to others in terms of what we *are* doing at this moment. (*Collected Papers*, I, 172-75) See above, n. 9.

36. *PP* 496-520, tr. 434-56; see also *SNS* 40-41, tr. 21.

37. *Being and Time*, par. 12.

38. *Ibid.*, par. 13.

39. *Ibid.*, pars. 19-20.

40. *Ibid.*, par. 21.

41. *Ibid.*, par. 14.

42. *Ibid.*, pars. 17-18, 32.

43. *Ibid.*, par. 16.

44. *Ibid.*, pars. 22-23. Merleau-Ponty explicitly identifies his view of the preobjective world with that of Heidegger in *SNS* 273, tr. 134.

45. *Ibid.*, par. 26.

46. See Alphonse de Waelhens, *Une Philosophie de l'ambiguité*, pp. 1-2; reprinted in the English translation of *The Structure of*

Behavior, pp. xviii-xix.

47. Ferdinand Alquié, "Une Philosophie de l'ambiguité: l'existentialisme de Maurice Merleau-Ponty," *Fontaine,* IX (1947), 47-70.

48. *Une Philosophie de l'ambiguité,* p. 397.

49. Edward Ballard, "On Cognition of the Pre-Cognitive," *Philosophical Quarterly,* XI (1961), 238-44.

50. Eugene Kaelin, *An Existentialist Aesthetic,* pp. 255-57.

51. *Ibid.,* pp. 320-21.

52. *Ibid.,* pp. 340-41.

53. *Ibid.,* p. 331.

54. *Ibid.,* pp. 352-53.

55. Alphonse de Waelhens, *Une Philosophie de l'ambiguité,* p. 173. Cf. *SNS* 186-87, tr. 93.

56. Stephan Strasser, *Phenomenology and the Human Sciences,* p. 262. Cf. *PP* 455, tr. 397; but also 448, tr. 391.

57. Moreau, *L'Horizon des esprits.*

58. Strasser, *Phenomenology and the Human Sciences,* pp. 218-23.

59. Kwant, *The Phenomenological Philosophy of Merleau-Ponty,* chap. 13. This critique is also pursued by Albert Dondeyne, *Contemporary European Thought and Christian Faith,* pp. 36-66, 108-25.

60. Alphonse de Waelhens, *Une Philosophie de l'ambiguité,* pp. 385-86, 392-94, 401-2. De Waelhens' general approach is followed by two other writers: André Hayen, S. J., "La Phénoménologie de M. Merleau-Ponty et la métaphysique," *Revue Philosophique de Louvain,* L (1952), 112-23; and R. Jolivet, "Le Problème de l'absolu dans la philosophie de M. Merleau-Ponty," *Tijdschrift voor Philosophie,*XIX (1957), 53-100.

CHAPTER III

1. Eugene Kaelin, *An Existentialist Aesthetic,* p. 339. Cf. Alquié, "Une Philosophie de l'ambiguité," pp. 51-52. On Bergson, see below, chap. 7.

2. Edward G. Ballard, "The Philosophy of Merleau-Ponty," *Tulane Studies in Philosophy,* IX (1960), 184-87.

3. Raymond Bayer, "Merleau-Ponty's Existentialism," *University of Buffalo Studies,* XIX (1953), 96.

4. Jean Grenier, "La Philosophie," *L'Arche,* III (1945), 136.

5. Alphonse de Waelhens, *Une Philosophie de l'ambiguité,* pp. 1-13, and *passim.* See also his article "Situation de Merleau-Ponty," *Les Temps Modernes,* XVII (1961), 377-98.

6. *Ideen zu einer reinen Phänomenologie und phänomenologischen philosophie* was first published in Volume I of the *Jahrbuch für Philosophie und phänomenologische Forschung* in 1913. The text was republished twice during Husserl's lifetime without change. An English translation by W. R. Boyce Gibson and a French translation by Paul Ricoeur have been made from this edition. A new critical edition appeared in 1952 in *Husserliana* III, ed. M. and W. Biemel. Another English translation, based on this critical text, is now in preparation.

Husserl continued his work on the *Ideen* throughout his life but was never enough satisfied with the results of his research to allow them to be published. *Ideen* II and *Ideen* III remained in manuscript until his death. These have since been published in *Husserliana* IV and V (1952).

7. Paul Ricoeur, "Introduction" to Husserl's *Idées directrices pour une phénoménologie,* p. xxxii. This is Ricoeur's translation of *Ideen* I. See also Paul Ricoeur, "Husserl" in Appendice to E. Bréhier, *Histoire de la philosophie Allemande,* pp. 183-96.

8. Spiegelberg, *The Phenomenological Movement,* I, 92. An account of this work is contained in Marvin Farber, *The Foundation of Phenomenology,* pp. 25-60.

9. A description of psychologism, as well as of Husserl's critique, may be found in *Realism and the Background of Phenomenology,* ed. Roderick Chisholm, pp. 13-17. See also Spiegelberg, The *Phenomenological Movement,* 1, 93-95; and Farber, *The Foundation of Phenomenology,* chap. 4.

10. Farber, *The Foundation of Phenomenology,* p. 146.

11. *The Phenomenological Movement,* I, 96.

12. See *Ideas,* trans. W. R. Boyce Gibson, p. 23.

13. "Introduction" to *Idées,* p. xxxiv.

14. The word "egology" is a neologism coined to describe Husserl's idea that there is a "pure consciousness" which remains as a phenomenological residue after the contents of consciousness have been placed in suspense. On this term and its development in Husserl, see Spiegelberg, *The Phenomenological Movement,* I, 140-41.

15. Originally delivered as lectures in Paris in 1929, they have been translated into English by Dorian Cairns.

16. Jean-Paul Sartre's interpretation of Husserl's understanding

of intentionality is based on its rendering in the first edition of the
Logische Untersuchungen. Sartre, in contending that consciousness
is always outside itself in the world, was returning to a descriptive
psychology from which Husserl was attempting to escape. See
"Une Idée fondamentale de la phénoménologie de Husserl: L'Intentionnalité," *Situations* I, 31-35. Sartre's Interpretation of the
phenomenological method will be discussed later in this chapter.

17. Or, as Paul Ricoeur says, *Ideen* I is ambiguous; one does
not know whether consciousness is receptive or creative. "Introduction" to *Idées*, p. xxx.

18. *Ibid.* The words "productive" and "creative" were used by
Eugene Fink in 1933 in his article on Husserl, which Husserl en-
dorsed completely. *Ibid.*, pp. xiii-xiv, xxix, xxxi-xxxiv, 188 n. l.

19. *Die Krisis der Europäischen Wissenschaften und die transzendentale Phänomenologie*, ed. Walter Biemel. Parts I-II of the
central group of *Krisis* lectures were published in *Philosophia*, I
(1936), 77-176. The third part was scheduled for publication in
that journal, but was never sent to the publisher. It appeared for
the first time in Biemel's critical edition of the lectures. Besides the
three central parts of the *Krisis* lectures, this edition includes
several other manuscripts relating to the same themes and period,
as, for example, the Vienna lecture delivered in May, 1935, several
months prior to the lectures delivered in Prague which form the
central *Krisis* group.

The contents of the *Krisis* lectures have been summarized in
English by Aron Gurwitsch in "Discussion: The Last Work of
Edmund Husserl," *Philosophy and Phenomenological Research*,
XVI (March, 1956), 380-99; XVII (March, 1957), 370-98. In ad-
dition, the Vienna lecture has been translated by Quentin Lauer,
S. J., in *Phenomenology and the Crisis of Philosophy*, pp. 149-92.

The first two parts of the central *Krisis* group have been translated into French by Edmund Gerrer as "La Crise des sciences
européennes et la phénoménologie transcendentale," *Les Etudes
Philosophiques*, IV (1949), 127-57, 229-301. The Vienna lecture
has been translated by Paul Ricoeur as "La Crise de l'humanité
européenne et la philosophie," *Revue de Métaphysique et de
Morale*, LV (1950), 225-58. Professor Ricoeur has also translated
some of Husserl's daily meditations dating from this period, "La
Philosophie comme prise de conscience de l'humanité," *Deucalion*
III, pp. 109-27.

20. Quoted in the introduction by Walter Biemal to "La
Philosophie comme prise de conscience de l'humanité," p. 113
(emphasis added).

21. The story of Merleau-Ponty's use of the Archives is told by H. L. Van Breda in "Maurice Merleau-Ponty et les Archives-Husserl à Louvain," *Revue de Métaphysique et de Morale*, LXVII (1962), 410-30. Van Breda says that Merleau-Ponty was the first person outside Louvain to request to see the unpublished manuscripts (p. 412). Jean Hering suggested to Merleau-Ponty that these manuscripts would aid his researches (see Merleau-Ponty's letter to Van Breda, *ibid*).

The fact that his study of Husserl's later philosophy began *after* he had completed *SC* tends to confirm the thesis I shall develop, namely, that Merleau-Ponty's phenomenological method was influenced by many thinkers of whom Husserl was only one, and that it was only later, when he rejected Marxism and Sartrian existentialism, that Merleau-Ponty defined his position in terms of his relation to Husserl. He refers to Husserl's later philosophy only a few times in his early writings: *SC* 236, n. 1, tr. 249, n. 56; Preface to *PP* (discussed in this section on Husserl); *PP* 318, n. 1, tr. 274, n. 1; 419, n. 1, tr. 365, n. 1; *SNS* 272-76, tr. 134-36.

22. *Krisis*, pars. 1-7.

23. It belongs to Western civilization alone in the sense that this ideal of infinite tasks based on rationalization is the special *telos* of Western civilization, that which animates it. (See the Vienna lecture,*Krisis*, pp. 318-22.) But insofar as the knowledge thus obtained is universally valid, it belongs to everyone.

24. The discussion in this paragraph is based on the Vienna lecture (*Krisis*, pp. 314-48). Husserl begins the second of the central *Krisis* lectures (par. 8) with a discussion of Euclidean geometry which expressed the Greek ideal of *epistémé*, in order to reveal how Galileo and his successors perverted their inheritance. I shall return to this discussion in connection with *Krisis* II.

25. *Krisis*, pp. 328, 331.

26. Paragraph 2 of the *Krisis* lectures carries as its title: "The positivist reduction of the idea of science to a simple science of facts; the crisis of science as the loss of its living signification." What Husserl has in mind here is not the crisis in the methodologies of the sciences themselves; he is saying nothing about that. Rather he is concerned about the relation of the particular sciences to man's total existence. The misunderstanding of that relation, from the side of science, has brought on what Husserl calls the "existential cantradition" (par. 7) in which we now live.

27. *Krisis*, par. 3

28. *Ibid.*, pars. 8-27.

29. See *ibid.*, par. 5.

30. See Paul Ricoeur, "Husserl et le sens de l'histoire," *Revue de Métaphysique et de Morale*, LIV (1949), 280-316. I found this article very helpful in clarifying both the significance of Husserl's turning from an "egology" to a philosophy of history and his interpretations of modern philosophy.

31. *Krisis*, par. 8.

32. *Krisis*, par. 9, which comprises almost half of the second *Krisis* lecture, is devoted to Galileo.

33. *Krisis*, pars. 10-21.

34. Husserl credits Descartes with having implicitly affirmed the notion of intentionality. (*Krisis*, par. 20)

35. *Krisis*, par. 23.

36. *Ibid.*, par. 24.

37. Husserl's discussion of Kant closes *Krisis* II (pars. 25-27) and opens *Krisis* III (pars. 28-32). On Husserl's belief that Hume was close to his own solution as the basis for his reservations about Kant's philosophy, see Ricoeur, "Husserl et le sens de l'histoire," pp. 305-6.

38. For an incisive critique of Husserl's view of the history of modern philosophy, see Ricoeur, *Ibid.*, pp. 308-16.

39. This statement of Husserl's aim makes it clear (as the title of his lectures should already have done) that his presentation of the *Lebenswelt* will be only a preliminary discussion ultimately aiming at the formulation of transcendental phenomenology. And such is in fact the case. The description of the *Lebenswelt* (pars. 33-38) leads into transcendental phenomenology by way of the *epoché* (pars. 39-44), the intuition of the essence of experience of the *Lebenswelt*—phenomenology of perception being chosen as the primary example (pars. 45-49), and the transcendental Ego (pars. 50, 52-55). The second part of *Krisis* III (pars. 56-73) deals with the relation of transcendental phenomenology to empirical psychology. The aim of the two parts converges insofar as the first part is concerned to show the inadequacy of the natural scientific view of the world, the second to show the inadequacy of the empirical psychological view of the mind, and both to show that transcendental phenomenology offers a more adequate account of both and, of course, of the relation between the two.

Since I have, however cursorily, already stated the essential points of Husserl's transcendental phenomenology, I shall not repeat them again. The point to be made here is that Husserl's intentions as well as his conception of transcendental phenomenology remained consistent with what it had been earlier. The question I shall have to raise is whether or not his return to the *Lebenswelt* to some degree made impossible the fulfillment of his intentions. The account of *Krisis* III presented here will be confined to a presentation of Husserl's account of the *Lebenswelt* and of the problems which it raises for his philosophy.

40. *Krisis*, par. 34, sec. *f*. The *Lebenswelt* becomes synonymous here with the idea of the world as the horizon of all experience. (See further, *Krisis*, pars. 47, 49) Horizon for Husserl always referred to the context in which experience takes place. But in his *Krisis* lectures the horizon itself is becoming the theme of his reflections. His desire to place all experience on rational foundations is readily apparent in this effort to reflect on the conditions for the possibility of any experience whatsoever, which is what is involved finally in the idea of the world as horizon. On Husserl's view of "horizon," see Ludwig Landgrebe, "The World as a phenomenological Problem," *Philosophy and Phenomenological Research*, I (1940), 38-58.

41. *Krisis*, pars. 35-37. This corrects an impression left in the Vienna lecture that the *Lebenswelt* as the prereflective world is finite and relative and therefore incapable of infinite rationalization in the manner in which we rationalize knowledge in the sciences. Now Husserl is insisting that the *Lebenswelt* itself can be made the theme of an infinite reflection.

42. What Husserl is suggesting here is that the *Lebenswelt* itself can be idealized in such a way as to clarify every other idealization as a partial idealization of the *Lebenswelt*. The idealization of the *Lebenswelt* is the *ultimate* idealization which will once for all constitute a firm foundation for philosophy. The possibility of this idealization, however, depends on Husserl's trancendental phenomenology through which the idealization is accomplished. And as will be suggested, the very idea of idealizing the *Lebenswelt* is contradictory.

43. *Krisis,* par. 51.

44. Paul Ricoeur, in *Histoire de la philosophie Allemande*, p. 196.

45. For example, Pierre Thévenaz, *What is Phenomenology?*, trans.James M. Edie, Charles Courtney, and Paul Brockelman, pp. 37-92.

The implications of this assertion by Thévenaz are quite complex. On the one hand, if this was the next logical step, Husserl

certainly never recognized it, even in the *Krisis* lectures. Historically speaking, therefore, it seems more accurate to distinguish between Husserl's actual *intentions* and the logical *implications* of
his views. It may be fair to say that the existential phenomenologists are faithfully carrying out the implications of Husserl's philosophy as expressed in the *Krisis* lectures. But it is much more
doubtful to say they are carrying out Husserl's intentions. On the
other hand, however, it is difficult to explain why the younger
generation of French philosophers, who were so self-consciously
reacting against idealistic rationalism, should have placed so much
confidence in Husserl, perhaps the most rationalistic philosopher
to appear in the twentieth century, unless they believed that, for
Husserl himself, there was much more in his philosophy than another formulation of classical rationalism.

46. Spiegelberg, "Husserl's Phenomenology and Existentialism,'
The Journal of Philosophy, LII (1960), 66-67. He does not, however, attempt to answer the question. Professor John Wild does
believe Husserl was influenced by Heidegger. See James M. Edie,
"Recent Work in Phenomenology," *American Philosophical Quarterly*, I (1964), 126-27.

47. It is the Husserl of the *Logische Untersuchungen* that Merleau-Ponty cites at this point. (*PP* iv, tr. x) Merleau-Ponty was
always predisposed toward the object-centeredness of descriptive
philosophy. He affirms it in his first published article: "Christianisme et ressentiment," p. 305.

48. In the last paragraph of the *Cartesian Meditations* (p. 157)
Husserl writes: "The Delphic motto, 'Know thyself!' has gained a
new signification. Positive science is a science lost in the world. I
must lose the world by *epoché*, in order to regain it by a universal
self-examination. 'Do not wish to go out,' says Augustine, 'go back
into yourself; truth dwells in the inner man.'"

49. *PP* viii, tr. xiv. Merleau-Ponty insisted on this point even in
his last writing: "The incompleteness of the reduction . . . is not an
obstacle to reduction, it is reduction itself, the rediscovery of
vertical being [= brute being or *Lebenswelt*]." (*VI* 232) On the
identification of description with a philosophy of being in his late
writings, see below, chap. 6.

50. *PP* xi, tr. xvi. Merleau-Ponty reaffirms this contention in his
last writing. See *VI* 70, 156. See also *SHP* 33, 35, tr. 73, 75.

51. On Merleau-Ponty's use of the term "world," see above,
chap. 2, n. 2.

52. *PP* xvi, tr. xx. Merleau-Ponty's understanding of "mystery"

here has affinities with Gabriel Marcel's use of the word. On this, see the following section of this chapter.

53. *The Phenomenological Movement*, II, 535.

54. Merleau-Ponty, "Christianisme et ressentiment," p. 305.

55. *Metaphysical Journal*, pp. 321-22.

56. *Ibid.*, p. 292.

57. *Ibid.*, pp. 73-74.

58. *Ibid.*, p. 287.

59. *Ibid.*, p. 30.

60. *Ibid.*, pp. 86, 137.

61. *Ibid.*, p. 137.

62. *Ibid.*

63. It is interesting to note, in relation to this conclusion, that, while Marcel has always been highly critical of Sartrian existentialism, he has never made a public statement, so far as I know, on his relation to Merleau-Ponty.

64. Merleau-Ponty, "Etre et avoir," pp. 107-9.

65. Spiegelberg, *The Phenomenological Movement*, I, 275. For a discussion of this relationship, see *Ibid.*, pp. 275-83, and the references cited.

66. The critical passage is quoted by Spiegelberg, *Ibid.*, p. 280.

67. It is significant that in *PP* the only two books by Heidegger listed in the bibliography are *Being and Time* and *Kant and the Problem of Methaphysics*, that is, precisely the two books in which *Dasein* represents a privileged access to Being.

68. Sartre, *Search for a Method*, trans. Hazel Barnes, p. 38. It was Raymond Aron who first mentioned phenomenology to Sartre (in 1932) and suggested that Sartre go to the French Institute—where Aron was then studying—the following year. See Simone de Beauvoir, *The Prime of Life*, trans. Peter Green, p. 112. But cf. Sartre, "Merleau-Ponty vivant," p. 306.

69. Spiegelberg, *The Phenomenological Movement*, II, 462-63.

70. Spiegelberg, *The Phenomenological Movement*, II, 529. See also Sartre, "Merleau-Ponty vivant," p. 306.

71. "Existentialism Is a Humanism," in Walter Kaufmann, editor, *Existentialism from Dostoevsky to Sartre*, p. 289.

72. Sartre never satisfactorily explained how the passage from the self as prereflective to the self as self is effected. Both usages are present in *Being and Nothingness* with no clear demarcation between them. The result is a lack of methodological clarity in Sartre's major work. On this see Maurice Natanson, *Literature, Philosophy, and the Social Sciences*, pp. 45-54.

73. Though, as we have already noted, his own predilection for an object-centered phenomenology was expressed even before this treatise by Sartre appeared. See above, n. 45.

74. This critique is better treated in relation to the context out of which it arose. Therefore, I simply note the point here. For an analysis of the critique, see below, chap. 5.

75. *The Imagination* (1936), trans. Forrest Williams. Merleau-Ponty's second published writing was a review of this book by Sartre ("L'Imagination," pp. 756-61). He confines himself for the most part to recounting the contents of the book (pp. 756-60), suggesting in a final paragraph that Sartre assumed positions in Husserl which were still in dispute in Germany (indication perhaps that he was reading rather widely in German phenomenology) and that his criticisms of Bergson may have been too severe. But he believes the book will assure Sartre an attentive audience. (But cf. VI 247)

76. On Sartre's view of intentionality in relation to Husserl, see above, n. 14.

77. Sartre, *The Imagination*, pp. 127-43.

78. *L'Imaginaire* (1940), translated anonymously as *The Psychology of Imagination*.

79. Sartre, *The Psychology of Imagination*, pp. 3-21.

80. *The Psychology of Imagination*, pp. 269-70 and following. This is related to Sartre's view of the emotions as a means of changing ourselves when we are unable, on account of external obstacles, to change the world. The emotions are "magical," the *illusion* of changing the world. *Sketch for a Theory of the Emotions* (1939), trans. Philip Mairet. Merleau-Ponty first accepted Sartre's view of the emotions and his idea that the unconscious is a species of bad faith (see *PP* 98-102, tr. 83-86; *SNS* 108-9, tr. 53), but later questioned this interpretation (see below, chap. 6).

81. See Alexandre Koyré, "Rapport sur l'état des études hégéliennes en France," *Revue d'Histoire de la Philosophie*, V (1931), 147-71.

82. *Le Malheur de la conscience dans la philosophie de Hegel.*

83. *Ibid.*, p. 143.

84. Koyré, "Rapport sur l'état des études hégéliennes en France," pp. 170-71.

85. Jean Hyppolite, "Les Travaux de jeunesse de Hegel d'après des ouvrages récents," *Revue de Métaphysique et de Morale*, XLII (1935), 399-426, 549-78.

In his later interpretation of the *Phenomenology of Mind*, Hyp-

polite contends that, whereas in his earliest writings Hegel looked
for the overcoming of the "unhappy consciousness" in a religious
concept of a new society, in the *Phenomenology of Mind* this reconciliation was to come through philosophy. Cf. also Auguste
Cornu, *The Origins of Marxian Thought.*

86. His lectures were compiled by Raymond Queneau, partly
on the basis of notes by students and partly on the basis of
stenographic accounts, and published as *Introduction à la lecture
de Hegel.* A second edition was published in 1962 which differs
from the first only by the addition of a long footnote on pp. 436-
37, altering the page numbers after that point. Page references
cited here will be from the second edition.

87. Iring Fetscher, "Der Marxismus im Spiegel der französischen
Philosophie," *Marxismus-Studien* (Tübingen, 1954), p. 181; and
Rudolf W. Meyer, "Maurice Merleau-Ponty und das Schicksal des
französischen Existentialismus," *Philosophische Rundschau,* III
(1955), 138.

88. *Introduction à la lecture de Hegel,* p. 257.

89. *Ibid.,* p 211.

90. *Ibid.,* pp. 192 ff.

91. *Ibid.,* p. 528.

92. *Ibid.,* p. 194.

93. *Ibid.,* p. 540.

94. *Ibid.,* p. 175; see also pp. 12, 30, 167, 178, 532.

95. *Ibid.,* p. 33.

96. *Ibid.,* pp. 163-64, 172-73.

97. *Ibid.,* pp. 153-54, 311.

98. *Ibid.,* p. 327.

99. Jean Wahl has written an excellent critique: "A propos de
l'introduction à la phénoménologie de Hegel par A. Kojève,"
Deucalion V, pp. 77-99.

100. Kojève, *Introduction à la lecture de Hegel,* p. 449; cf. p.
38.

101. *Ibid.,* p. 470.

102. See, for example, Jean-F. Lyotard, *La Phénoménologie,* pp.
42-46; see also S 196-97, tr. 156; SNS 274-75, tr. 135.

103. See Kojève, *Introduction,* pp. 549 and 575, n. 1, where
Heidegger's views are explicitly mentioned.

104. *Ibid.,* p. 30.

105. *Ibid.,* pp. 180 ff.

106. See for example, *Ibid.,* pp. 12, 30, 167, 175, 178, 532.

107. Jean Wahl, "A propos de l'introduction à la phénoménologie de Hegel par A. Kojève," pp. 93-99.

108. Simone de Beauvoir, *The Prime of Life*, p. 363.

109. *SNS* 257-60, tr. 127-28. Marx's remarks in his early writings reflect this same perspective. See Erich Fromm, ed., *Marx's Concept of Man*, pp. 186-89. On this treatise, see the following note.

110. These manuscripts, although not published in German until 1932, were translated into French in 1927 from a Russian manuscript, and published first in a journal and then in book form. I have learned this through a personal communication from the translator, Norbert Guterman. Professor Paul Ricoeur has emphasized to me the importance of Marx's early manuscripts for French thinkers. However, the early translation is listed in none of the major bibliographies of Marxism or of philosophy in France. Even more significantly perhaps, it is not mentioned by Auguste Cornu in a dissertation he wrote on the young Marx in 1934: *Karl Marx: l'homme et l'oeuvre*. Perhaps the best conclusion is that this early translation was not widely read, or at least that the milieu was not yet prepared for Marx. But with the revival of Hegel, and particularly with Kojève's interpretation of Hegel, the young Marx soon became a center of attention.

These manuscripts have recently been translated into English by T. B. Bottomore in Erich Fromm, ed., *Marx's Concept of Man*. They are also available from the Foreign Languages Publishing House in Moscow.

111. *Ibid.*, pp. 101, 183.

112. *Ibid.*, pp. 142-43, 151.

113. "The positive supersession of *private property* as the appropriation of *human* life, is therefore the *positive* supersession of all alienation, and the return of man from religion, the family, the state, etc., to his *human*, i.e., *social* life." *Ibid.*, p. 128, emphasis in text.

114. *Ibid.*, p. 127, emphasis in text.

115. *Ibid.*, p. 107, emphasis in text. See *SNS* 240 ff., tr. 119 ff.

116. This is not to say that Marx's position is without equivocation even in these early writings. For in dividing all men into two "classes," the exploiters and the exploited, Marx was already erecting new abstractions in place of those he had abandoned. Not "concrete" man, but man as the reflection of a class image, was becoming his norm. (See *Ibid.*,p. 131) This remark is made with the wisdom of hindsight. It does not mean that this process of abstraction necessarily follows from these early writings, but only that historically speaking it did follow. As we shall see, Merleau-Ponty, who recognized some equivocations in Marx from the be-

ginning, finally had to admit that the equivocations were present even where he had formerly believed they were not.

On this problem of the extent to which Marx's philosophy was ever a "concrete" philosophy, see Daniel Bell, *The End of Ideology*, pp. 365-66. Bell's book was originally published by the Free Press in 1960. The citations here, however, are based on the Collier paperback edition published in 1961.

117. *Ibid.*, p 140.

118. *Ibid.*, p. 129, emphasis in text. Merleau-Ponty insists on this as the essential character of Marxism. It is already implicit in *PP* and becomes explicit in his early postwar essays. (See *SNS* 211-12, tr. 106; 272, tr. 134; *HT* 206)

119. *Ibid.*, pp. 135, 149. As for Marx so for Merleau-Ponty at this time action will take the form of expropriating the expropriators, i.e., of revolution. (See *SNS* 229, tr. 114)

120. "Metaphysics begins from the moment when, ceasing to live in the evidence of the object—whether it is the sensory object or the object of science—we apperceive the radical subjectivity of all our experience as inseparable from its truth value. It means two things to say that our experience is our own: both that it is not the measure of all imaginable being in itself and that it is nonetheless co-extensive with all being of which we can form a notion. This double sense of the *cogito* is the basic fact of metaphysics: I am sure that there is being—on the condition that I do not seek another sort of being than being-for-me." (*SNS* 186-87, tr. 93; cf. *SNS* 190-91, tr. 95) See the discussion of this passage in Alphonse de Waelhens, *Une Philosophie de l'ambiguïté*, pp. 387-89, where it is argued that Merleau-Ponty is too narrowly humanistic at this point. It is to this kind of criticism that the later phases of Merleau-Ponty's metaphysical philosophy attempt to respond, as we shall see.

CHAPTER IV

1. This story has recently been dramatically told in *Is Paris Burning?* by Larry Collins and Dominique Lapierre.

2. "La Guerre a eu lieu," reprinted in *SNS* 308, tr. 152; see *SNS* 205-6, tr. 103, also written in 1945; and *S* 279, tr. 221, written in 1949.

3. Alexander Werth, *France: 1940-1955*, pp. 246, 247.

4. "Conseil National de la Résistance," which represented eight resistance movements, six political parties, and the two trade union

movements. Its representatives drew up a plan of action for the period following the liberation. Dorothy Pickles, *France Between the Republics*, Appendix 9. See also Werth, *France*, pp. 220 ff.

5. See on this Merleau-Ponty, *HT* 3; Jules Monnerot, "Liquidation et justification," *La Nef*, IV (February, 1947), 9; and Roland Caillois, "Destin de l'humanisme marxiste," *Critique*, IV (March, 1948), 244.

6. There is nothing in the articles not in the book, but the book contains material not in the articles: pp. 56-58, 76-100 (chapter on Trotsky), 103-4, 109-11, 119-22, 132-35, and 196-201 (Merleau-Ponty's political platform). There was no change in Merleau-Ponty's position between the publication of the articles and the appearance of his book except that some of his additions, perhaps in reaction against the position of his critics, are stated in more uncompromising terms. This is especially true of the additions on pp. 119-22 and 132-35 where Merleau-Ponty, in discussing the proletariat as that which distinguishes Marxism from fascism and renders all comparisons between the two false, asserts that the proletariat is the carrier of a universal meaning in history and that it is the true inheritor of western liberalism. These remarks, made during the height of controversy, Merleau-Ponty was to deny later, while Sartre was to avow them with increasing vigor.

7. *HT* 37-38, especially 38, n. 1.

8. *HT* ix-xvii. Cf. *S* 402, tr. 323, also written in 1947.

9. *HT* xvii. Merleau-Ponty made this same point again in 1948 in "Le 'Manifeste Communiste' à cent ans," *Le Figaro Littéraire*, April 3, 1948. It is important to note this inasmuch as Merleau-Ponty will reject it later.

10. *HT* xxi-xxii; cf. *SNS* 327-41, tr. 160-67. To this should be added the widespread and probably well-founded belief that, had the left wing attempted to rule alone, the British and Americans would have intervened to prevent it. (*SNS* 348, tr. 170; and Sartre, "Merleau-Ponty vivant," p. 314) Thus, Merleau-Ponty's position involves an equivocation also, inasmuch as he realized that political forces outside France made the alternative he proposed within France an impossibility. This equivocation is the clue to the later transformations in his views. For it led him to an "attentisme marxiste," the expectation and hope for a proletarian revolution, a hope which events subsequent to 1947 completely shattered.

11. The book was originally published by the Macmillan Co. in 1941. The citations here, however, are based on the paperback edition published by the New American Library in 1961.

12. Arthur Koestler, *The Yogi and the Commissar and Other Essays*, pp. 13-22, 198-223. The book was first published by the Macmillan Co. in 1945. The citations here, however, are based on the paperback edition published by Collier Books in 1961.

13. In the first of two essays entitled "The Yogi and the Commissar," he suggests that no synthesis is possible. (p. 18; see also *Darkness*, p. 208) In the second, however, he argues that our only salvation lies in the attempt to effect a synthesis. (pp. 222-23) Since for Koestler the political arena is by and large inhabited by the commissar (see *Darkness*, p. 137), a synthesis would require a concerted effort to introduce the contemplative or yogi ideal into Western education. (pp. 221-22) Merleau-Ponty is thus correct when he says that Koestler leans toward the position of the yogi. (*HT* 177 ff.)

14. Two alternatives were open to Rubashov in Koestler's view: "Either the cut connection (Man-Universe) is re-established and as an act of atonement the Man-Society connection broken off; this is the classical case of the Revolutionary turning into a Mystic, the total jump from Commissar to Yogi. Or the connection is *not* re-established—then the dead cord coils up and strangles its owner. This is the equally classical case of the ex-revolutionaries whose souls died of suffocation." (*The Yogi and the Commissar*, p. 18) Rubashov experiences both alternatives, though in the end he dies a "suffocated" revolutionary rather than a yogi.

15. *Darkness*, p. 47.

16. *Ibid.*, p. 77.

17. *Ibid.*, pp. 58-59, 213, 217.

18. *Ibid.*, pp. 79 ff.

19. *Ibid.*, pp. 146-47, 196-97, 211; see below n. 26.

20. *Ibid.*, p. 56.

21. *Ibid.*, p. 92.

22. See Sartre, "Merleau-Ponty vivant," p. 315.

23. *Report of Court Proceedings in the Case of the Anti-Soviet "Bloc of Rights and Trotskyites."* Hereafter in the notes, this document will be referred to as *Report*.

Merleau-Ponty records as a well-known fact that Rubashov combined the physical traits of Zinoviev and the moral traits of Bukharin. (*HT* 27, n. 1) Koestler himself says "the life of the man N. S. Rubashov is a synthesis of the lives of a number of men who were victims of the so-called Moscow trials." *Darkness*, p. vi. See also Peter Viereck's "Foreword," pp. ix-x.

24. The situation of the revolutionary is analogous to that of

the heretic in the church. Merleau-Ponty writes in this regard: "Like the Church, the Party will perhaps rehabilitate those it has condemned when a new phase of history will have changed the meaning of their conduct." (*HT* 74; cf. *Darkness*, p. 201) This is a prophetic comment inasmuch as the trials were disavowed by the Russian government in the anti-Stalinist reaction of the 1950s. This is undoubtedly why the French Communists, who reacted negatively to Merleau-Ponty's book in 1948, see nothing harmful in it today. See Sartre, "Merleau-Ponty vivant," p. 322; and Georg Lukacs' introduction to the 1960 edition of his *Existentialisme ou marxisme?*, p. 7.

25. On the admittance of objective guilt, see *Report*, pp. 34, 36, 370, 381, 768. On the simultaneous maintenance of subjective *Report*, pp. 34, 36, 370, 381, 768. On the simultaneous maintenance of subjective innocence, see *Report*, pp. 383, 413, 424, 433, 770.

26. *HT* 71. Eric Hoffer contends that those who confessed at the Moscow trials did so because, having forsaken the past and everything outside Russia, they could avoid complete isolation only by agreeing to the Party's condemnation. To have renounced the Party would have been to cut themselves completely off from humanity. (*The True Believer*, pp. 62-63. The book was originally published by Harper and Bros. in 1951. The citations here, however, are to the paperback edition published by the New American Library in 1958.) This is another of many possible interpretations and is psychologically as tenable as the theories of either Koestler or Merleau-Ponty.

27. Hannah Arendt's study, *Eichmann in Jerusalem*, provides an interesting corroboration of Merleau-Ponty's argument. She writes: "The defense would apparently have preferred him [Eichmann] to plead not guilty on the grounds that under the then existing Nazi legal system he had not done anything wrong, that what he was accused of were not crimes but 'acts of state,' over which no other state has jurisdiction (*par in parem imperium non habet*), that it had been his duty to obey and that, in Servatius' [his lawyer's] words, he had committed acts 'for which you are decorated if you win and go to the gallows if you lose.' (Thus Goebbels had declared in 1943: 'We will go down in history as the greatest statesmen of all times or as their greatest criminals')" (pp. 21-22). Later she adds the comment: "Aggressive warfare is at least as old as recorded history, and while it had been denounced as 'criminal' many times before, it had never been recognized as

such in any formal sense [prior to the Nuremberg Trials]" (p. 255; see also pp. 256-57). Miss Arendt's book was first published by the Viking Press in 1963. A revised edition appeared in 1964. The citations here are to the revised edition reissued as a Compass paperback in 1965.

See also, on this point, Roland Bainton, *Christian Attitudes Toward War and Peace*, p. 243.

28. *SNS* 230, tr. 114. Many commentators have noted an ambiguity in Marx at this point. But insofar as Merleau-Ponty includes Lenin and Trotsky in his definition of "classical Marxism" the equivocation is removed. For they clearly affirmed the necessity of violence. During this period Merleau-Ponty believed the only effective proletarian revolution in France would be a violent one. *SNS* 219-21, tr. 109-10; 230-34, tr. 114-16,

29. *HT* 135; see also *AD* 101-3. Later, Merleau-Ponty will describe the Hungarian Revolution of 1956 as a manifestation for all to see of the internal contradictions within communism itself, inasmuch as violent repression was applied in this case, not against the oppressors, but against the *proletariat*. *S* 366-85, tr. 293-308,

30. *HT* 165, tr. 213. The italics are in the French text, though they were omitted in the copyrighted English translation. The sentence in brackets is a departure from the copyrighted translation. The latter reads: "After that there are no more dreams or experiences." But the French text reads: "Après quoi, il n'y a plus que rêveries ou aventures."

31. See above, chap. 3, n. 116.

32. Merleau-Ponty's remarks in *HT* xxvi-xl are directed to these critics, though none of them is mentioned by name.

33. Jules Monnerot admits this as a factor motivating his response after Merleau-Ponty's first article. ("Réponse aux *Temps Modernes*," *La Nef*, IV (December, 1947), 32-33; cf. *HT* xxvi)

34. Jean-Daniel Martinet, "Les Intellectuels et le goût du pouvoir," *La Révolution Prolétarienne*, CCCIII (May, 1947), 43, 45. He also refers to Aimé Patri who makes the same accusation in "La Philosophie de la police politique," *Masses* 7-8 (1947). Peter Viereck, who should have known better since he was not reading Merleau-Ponty in the political atmosphere of France in 1947, follows this same line of reasoning in his foreword to the Signet edition of Koestler's *Darkness*, p. xii.

35. Robert Campbell, "Monsieur Merleau-Ponty et ses lecteurs," *Paru*, XXXVII (December, 1947), 49; Aimé Patri, "Humanisme et Terreur," *Paru*, XLII (May, 1948), 61; Jules Monnerot, "Liquidation et justification," *La Nef*, IV (February, 1947), 10; Christianus,

"Sainte Antigone," *La Vie Intellectuelle*, XV (January, 1947), 4; Martinet, "Les Intellectuels et le goût du pouvoir," p. 45. Even Albert Camus was of this opinion: see Sartre, "Merleau-Ponty vivant," p. 323.

36. Martinet, "Les Intellectuels et le goût du pouvoir," pp. 43-44; Christianus, "Sainte Antigone," pp. 1-4; Jules Monnerot, "Réponse aux *Temps Modernes*," *La Nef*, IV (December, 1947), 32-43; and Emmanuel Berl, *De L'Innocence*, p. 12.

37. Georg Lukacs, *Existentialisme ou marxisme?*, p. 201; see pp. 196-203. This contention is repeated in Roger Garaudy, *et al.*, *Mésaventures de l'anti-marxisme: Les malheurs de M. Merleau-Ponty*, p. 12.

38. Emmanuel Berl, *De L'Innocence*.

39. The book was Kravchenko's *I Chose Freedom*. On this case see Alexander Werth, *France*, pp. 436 ff.

40. Sartre and Merleau-Ponty refused to attend this rally. (Sartre, "Merleau-Ponty vivant," p. 330)

41. This remained the policy of *Les Temps Modernes* even after Sartre and Merleau-Ponty disavowed the R. D. R. See, for example, Merleau-Ponty's article on the Soviet concentration camps in the January, 1950, issue of the journal (reprinted in S 330-43, tr. 263-73), to which Sartre added his signature.

42. Sartre, "Merleau-Ponty vivant," p. 338.

43. *Ibid.*, pp. 347-48.

44. Alexander Werth, *Lost Statesman: The Strange Story of Pierre Mendès-France*, pp. 151-55, especially p. 153.

45. This discussion is based on two essays Merleau-Ponty devoted to Trotsky: HT 76-105; AD 101-29; see also S 322-28, tr. 256-60.

46. Merleau-Ponty analyzes this book, and Lukacs' evolution since its publication, in AD 43-99. Lukacs, in a letter written to the editors of *Cahiers du Communisme* and published in *Mésaventures de l'anti-marxisme*, pp. 158-59, objects to Merleau-Ponty's analysis, not because Lukacs felt that it was inaccurate, but because he had passed beyond the opinions expressed in it. Because of this latter fact, he considered Merleau-Ponty "dishonest" in his use of it. Merleau-Ponty's whole point is that we must try to understand *why* Lukacs passed beyond.

47. SNS 201-2, tr. 101; 217, tr. 108; 229, tr. 114; 249, tr. 123-24; 300 ff., tr. 148 ff. (all written in 1945). See also HT 170 (written in 1947), where, however, the illustration used to confirm his point is inappropriate.

48. See above, p. 101.

49. "Le 'Manifeste Communiste' à cent ans," *Le Figaro Litté-raire*, April 3, 1948.

50. *AD* 309. In 1945 Merleau-Ponty had criticized a right-wing intellectual precisely for justifying a "fascism in thought" which was not guilty of (and could transcend) the historical errors of real fascism. (*SNS* 197-202, tr. 99-101) In 1955 he applied this same critique to his own brand of Marxism.

51. His reassessment led him to the adoption of a platform which included six major points: (1) insofar as classes exist there should be a class struggle; (2) the means for this struggle [the strike] should also exist; (3) the Communist Party, as one which stands outside the rules of democratic play, should be legal (this brought from one of his communist critics the remark: "Thanks all the same." Garaudy, *et al.*, *Mésaventures de l'anti-marxisme*, p. 140); (4) revolutionary movements are justified insofar as they reveal the fact that society does not permit the proletariat to live; (5) there should be a parliament, but one which does not try to mask the true problems; (6) the noncommunist left ought to maintain a spirit of criticism against every proletarian regime as well as against every liberal one. (*AD* 302-5)

52. Merleau-Ponty had denied this in 1945: *SNS* 233-34, tr. 116.

53. These points are made in an article intended as an explication of the results to which he had been led in *AD*: "Ou va l'anti-communisme?," *L'Express*, June 25, 1955, p. 12. See also "La France va-t-elle se renouveler?," *L'Express*, October 23, 1954, p. 4.

54. *S* 408-18, tr. 328-36; 423-35, tr. 341-50. This is a dramatic reversal of the position he held in 1947, when he criticized François Mauriac for maintaining a similar position. See *S* 402-7, tr. 323-27.

CHAPTER V

1. See Merleau-Ponty, "Christianisme et ressentiment," pp. 303-6; and Sartre, "Merleau-Ponty vivant," pp. 305-6, and *Situations*, I, 31.

2. "I always found, I still find, that the Truth is one; on points of detail it appeared to me, then, that I had to abandon my views if I was unable to convine the interlocuter to abandon his. Merleau-Ponty, on the contrary, found his security in the multiplicity of perspectives: he saw [in this multiplicity] facets of being." Sartre, "Merleau-Ponty vivant," pp. 307-8.

3. Sartre calls Merleau-Ponty the "lieur," one who binds men together. *Ibid.*, p. 307.

4. See Sartre, "Merleau-Ponty vivant," pp. 319-21.

5. Such was not the case when Sartre broke with Camus during this same period.

6. See "Existentialism Is a Humanism," in Walter Kaufmann, ed., *Existentialism from Dostoevsky to Sartre*, pp. 287-311.

7. See *ibid.*; and *Literature and Existentialism*, trans. by Bernard Frechtman, *passim*.

8. See "Existentialism Is a Humanism"; and "Materialism and Revolution," in *Literary and Philosophical Essays*, trans. by Annette Michelson, pp. 198-256.

9. "Les Mouches," *Confluences*, III (September-October 1943), 515-16.

10. See, for example, Gabriel Marcel, "Existence and Human Freedom," in *The Philosophy of Existentialism*, trans. by Manya Harari, p. 90. (Written in January, 1946.) This book was originally published by the Philosophical Library in 1956. Citations here, however, refer to The Citadel Press paperback edition, published in 1961.

11. *SNS* 87, tr. 43. The Marxist emphasis is clear here.

12. *SNS* 84, tr. 41. It is fair to say that Merleau-Ponty is reading his own viewpoint into Sartre here. The same is true in *SNS* 85, tr. 42, in his discussion of Sartre's novel *The Age of Reason*.

13. *SNS* 144, tr. 72-73; cf. *VI* 135. But see below pp. 134 and 288, n. 63.

14. *Being and Nothingness*, pp. 440-41.

15. This is the case despite the observation made in chap. 3 that in Sartre's view the self emerges in time through its acts, for the emphasis in *Being and Nothingness* is on the world as it is constituted by the self, not on the unfolding of a self simultaneously and in relation to the world.

16. See "Existentialism Is a Humanism," pp. 291-92; and *Anti-Semite and Jew*, trans. George J. Becker, p. 153. (Written in 1946.)

17. Many commentators have drawn attention to this fact. See, for example: Maurice Natanson, *A Critique of Jean-Paul Sartre's Ontology*; Stephen Strasser, *Phenomenology and the Human Sciences*, trans. Henry J. Koren, pp. 42-55; Alphonse de Waelhens, *Une Philosophie de l'ambiguité*, pp. 2-8; Jean Wahl, *A Short History of Existentialism*, trans. Forrest Williams and Stanley Maron, p. 30.

18. Jean Wahl believes new possibilities emerged for existentialism with the appearance of *Phenomenology of Perception*,

because "the impasse, which in *Being and Nothingness* seemed to hinder the thought of Sartre from going toward more and more positive results, seems no longer to be the necessary final point of an existentialist meditation." See Marvin Farber, ed., *Philosophical Thought*, pp. 41-42.

19. "Le Langage indirect et les voix du silence," *Les Temps Modernes*, VII (1952), 2113-44; VIII (1952), 70-94. These articles have been reprinted in S 49-104, tr. 39-83, and will be discussed in chap. 8.

The articles are said to be an extract from a book in preparation entitled *La Prose du monde*, though the book never appeared. Merleau-Ponty mentioned this book again during this same period in a personal communication to Martial Gueroult. See "Un Inédit de Maurice Merleau-Ponty," *Revue de Métaphysique et de Morale*, LXVII (1962), 407 ff.

20. See above, p. 107.

21. Sartre's first article, "Les Communistes et la Paix, I," was published in July, 1952 (*Les Temps Modernes*, VII, 1-50); and his second, "Les Communistes et la Paix, II," in October-November, 1952 (*Les Temps Modernes*, VIII, 695-763). Claude Lefort responded to these two articles in "Le Marxisme et Sartre" in March, 1953 (*Les Temps Modernes*, VIII, 1541-70); Sartre replied in the same issue ("Réponse à Lefort," pp. 1571-1629). Lefort's second article, "De la Réponse à la question," was published in February, 1954 (*Les Temps Modernes*, IX, 157-84). Sartre's final article, "Les Communistes et la Paix, III," was published one month later, in March, 1954 (*Les Temps Modernes*, IX, 1731-1819).

22. Sartre, "Merleau-Ponty vivant," pp. 355-57. I have been unable to identify the article in *Les Temps Modernes* to which Sartre refers in recording this incident.

23. His "adhesion" was on his own terms. Near the beginning of his second article he wrote: "The end of this article is to declare my agreement with the communists on precise and limited subjects in reasoning from *my* principles and not *theirs*; one will see why." ("Les Communistes et la Paix, II," p. 706.)

24. Here Sartre is renouncing the position he had held between 1945 and 1952. See "Merleau-Ponty vivant," pp. 352-53.

25. This is a summary of "Les Communistes et la Paix, I."

26. "Les Communistes et la Paix, II," pp. 696-705.

27. This is a highly condensed summary of the main argument in "Les Communistes et la Paix, II," pp. 706 ff.

28. See above, chap. 3, n. 116.

29. Merleau-Ponty disagrees with Lefort here, believing, as he attempted to show in *Les Aventures de la dialectique*, that Stalinist bureaucratization was the result of more basic weaknesses.

30. This is a summary of Lefort's article, "Le Marxisme et Sartre."

31. To which Lefort replies later that Sartre also is an intellectual and, moreover, one with less political experience and involvement to his credit than the one he is criticizing.

32. This is a summary of Sartre's "Réponse à Lefort."

33. This is a summary of Lefort's article, "De la Réponse à la question."

34. At the end of the article Sartre indicates that another is to follow, but this promise was never fulfilled.

35. Sartre calls this "economic Malthusianism." Merleau-Ponty, commenting on this idea, remarked that it could be intended only in a symbolic way, not literally (*L'Express*, December 4, 1954, pp. 3-4). One wonders, however, whether this is actually the case. Sartre speaks as if he subscribes to the conspiracy theory of history, such as the one underlying the Moscow trials of 1937-38. See further the following note.

36. One wonders how the bourgeoisie is responsible for the divisions within the union movement. It seems that, having rejected the bourgeoisie, Sartre is determined to make them responsible for all the ills of society. His line of reasoning is not far removed from that of many right-wing groups in the United States which blame "communism" for whatever they happen to dislike in the society. In both cases, the reasoning used is based on ideological premises which do not necessarily correspond to the actual situation.

37. This is a summary of "Les Communistes et la Paix, III."

38. He answers Sartre's personal attack against Lefort, making four points: (1) There are easier ways to immerse oneself in the bourgeoisie than the way Lefort has chosen! (2) Sartre falls under the same criticism since he also is not a member of the proletariat (a criticism which echoes that of Lefort). (3) Sartre's accusation would be valid only *if* Lefort first accepted Sartre's view of consciousness, which he does not. (4) Sartre is really trying to affirm his own good faith, which is difficult for him to do since he has not joined the Communist Party. But he has been more indulgent with himself than with Lefort! (*AD* 214-16)

39. *AD* 155-75. Writing one year later in *Les Philosophes*

célèbres, Merleau-Ponty asserts that there is a basis in *Being and Nothingness* for the reciprocal determination of freedom and things. (S 196 tr. 155). See above, pp. 119 and 283, n. 13.

40. Lefort had also remarked that Sartre accepted Bolshevism without adopting its *raison d'être,* namely, its philosophy of the end of history. Merleau-Ponty's "attentisme marxiste" ended when, as we saw in the last chapter, he abandoned any notion of a universal history.

41. *AD* 206-9. Merleau-Ponty had suggested this criticism in 1945, but here it becomes much sharper and more explicit.

42. *AD* 255-58. Merleau-Ponty says it is not Sartre but the world which has changed. Sartre says precisely the same thing in trying to explain the reversals in Merleau-Ponty's political positions. See "Merleau-Ponty vivant," pp. 352-53.

43. "Merleau-Ponty vivant," p. 370. The article to which Sartre refers is Simone de Beauvoir, "Merleau-Ponty et le pseudo-sartrisme," *Les Temps Modernes,* X (April-May, 1955), 2072-2122.

44. See above, pp. 70-71.

45. "Merleau-Ponty et le pseudo-sartrisme," pp. 2074, 2080. Mlle de Beauvoir points out that Sartre does affirm a social world (cf. "Réponse à Lefort," p. 1581), and that Merleau-Ponty even admits this. (*AD* 186-87) The question, however, is not whether Sartre affirms a social field, but what significance can be attached to his affirmation. It is Merleau-Ponty's contention that within Sartrian ontology none can. It is never clear whether Mlle de Beauvoir is defending Sartre's description of the social world or his ontology. She admits that there are difficulties in reconciling the two (pp. 2121-22), but never raises the question of their ultimate compatibility.

46. Presumably in a classless society this necessity would disappear.

47. She cites "Les Communistes et la Paix, II," p. 717: "The historical ensemble decides at each moment concerning our powers, it prescribes their limits with regard to our field of action and our *real* future. . . . From there, we decide in our turn concerning our relations with others, that is to say, the meaning of our lives and the value of our death. It is in this framework that our *Me* finally appears, that is . . . a decision concerning the relative importance of what one improperly calls 'particular interest' and 'general interest', which can be altered at any moment."

48. "Les Communistes et la Paix, III," p. 1801: "It matters little whether the strikers or the demonstrators have a will to make the

revolution: objectively every demonstration of the masses is revolutionary."

49. "Merleau-Ponty et le pseudo-sartrisme," p. 2096. The question, however, is to know how a humanism of need becomes the basis for establishing political power. By pure action or not?

50. *Ibid.*, p. 2097. We have already seen the ambiguity involved in this point.

51. *Ibid.*, p. 2098. Again, however, the question is whether or not this is a correct interpretation of Marx, and this question is not broached. Moreover, does it not raise again the question of the centrality of "pure action" and "creation *ex nihilo*"?

52. *Ibid.*, p. 2100. "Les Communistes et la Paix, III," p. 1808, is cited in support of this contention. But that passage reads as follows: "How does one decide if one has not gathered information, taken soundings and consulted statistics. The masses do not cease *to give signs*; the militant must interpret them. He no longer has time to invoke I do not know what confused knowledge which is born with engagement, nor to support his decisions on some creative intuition. Being an object by nature, the masses become *the proper object* of the militant and there is a technique of the masses as there is of navigation." This passage reads as if the leader, instead of going in the direction the masses wish him to go, convinces the masses that they want to go in the direction he has determined to be the proper one.

53. "Merleau-Ponty et le pseudo-sartrisme," pp. 2115-22.

54. *Ibid.*, pp. 2121-22.

55. Simone de Beauvoir, "'La Phénoménologie de la perception' de M. Merleau-Ponty," *Les Temps Modernes*, I (November, 1945), 366, 367.

56. Simone de Beauvoir, *The Ethics of Ambiguity*, trans. Bernard Frechtman, pp. 41-72. Citations here are to the Citadel Press paperback edition, published in 1962.

57. "Merleau-Ponty vivant," pp. 357-58.

58. These discussions were later published: "Rencontre Est-Ouest à Venise," *Comprendre*, XVI (September, 1956), 202-301 (discussions held March 26-31, 1956). We shall have occasion to refer to them later.

59. "Merleau-Ponty vivant," pp. 370-72.

60. *Ibid.*, p. 363.

61. The book was published in 1960 as *Critique de la raison dialectique*. It includes an introductory essay, "Questions de méthode," which has been independently translated as *Search for*

a Method by Hazel Barnes. This introductory essay was originally written in 1956 for a Polish publication, was revised and published in *Les Temps Modernes* in 1957, and was included in the larger book in this revised form in 1960. The entire *Critique* will eventually be published in English translation.

62. In addition to what has already been said on this point, see Paul Ricoeur, "Hommage à Merleau-Ponty," *Esprit*, June, 1961, p. 1119.

63. *VI* 118. Presumably he is referring to *Critique de la raison dialectique* (see above, n. 61), though he does not mention it by name.

64. Sartre's essay has recently been translated by Benita Eisler in *Situations*, pp. 115-73. The conclusions Sartre reaches and to which Merleau-Ponty makes special reference may be found in the translated essay, pp. 124, 125, 172, 173.

CHAPTER VI

1. Near the end of his life he wrote: "History has gnawed the frames in which conservative thought placed it, but also the frames in which revolutionary thought placed it." (*ACF 1959*, 231)

2. The first occurrence of the phrase "an opening to being" appears in Merleau-Ponty's lecture in Geneva in 1951. (S 304, tr. 239)

3. See "Textes et commentaires sur la dialectique," *ACF 1956*, 179-80, which deals with dialectic from Zeno to Hegel. S 197-200, tr. 156-58, deals with the problem in some modern philosophical traditions. On the significance of Merleau-Ponty's interest in the history of philosophy after 1955, see the following chapter.

4. See below, n. 22.

5. S 198, tr. 157. Cf. *SNS* 250, tr. 124 (written in 1945) for a similar remark with respect to political thought.

6. "Rencontre Est-Ouest à Venise," *Comprendre*, XVI (1956), 212-17.

7. *ACF 1954*, 180-87; *L'Express*, January 29, 1955, p. 4; *AD* 15-42. The chapter on Weber in *AD* 15-42 has been translated in *The Primacy of Perception and other Essays*, pp. 193-211. It is the only chapter in the book that has been translated.

8. S 123-42, tr. 98-113 (written in 1951); S 143-57, tr. 114-25 (written in 1954); *ACF 1955*, 157-60.

9. *From Max Weber: Essays in Sociology*, trans. and ed. by H. H. Gerth and C. Wright Mills, p. 127. The passage is discussed by Merleau-Ponty in *AD* 40-41.

10. Claude Lefort has described this double aspect of Merleau-

Ponty's view of nature well. See "L'Idée d''être brut' et d''esprit sauvage'," *Les Temps Modernes*, XVII (1961), 273.

11. *The Rationality of Faith*, p. 24; see also p. 27 and *passim*.

12. *Ibid.*, pp. 16-17.

13. S 242-49, tr. 192-97. See also *VI* 31-35; and *SHP* 1-3, tr. 43-45. Husserl made this same criticism of Einstein in his Vienna lecture. See *Krisis*, pp. 342-43.

14. The examples used to illustrate the idea of an "institution" in his course lectures were Proust's description of love and the nature of painting. Proust, looking at love as a symbol of relational existence, first characterized it as a habit, a transfer in adulthood from a manner of loving learned in childhood. In order to become genuine love, Proust believed, this habit must be broken. However, the habit cannot be completely broken without annulling the past entirely. Hence he is driven to recognize that love is never *only* a habit, just as it is never *entirely removed* from habit. The past is a preparation for the present, but the present carries something new regardless of how much of the past can be recognized in it. The same is true of painting. A painter interrogates his past, imitates it, and becomes related to his predecessors in a unitary experience. But his interrogation involves the novelty of his own present since his relationship to his past does not anticipate the peculiar style which his own work will assume. (For an excellent discussion of Merleau-Ponty's use of "institution" in relation to aesthetic theory, see Kaelin, *An Existentialist Aesthetic*, pp. 342-45.) It is clear from Merleau-Ponty's use of the term that it was operative in his thought before he defined it. Indeed, the example chosen to illustrate the idea in the text above suggests that many ideas discussed by Merleau-Ponty may properly be called institutions in his sense of the term.

15. This analysis, though richer in its implications, may be compared with S 123 ff., tr. 98 ff.

16. *VI* 157. In every case, however, it is not the meaning of being about which we are asking but the meaning of things in the presence of being. The question "What is Being?" is not a philosophical question until it aims at the being of signification and signification in being. (*VI* 160) Involved in this asking is also the question of what it means to ask and respond, since the person asking the questions is involved in his questions and brings a meaning to them.

17. *SHP* 50-51, tr. 90-91; S 135, tr. 107-8; "Préface" to A. Hesnard, *L'Oeuvre de Freud*, pp. 9-10.

18. In addition to *SHP*, the relevant texts here are: "Le Pro-

blème de la passivité: le sommeil, l'inconscient, la mémoire," *ACF 1955*, 161-64; and "Préface," to A. Hesnard, *L'Oeuvre de Freud*, pp. 5-10. See also "Nature et Logos: le corps humain," *ACF 1960*, 175-76.

19. See above, pp. 20-21, and the text to which it refers: *PP* 98-99, tr. 83.

20. "Préface," to A. Hesnard, *L'Oeuvre de Freud*, p. 8. J.-B. Pontalis, in an article on Merleau-Ponty's view of the unconscious written after Merleau-Ponty's death, emphasizes the distinction even in *SC* between Merleau-Ponty and the Sartrian denial of the unconscious. However, he notes the ambiguities in Merleau-Ponty's early interpretation and contends that in his later lectures (cited in the text above) Merleau-Ponty explicitly recognized the unconscious as incapable of being reduced either to a phenomenological description based on intentionality or to some form of consciousness. His problem was how to relate the unconscious to conscious thought. And his solution was similar to that of Jacques Lacan, namely, to recognize the unconscious as possessing an intentionality of its own, different from the intentionalities of the subject, but in a dynamic relationship to those intentionalities. Thus the conscious and the unconscious are two structures which belong in different ways to the same phenomenon, and do not, as in Freud's view, belong to different phenomena altogether. "Note sur le problème de l'inconscient chez Merleau-Ponty," *Les Temps Modernes*, XVII (1961), 287-303, especially 298-303. See also Pontalis' note on the Freudian concept of the unconscious in *PC* 443.

It might also be added that the denial of the unconscious is the starting-point of the Marxist critique of Freud as, for example, that of Georges Politzer. (Cf. *PC* 443) There may be some connection between the Marxist and Sartrian positions at this point, as well as between their respective critiques and Merleau-Ponty's progressive separation of his own viewpoint from them.

21. The relevant essay here is "De Mauss à Claude Lévi-Strauss," in *S* 143-57, tr. 114-25 (first published in *La Nouvelle Revue Française*, VII [1959], 615-31). See also *SHP* 46-47, tr. 85-86.

22. Merleau-Ponty elaborated the implications contained in this statement in the book on which he was working at the time of his death. (*VI* 17-30) The task of philosophy, he begins by saying in that work, is to describe the interconnections between the *we* who see, the *thing* that is seen, and the *world* in which it is seen. In

order to do this, it is necessary, not only that we perceive, but that we *learn* to perceive, that is, that we learn to interrogate the we who see, the thing seen, and the world. Philosophy is therefore at once involved in paradoxes. It is true both that we see the world and that the world we see is an enigma. This being the case, it is necessary to say that each of us inhabits a private world not open to others, and that we do not all perceive the same "world." The common world (*koinos kosmos*) is not the world we perceive. The question therefore arises as to that on which our perceptions open. We can say that they open on the lives of others. For we are always living in the presence of other lives, and at times we realize that the life of another breaks through our private world, placing us in his world. It makes no difference whether the red color I see is the same as the red color he sees; it is still true that my private world has ceased to be my private world. At the same time, however, it must be granted that this connection with others is based on external things; and the thing that I see is still the thing that *I* see, even if it belongs to the other's world also. "It is therefore very true that the 'private worlds' communicate, that each of them is given its title as variant of a common world. ... But in one case as in the other, the certitude, as irrestible as it is, remains absolutely obscure; we can live it, we cannot think it or formulate it or erect it into a thesis. Every attempt at elucidation leads us back to dilemmas." (*VI* 27) In the final analysis, therefore, the world is both visible and invisible. We are all open to a common visible world. But this cannot gainsay the fact that each of us also inhabits an invisible private world from which there is no apparent transition to the world of others. The unity we live is therefore the unity we seek; it will never be wholly given to us. Cf. *OE* 201, tr. 166; 224, tr. 187.

23. S 157-58, tr. 124. In accordance with the expanded notion of the "philosophy of nature" which he developed, particularly after 1955, Merleau-Ponty began to turn his attention to the sciences of life as well as to the sciences of man. In his course summary for 1958 he wrote: "In the second half of the year we have ... tried to establish the conception of the being of life which is immanent in the science of today. The sciences of life also continually introduce 'operational' concepts whose obscurity ought to be, not dissipated, but circumscribed and meditated on by philosophy." (*ACF 1958*, 217) Unfortunately, we do not have the results of his meditation, but only the areas about which he lectured. These are worth recording: the concept of behavior as found

292   NOTES   [pp. 166-172]

in Coghill and Gesell; the concepts of *Umwelt, Merkwelt, and Wirkwelt* introduced by J. von Uexküll in the study of inferior behavior; the notion of the inertia of the body in so-called superior behaviors, studied by Lorenz, whose source of inspiration was Uexküll; the notion of animal types (*die Tiergestalt*) developed by Portmann; the extent to which one or several "meanings" can be attributed to animals, as examined in specific works, such as Chauvin's work on the pilgrim locusts and the study of bees by von Frisch; and interpretations of embryology such as those of Speemann and Driesch. (*ACF 1958*, 217-19)

CHAPTER VII

1. The lecture was delivered at the Rencontres Internationales in Geneva in 1951. It is reprinted in S 284-308, tr. 224-43. The discussion following the lecture is not reprinted with the lecture, but may be found in *Rencontres Internationales de Genève*, pp. 215-52. The quotation above may be found on p. 246.

2. See *VI* 65, 70-71, 170-71, 184, 195, 203.

3. He expresses reservations in several places regarding Husserl's view of essences and his view of transcendental subjectivity in the *Cartesian Meditations* (*VI* 155, 225, 288, 291-92), but he gives greatest attention to those aspects of Husserl's thought which drive toward the interworld between subject and object and fundamentally alter the notion of a total rationality. (*VI* 221-22, 226, 233, 237, 239, 244-46, 284, 296, 297, 312, 321)

4. S 201-28, tr. 159-81. See also *ACF 1959*, 233-35; *ACF 1960*, 169-73; *VI* 219.

5. S 202, tr. 160. see also *ACF 1960*, 169.

6. S 223, tr. 177. In the last course Merleau-Ponty taught at the Collège de France, he translated and commented upon a text of Husserl's on geometry, showing that for Husserl geometry is not simply an "ideal" construction, an eternal idea which belongs to consciousness and is derivable from it *alone*, but rather that geometry belongs to history, joining the person learning it to the past through which it has been acquired and to the present and future to which it opens one. The human relationship to geometry illustrates the intersection (or circularity) of historical and natural being in man. *ACF 1960*, 169-70; cf. *PP* 455, tr. 397.

7. In one of the last essays he wrote before his death, Merleau-Ponty states that Husserl abandoned the idea of a "phenomenological positivism" according to which consciousness and its objects are perfectly adjusted to one another, and openly acknowledged

the "latency" or "hiddenness" present in our consciousness of things. He remarks: "Every consciousness is consciousness of something or of the world, but this *something*, this *world*, are no longer, as 'phenomenological positivism' appeared to teach, an object which is what it is, exactly adjusted to acts of consciousness. Consciousness is now the 'soul of Heraclitus', and Being, which is around it rather than before it, is a frenzied Being, by definition hidden, Husserl says sometimes: a 'pre-being'." "Préface" to A. Hesnard, *L'Oeuvre de Freud*, p. 8.

This use of the idea of "phenomenological positivism" is to be distinguished from its earlier designation in *Phenomenology of Perception* (xii, tr. xvii) as the doctrine according to which every (essential) possibility of reflection must be based on the world or things in the world that are experienced, a view attributed to Husserl in Merleau-Ponty's Sorbonne lectures of 1951. (*SHP* 9, tr. 50) In this latter sense, "phenomenological positivism" means "world-centeredness" and never ceased to be accepted by Merleau-Ponty. He is not inconsistent in his late text; he is simply using the term in a different manner.

8. Not matter, mind, or substance, but element in the pre-Socratic sense, a designation of being-itself. See *OE* 198, tr. 164.

9. This judgment, of course, does not hold true of Marx, about whom Merleau-Ponty had more to say during these years than about anyone else.

10. 'Christianisme et ressentiment," *La Vie Intellectuelle*, VII (1935), 278-306.

11. *Ibid.*, p. 289. It is more likely that Merleau-Ponty already regarded as his own point of view what he here finds in Scheler. But if there is at least an indirect influence of Scheler on Merleau-Ponty, it is to be found at this point.

12. *Ibid.*, pp. 304-5.

13. See, for example in 1951, S 122, tr. 97; S 286, tr. 225; in 1956, S 193, tr. 153; S 197, tr. 156; in 1959, S 202, tr. 160; *VI* 154, 222, 223-24, 239, 249, 258, 269; in 1960, *VI* 281, 303, 319.

14. *EP* 47-57, tr. 33-41. This conclusion is also substantiated by remarks Merleau-Ponty made in "Forum," *L'Express*, October 9, 1954, p. 3.

15. See above, chap. 1, n. 3.

16. "But between this perception of matter and matter itself there is but a difference of degree and not of kind, pure perception standing towards matter in the relation of the part to the whole." *Matter and Memory*, p. 58.

17. Merleau-Ponty, "L'Imagination," p. 761. Cf. *S* 232, tr. 185. See *Matter and Memory*, pp. 1-7, and the discussion of Bergson's theory of the body, above, pp. 24-25.

18. On the first point, see above, pp. 20-21, and see *PP* 93-94, n. 2, tr. 78-79, n. 2; 211, tr. 181. On the second point, see *PP* 76, tr. 62.

19. *PP* 69-70, tr. 57. Merleau-Ponty's reservations with respect to Bergson's method at this point are similar to the hesitation with which he read Marcel. See above, pp. 66-67.

20. See *EP* 89-91, tr. 66-67; *ACF 1953*, 146; *VI* 165, 207-8.

21. *VI* 249. It would be interesting and perhaps instructive to compare the dualisms of Bergson and Sartre.

22. Cf. Eugene Kaelin, *An Existentialist Aesthetic*, p. 339.

23. Jean Hyppolite remarked in a lecture on Merleau-Ponty after the latter's death: "We have been less just to Bergson whose influence was, nevertheless, so profound on our generation. Perhaps the Bergsonian philosophy appeared to us still—despite its discovery of temporality, its quest for the immediate—too contemplative, too serene to respond to the requirements of our historical existence." *Sens et existence*, p. 4. This absence of a genuinely *social* (historical) perspective is behind much of Merleau-Ponty's criticism of Bergson. See *S* 236-40, tr. 188-90.

24. Questioned once as to whether this conception of philosophy as "pure interrogation" did not leave one in a state of dizziness, Merleau-Ponty replied: 'Philosophy is not a hospital. If men are dizzy and wish to take drugs against dizziness, I do not hinder them, but I say: these are drugs." "La Connaissance de l'homme au XXe siècle," p. 247.

CHAPTER VIII

1. In a lecture delivered in 1948, "L'Homme et l'objet," summarized by Jean-Louis Dumas, "Les Conférences," *La Nef*, V (August, 1948), 150-51, Merleau-Ponty says that this attribution of an expressive character to the object itself stands in contrast to classical views in which the object was under control of the understanding, and he suggests that this difference reflects the transformation of classical humanism by contemporary humanism. The elements of a new humanism which Merleau-Ponty sees illustrated in painting are (1) that man is in a living relationship with matter, (2) that this relationship takes many forms and therefore can never lead to any notion of a humanity wholly made, (3) that humanity is free, inventive, without stability, and menaced by the world, (4) that being-in-the-world is no longer intelligible in terms of laws, but

has the character of astonishment and mystery, and (5) that artistic creation today does not disclose either a finality or a preestablished harmony, but rather a movement in which form takes possession of matter without ceasing. See also *OE* 202, tr. 167-68; 204 ff., tr. 169 ff., 216, tr. 180.

It is evident here that Merleau-Ponty is applying to a philosophy of art the major ideas already elucidated in his phenomenology of perception and in his political philosophy.

2. See above, chap. 2, n. 9.

3. Some programmatic remarks made in *SNS* 172-76, tr. 86-88 (1947) hinted at future developments, but did not add to what had been said earlier.

4. See *SHP*, tr. 38-45, tr. 78-85; *S* 294-98, tr. 231-35; *S* 128-33, tr. 102-6; and *S* 105-22, tr. 84-97, respectively.

5. *S* 49-59, tr. 39-47; 95-104, tr. 76-83

6. "Le Monde sensible et le monde de l'expression," *ACF 1953*, 145-50; "Recherches sur l'usage littéraire du langage," *ACF 1953*, 150-55.

7. "Le Problème de la parole," *ACF 1954*, 175-79.

8. H.-J. Pos, "Phénoménologie et Linguistique," *Revue Internationale de Philosophie*, I (January, 1939), 354-65. Cf. references to Pos in *S* 106, tr. 85; 107-8, tr. 86; 131, tr. 104; *SHP* 40, 42, tr. 80, 82.

9. *Cours de linguistique generale*. The lectures were compiled from students' notes after Saussure's death in 1913. They have recently been translated into English: *Course in General Linguistics*, trans. Wade Baskin. Merleau-Ponty mentions Saussure for the first time in 1947 (*SNS* 173, tr. 87), but only in passing.

10. *Course in General Linguistics*, p. xi.

11. *Ibid.*, pp. 65 ff.

12. This point had already been made in *Phenomenology of Perception*. See above, p. 23. See also *S* 49-50, tr. 39-40; 54, tr. 43; 117-21, tr. 93-97; *ACF 1954*, 175.

13. *Course in General Linguistics*, pp. 9-15.

14. *Ibid.*, pp. 101 ff.

15. *Ibid.*, pp. 140 ff.

16. *Ibid.*, pp. 90-95.

17. Indeed, as Merleau-Ponty had pointed out in *Phenomenology of Perception*, apparently before he had read Saussure, words can have several levels of meaning, depending on the form of relationship between consciousness and object in the body-subject. *PP* 228, tr. 194.

18. See "Recherches sur l'usage littéraire du langage," *ACF 1953*, 150-55. See also S 294-98, tr. 231-35.

Eugene Kaelin states (*An Existentialist Aesthetic*, p. 326) that Merleau-Ponty never recognized the extent to which Valéry was dealing with the same problems he was. Professor Kaelin was apparently unaware that Merleau-Ponty devoted course lectures to Valéry as far back as 1953.

19. The articles have been reprinted in S 49-104, tr. 39-83. See above, chap. 5, n. 19.

20. André Malraux, *The Voices of Silence*, p. 19.

21. *Ibid.*, p. 65.

22. *Ibid.*, chap. 1 and p. 557.

23. *Ibid.*, pp. 280, 334, 346-47, 355.

24. *Ibid.*, chap. 2 and p. 623.

25. *Ibid.*, pp. 601-2.

26. *Ibid.*, pp. 45-46, 101, 117, 119, 120.

27. *Ibid.*, pp. 76, 475, 576, 630, 631, 641-42.

28. In an earlier essay on art (1945), Merleau-Ponty had suggested that for metaphysicians and novelists this loss of faith in a fixed conception of being meant that rationality could no longer be imposed upon existence but must be described *in* existence. He cites examples both from literature and from philosophy to show that past writers have not successfully brought facts and essences together because they have talked of something other than the "human situation." He suggests that Simone de Beauvoir's novel, *L'Invitée* (translated as *She Came to Stay*), is an attempt to describe the contemporary lived world in which there is no fixed and certain notion of being, a world in which our relationships with others must be established without a universal conception of being or of human nature or of principles of morality applicable to every situation. (*SNS* 51-81, tr. 26-40. See also *PP* 341-42, tr. 295-96)

The attitude reflected in this early article was qualified later by Merleau-Ponty's historical analysis of the philosophy of nature since Descartes, in which he contended that modern philosophers were all attempting to bridge the gap between man and nature, even if they failed to do so. See above, pp. 152-53.

29. In the English translation, "one hundred fifty" is mistranslated "five hundred". (*SNS* 15, tr. 9)

30. "Forum," *L'Express*, October 2, 1954, p. 3.

31. "Forum," *L'Express*, October 9, 1954, p. 3.

32. "Notes sur 'Les Cahiers de la Pléiade'," *Les Temps Modernes*, III (December, 1947), 1152.

33. See further on this point, "Rencontre Est-Ouest à Venise," pp. 212-13, 226.

Sartre indicates in his article, "Merleau-Ponty vivant," p. 307, that he and Merleau-Ponty were concerned in the early 1940s (within the Resistance movement) to define the freedom to write and that it was through this defense that they discovered the other political issues.

34. See above, on p. 173, the quotation from *VI* 189. See also *VI* 203-4.

CHAPTER IX

1. "Merleau-Ponty vivant," p. 315.

2. See above, p. 116.

3. Colette Audry, "La Vie d'un philosophe," *L'Express*, May 11, 1961, p. 34. She states that this version of the event is that of Jean Lacroix. In his own account of the incident, Merleau-Ponty leaves room for this ambiguity inasmuch as he does not say what the "vulgar" nature of the songs was. (*SNS* 83, tr. 41)

4. "La Connaissance de l'homme au XXe siècle," p. 250.

5. Merleau-Ponty, "Christianisme et ressentiment," p. 302.

6. See above, pp. 174-75.

7. "Christianisme et ressentiment," pp. 303-4.

8. *Ibid.*, p. 250, emphasis added. Implying, as he does here, that his "atheism" is not intrinsic to his philosophical program, Merleau-Ponty, as we shall see momentarily, understood himself better than some do of his critics. See, for example, Albert Dondeyne, who writes that Merleau-Ponty declares "the existence of God ... irreconcilable with the contingency of history and the autonomy of human freedom." *Contemporary European Thought and Christian Faith*, p. 26. See also p. 111.

9. In his article on Merleau-Ponty after the latter's death, Sartre comments that, despite what many thought, Merleau-Ponty never abandoned humanism. He attributes Merleau-Ponty's openness to religion to his desire to leave the past a chance to speak once again (a past represented for him by his mother)! "Merleau-Ponty vivant," pp. 367-68. Sartre certainly would not have mentioned the matter had there not been cause for wondering whether in fact Merleau-Ponty had adopted a more "religious" position.

10. It is in this sense that Merleau-Ponty said the fault of man is a happy fault. (*SNS* 193, tr. 96-97) This interpretation is ques-

tioned, from the point of view of Roman Catholic theology, by R. Jolivet, "Le Problème de l'absolu dans la philosophie de M. Merleau-Ponty," pp. 85 ff.

11. S 88, tr. 70-71. A similar statement appears in Merleau-Ponty's inaugural lecture two years later: "There is . . . perhaps in every theology since Christianity, an ambiguity thanks to which we never know if it is God who sustains men in their human being or if it is the inverse, since in order to know His existence it is necessary to pass through ours, and this is not an optional detour. (EP 38, tr. 26)

12. See Henri de Lubac, S.J., *The Drama of Atheist Humanism*, trans. Edith M. Riley; and Jacques Maritain, *True Humanism*, trans. Margot Adamson.

13. Later he remarked, in relation to this point: "Unlike the atheism of 1900, contemporary 'atheism' does not claim to explain the world 'without God'. It claims that the world is inexplicable, and in its view the rationalism of 1900 is a secularized theology." (S 191, tr. 151)

14. "La Notion de philosophie Chrétienne," *Bulletin de la Société française de Philosophie*, XXXI (March-June, 1931), 37-93. Etienne Gilson presented the theses for discussion. The other participants were Emile Bréhier, Jacques Maritain, Léon Brunschvicg, Edouard Le Roy, and Raymond Lenoir. Maurice Blondel and Jacques Chevalier wrote letters to the editor of the journal on the issues discussed in the debate, and these were added to the debate itself as an appendix. The substance of the theses presented by Gilson may be found in English in his' Gifford lectures, *The Spirit of Medieval Philosophy*, trans. A. H. C. Downes, chaps. 1-2.

15. "La Notion de philosophie Chrétienne," pp. 37-49. As is well known, in his Gifford lectures of 1931-32 (see preceding note), he undertook such an historical analysis of medieval philosophy and concluded that there was an influence of Chistianity upon philosophy, thus establishing the theoretical possibility of a Christian philosophy.

16. *Ibid.*, pp. 49-59. The exchanges between Gilson and Bréhier on the Christian origin or reinterpretation of such ideas as the *Logos* and creation are extremely interesting. In my opinion, Gilson had much the better of the argument, especially as regards the idea of creation. Merleau-Ponty also believed this to be the case. See S 178-79, tr. 141-42.

17. *Ibid.*, pp. 59-72.

18. *Ibid.*, pp. 73-77. Gilson's exchange with Brunschvicg (pp. 77-

82) suggests that Brunschvicg's critique, particularly as it relates to Thomism, is based on his own "dogmatic" position rather than on historical considerations.

19. *Ibid.*, pp. 86-92, especially p. 88.

20. However, see his remarks in *ACF 1958*, 213 ff.

CHAPTER X

1. This interpretation questions the validity of efforts to isolate "cognitive" and "precognitive" experience and on the basis of their isolation to say that Merleau-Ponty cannot move from the one to the other without contradiction.

2. Merleau-Ponty was consistent in demanding of Marxism what he had earlier demanded of the Church, that it translate its values into facts. The lesson he learned in each case was that values cannot be *completely* translated into facts. The problem at this point is knowing when the realization of the values affirmed is no longer concretely intended by the group espousing them. This was the problem Merleau-Ponty never satisfactorily resolved.

3. Jacques Maritain, as noted earlier, has stated that it is essential to Roman Catholicism as well to criticize continually the various idols of culture. See above, p. 227.

Bibliography

Primary Sources:
Books, Articles, and Lectures by Merleau-Ponty

1935

"Christianisme et ressentiment," *La Vie Intellectuelle*, 7, 278-306. Review of Max Scheler's book *Ressentiment*.

1936

"Être et avoir," *La Vie Intellectuelle*, 8 (October 10), 98-109. Review of Gabriel Marcel's book *Être et avoir*.

"L'Imagination," *Journal de Psychologie Normale et Pathologique*, 33:9-10 (November-December), 756-61. Review of Jean-Paul Sartre's book *L'Imaginaire*.

1942

La Structure du comportement. Paris, Presses Universitaires de France. Second edition with an introductory essay by Alphonse de Waelhens, 1949. English translation of second edition: *The Structure of Behavior*. Translated by Alden L. Fisher. Boston, Beacon Press, 1963.

1943

"Les Mouches," *Confluences*, 3:25 (September-October), 514-16. Review of Jean-Paul Sartre's play *Les Mouches*.

1945

Phénoménologie de la perception. Paris, Gallimard. English translation of the Preface by John F. Bannon, *Cross Currents*, 6 (1956), 59-70. English translation of entire book: *Phenomenology of Perception*. Translated by Colin Smith. New York, Humanities Press, 1962; London, Routledge and Kegan Paul, 1962.

"Le Roman et la Métaphysique," *Cahiers du Sud*, 22:270 (March-April), 194-207; also in *Sens et non-sens* (1948).

"La Guerre a eu lieu," *Les Temps Modernes*, 1:1 (October), 48-66; also in *Sens et non-sens*.

"La Querelle de l'existentialisme," *Les Temps Modernes*, 1:2 (November), 344-56; also in *Sens et non-sens*.

"Le Doute de Cézanne," *Fontaine*, 8:47 (December), 80 ff.; also in *Sens et non-sens*. Abridged English translation in *The Partisan Review*, 13:4 (September-October, 1946), 464-78.

1946

"Pour la vérité," *Les Temps Modernes*, 1:4 (January), 577-600; also in *Sens et non-sens* (1948).

"Le Cult du héros," *Action*, No. 74 (February 1), 12-13; also in *Sens et non-sens*, under title "Le Héros, l'homme."

"Autour du marxisme," *Fontaine*, 9:48-49 (February), 309-31; also in *Sens et non-sens*.

"Foi et bonne foi," *Les Temps Modernes*, 1:5 (February), 769-82; also in *Sens et non-sens*.

"L'Existentialisme chez Hegel," *Les Temps Modernes*, 1:7 (April), 1311-19; also in *Sens et non-sens*.

Wahl, Jean. "A propos d'une conférence de Maurice Merleau-Ponty sur les aspects politiques et sociaux de l'existentialisme," *Fontaine*, 9:51 (April), 678-79. Lecture delivered March 23, 1946, at the Institut d'Etudes Politiques de l'Université de Paris. This is Wahl's summary. So far as I know, the lecture itself is not available.

"Marxisme et philosophie," *Revue Internationale*, 1:6 (June-July), 518-26. Also in *Sens et non-sens* (1948). Abridged translation, "Marxism and Philosophy," in *Politics*, 4:4 (July-August, 1947) 173-75.

"Le Yogi et le prolétaire," *Les Temps Modernes*, 2:13 (October), 1-29. Contains material used in Part I, chapters 1-2, of *Humanisme et terreur* (1947).

"Crise de conscience européenne," *La Nef*, 3:24 (November), 66-73. A reprint of remarks made in a discussion following a lecture at the Rencontres and first published in *Rencontres Internationales de Genève* (Neuchâtel, Editions de la Baconnière, 1946), pp. 74-77.

"Deux philosophies de l'Europe (Marxisme-Existentialisme)," *La Nef*, 3:24 (November), 87-98. A reprint of remarks made at the Rencontres in a discussion following a lecture and first published in *Rencontres Internationales de Genève* (Neuchâtel, Editions de la Baconnière, 1946), pp. 252-56.

"Le Yogi et le prolétaire," *Les Temps Modernes*, 2:14 (November), 253-87. Contains material used in Part I, chapter 2, and in Part II, chapter 1, of *Humanisme et terreur*.

"Le Primat de la perception et ses conséquences philosophiques," *Bulletin de la Société Française de Philosophie*, 41:4 (October-December, 1947), 119-53. The lecture was delivered on November 23, 1946. English translation by James M. Edie in *The Primacy of Perception and Other Essays*, edited by James M. Edie (Evanston, Northwestern University Press, 1964), pp. 12-42.

1947

"Le Yogi et le prolétaire," *Les Temps Modernes*, 2:16 (January), 676-711; contains material used in Part II, chapters 1-2, of *Humanisme et terreur* (1947).

"Indochine S.O.S.," *Les Temps Modernes*, 2:18 (March), 1039-52 (unsigned editorial). Also in *Signes* (1960) under the title "Sur l'Indochine."

"Pour les rencontres internationales," *Les Temps Modernes*, 2:19 (April), 1340-44.

"Apprendre à lire," *Les Temps Modernes*, 2:22 (July), 1-27. Contains material used in the Preface of *Humanisme et terreur*.

Humanisme et terreur. Paris, Gallimard. English translation of Part II, chapter 2, by Nancy Metzel and John Flodstrom, in *The Primacy of Perception and Other Essays* (1964), pp. 211-28.

"Le Métaphysique dans l'homme," *Revue de Métaphysique et de Morale*, 52:3-4 (July-October), 290-307. Also in *Sens et non-sens*.

"Le Cinéma et la nouvelle psychologie," *Les Temps Modernes*, 3:26 (November), 930-43. Also in *Sens et non-sens*.

"En un combat douteux," *Les Temps Modernes*, 3:27 (December), 961-64 (editorial signed T.M.).

"Lecture de Montaigne," *Les Temps Modernes*, 3:27 (December), 1044-60. Also in *Signes* (1960).

"Notes sur 'Les Cahiers de la Pléiade, avril 1947'," *Les Temps Modernes*, 3:27 (December), 1151-52.

La Liberté chez Leibniz. Cours de l'Université de Lyon. Lyon, Année scolaire. (Unpublished.)

1948

Sens et non-sens. Paris, Nagel. English translation: *Sense and Non-Sense*. Translated by Hubert L. Dreyfus and Patricia Allen Dreyfus. Evanston, Northwestern University Press, 1964.

"Un Auteur scandaleux," *Le Figaro Littéraire* (January 3). Also in
Sens et non-sens.

"Le 'Manifeste communiste' à cent ans," *Le Figaro Littéraire*
(April 3).

"Complicité objective," *Les Temps Modernes*, 4:34 (July), 1-11
(editorial signed T.M.).

"Communisme et anticommunisme," *Les Temps Modernes*, 4:34
(July), 175-88. Also in *Signes* (1960), under title "La Politique
paranoiaque."

Dumas, J.-L. "Les Conférences," *La Nef*, 5:45 (August), 150-51.
A summary by M. Dumas of a lecture given by Merleau-Ponty
entitled "L'Homme et l'objet." So far as I know, the lecture
itself is not available.

Ame et corps chez Malebranche, Maine de Biran, Bergson. Cours de
l'Université de Lyon. Lyon, Année scolaire. (Unpublished.)

Langage et communication. Cours de l'Université de Lyon. Lyon,
Année scolaire. (Unpublished.)

1949

"Humanisme surréaliste et humanisme existentialiste." Lecture
delivered at the Collège Philosophique, 1949. I have not been
able to locate it in any publication.

"Note sur Machiavel," *Les Temps Modernes*, 5:48 (October), 577-
93. Also in *Signes* (1960).

"Commentaire (à propos de Georg Lukacs)," *Les Temps Modernes,*
5:50 (December), 1119-21. Also in *Signes*, under title "Marxisme
et superstition." The editorial was preceded by an article on
Lukacs of F. Ernal.

1950

"Les Jours de notre vie," *Les Temps Modernes*, 5:51 (January),
1153-68. Also in *Signes* (1960), under title "L'URSS et les
camps." The editorial is co-signed by Sartre.

"Mort d'Emmanuel Mounier," *Les Temps Modernes*, 5:54 (April),
1906.

"Réponse à C. L. R. James," *Les Temps Modernes*, 5:56 (June),
2292-94 (signed T.M.).

"L'Adversaire est complice," *Les Temps Modernes*, 5:57 (July), 1-11
(editorial signed T.M.).

1951

"Le Philosophe et la sociologie," *Cahiers Internationaux de Sociologie*, 10, 55-69. Also in *Signes* (1960). In addition to the Eng-

lish translation in *Signs* (1964), this essay has been translated by
Harvey G. Rabbin in *Philosophy of the Social Sciences*, edited
by Maurice Natanson (New York, Random House, 1963), pp.
487-505.

"La Connaissance de l'homme au XXe siècle," in *Rencontres Internationales de Genève* (Neuchâtel, Editions de la Baconnière),
pp. 57-75; discussion of the lecture, pp. 215-52. Also in *Signes*,
under title "L"Homme et l'adversité," but without the discussion.

Les Relations avec autrui chez l'enfant, Cours de Sorbonne. Paris,
Centre de Documentation Universitaire. English translation by
William Cobb in *The Primacy of Perception and Other Essays*
(1964), pp. 96-155.

*Les Sciences de l'homme et la phénoménologie: Introduction et
première partie*, Cours de Sorbonne. Paris, Centre de Documentation Universitaire. English translation by John Wild in *The
Primacy of Perception and Other Essays*, pp. 43-95.

1952

"Sur la phénoménologie du langage," in *Problèmes actuels de la
phénoménologie*, edited by H. L. Van Breda (Paris, Desclée de
Brouwer). Also in *Signes* (1960).

"Le Langage indirect et les voix du silence," *Les Temps Modernes*,
7:80 (June), 2113-44; 8:81 (July), 70-94. Also in *Signes*.

1953

"Un Inédit de Maurice Merleau-Ponty," *Revue de Métaphysique
et de Morale*, 67:4 (October-December, 1962), 401-9. A personal
communication to Martial Gueroult written by Merleau-Ponty
late in 1952 or early in 1953 after his appointment to the faculty
of the Collège de France, and submitted for publication by M.
Gueroult after Merleau-Ponty's death. English translation by
Arleen B. Dallery in *The Primary of Perception and Other
Essays* (1964), pp. 3-11.

Eloge de la philosophie. Paris, Gallimard. English translation: *In
Praise of Philosophy*. Translated by James M. Edie and John
Wild. Evanston, Northwestern University Press, 1963.

"Le Monde sensible et le Monde de l'expression," in *Annuaire du
Collège de France* (Paris, Imprimerie Nationale), pp. 145-50.
This and following citations of the *Annuaire* represent Merleau-
Ponty's summaries of courses given at the Collège de France.

"Recherches sur l'usage littéraire du langage," in *Annuaire du
Collège de France* (Paris, Imprimerie Nationale), pp. 150-55.

1954

"Le Problème de la parole," *Annuaire du Collège de France* (Paris, Imprimerie Nationale), pp. 175-79.

"Matériaux pour une théorie de l'histoire," in *Annuaire du Collège de France* (Paris, Imprimerie Nationale), pp. 180-87.

"Forum," *L'Express,* October 2, p. 3.

"Forum," *L'Express,* October 9, p. 3.

"Sur l'érotisme," *L'Express,* October 16, pp. 3-4. Also in *Signes* (1960).

"La France va-t-elle se renouveler?," *L'Express,* October 23, pp. 3-4.

"Les Femmes sont-elles des hommes?," *L'Express,* November 6, p. 4.

"Les Peuples se fâchent-ils?," *L'Express,* December 4, pp. 3-4.

"Sur les faits divers," *L'Express,* December 18, pp. 3-4. Also in *Signes.*

1955

Les Aventures de la dialectique. Paris, Gallimard. English translation by Nancy Metzel and John Flodstrom of chapter 1 in *The Primacy of Perception and Other Essays* (1964), pp. 193-210.

"L''Institution' dans l'histoire personnelle et publique," in *Annuaire du Collège de France* (Paris, Imprimerie Nationale), pp. 157-60.

"Le Problème de la passivité: le sommeil, l'inconscient, la mémoire," in *Annuaire du Collège de France* (Paris, Imprimerie Nationale), pp. 161-64.

"Sur l'abstention." Also in *Signes* (1960). I have been unable to trace the first appearance of this article.

"D'Abord comprendre les communistes," *L'Express,* January 8, pp. 8-9.

"A quoi sert l'objectivité?," *L'Express,* January 29, p. 4.

"Comment répondre à Oppenheimer?," *L'Express.* February 19, p. 3.

"Sur Claudel," *L'Express,* March 5, pp. 3-4. Also in *Signes.*

"M. Poujade a-t-il une petite cervelle?," *L'Express,* March 19, p. 3.

"Les Papiers de Yalta," *L'Express,* April 9, pp. 3-4. Also in *Signes.*

"Einstein et la crise de la raison," *L'Express,* May 14, p. 13. Also in *Signes.*

"Où va l'anticommunisme?," *L'Express,* June 25, p. 12.

"L'Avenir de la Révolution," *L'Express,* August 27, pp. 7-10. Also in *Signes.*

1956

Les Philosophes célèbres (editor). Paris, Lucien Mazenod. Merleau-Ponty wrote introductions for each of the major sections in this book, all but two of which are reprinted in *Signes* (1960).

"Christianisme et philosophie," in *Les Philosophes célèbres*, pp. 104-9. Also in *Signes*.

"La Découverte de l'histoire," in *Les Philosophes célèbres*, pp. 250-51.

"La Découverte de la subjectivité," in *Les Philosophes célèbres*, pp. 186-87. Also in *Signes*.

"Existence et dialectique," *Les Philosophes célèbres*, pp. 288-91. Also in *Signes*.

"Les Fondateurs," in *Les Philosophes célèbres*, pp. 44-45.

"Le Grand rationalisme," in *Les Philosophes célèbres*, pp. 134-37. Also in *Signes*.

"L'Orient et la philosophie," in *Les Philosophes célèbres*, pp. 14-18. Also in *Signes*.

"Avant-propos," in *Les Philosophes célèbres*, pp. 7-14. Also in *Signes*, under title "La Philosophie et le 'dehors'."

"La philosophie dialectique," in *Annuaire du Collège de France* (Paris, Imprimerie Nationale), pp. 175-79.

"Textes et commentaires sur la dialectique," in *Annuaire du Collège de France* (Paris, Imprimerie Nationale) pp. 179-80.

"Rencontre Est-Ouest à Venise," *Comprendre*, 16 (September), 202-301. Public discussions held in nine sittings, March 26-31, 1956. A condensed account with excerpts can be found in "Entre Merleau-Ponty, Sartre, Silone et les écrivains sovietiques: premier dialogue est-ouest à Venise," *L'Express*, October 19, pp. 21-24.

"Sur la destalinisation," *L'Express*, November 23, pp. 13-17. Also in *Signes*.

1957

"Le Concept de Nature," in *Annuaire du Collège de France* (Paris, Imprimerie Nationale), pp. 201-17.

"La Psychoanalyse et son enseignement," *Bulletin de la Société Française de Philosophie*, 51:2 (April-June), 65-104. A discussion in which Merleau-Ponty makes one comment, on pp. 98-99.

1958

"Le Concept de Nature (suite): L'Animalité, le corps humain, passage à la culture," in *Annuaire du Collège de France* (Paris,

Imprimerie Nationale), pp. 213-19.

"Du moindre mal à l'union sacrée," *Le Monde,* June 5. Also in *Signes* (1960) under the title "Sur le 13 mai 1958."

"La Démocratie peut-elle renaître en France?" (interview) *L'Express,* July 3, pp. 15-17. Also in *Signes* under the title "Demain . . ."

"Sur Madagascar" (interview), *L'Express,* August 21. Also in *Signes.*

1959

"Le Philosophe et son ombre," in *Edmund Husserl 1859-1959.* Edited by H. L. Van Breda and J. Taminiaux. The Hague, Martinus Nijhoff. Also in *Signes* (1960).

"Réflexions générales sur le sens de cette tentative (l'ontologie de la Nature) et sur la possibilité de la philosophie aujourd'hui," in *Annuaire du Collège de France* (Paris, Imprimerie Nationale), pp. 229-37.

"Bergson se faisant," *Bulletin de la Société Française de Philosophie,* 54:1 (January-March), 1960. Also in *Signes.* The lecture was first delivered at the Bergson Congress, May 17-20, 1959. Another translation of Merleau-Ponty's lecture may be found in *The Bergsonian Heritage,* edited by Thomas Hanna (New York, Columbia University Press, 1962), pp. 133-49.

"De Mauss à Claude Lévi-Strauss," *La Nouvelle Revue Française,* 7:82 (October), 615-31. Also in *Signes.*

1960

Signes. Paris, Gallimard. English translation: *Signs.* Translated by Richard C. McCleary. Evanston, Northwestern University Press, 1964.

"Husserl aux limites de la phénoménologie," in *Annuaire du Collège de France* (Paris, Imprimerie Nationale), pp. 169-73. A translation and commentary on texts of Husserl's latest period.

"Nature et Logos: le corps humain," in *Annuaire du Collège de France* (Paris, Imprimerie Nationale), pp. 173-76.

"Préface," to *L'Oeuvre de Freud* by Dr. Hesnard (Paris, Payot), pp. 5-10.

"La Volonté dans la philosophie de Malebranche," *Bulletin de la Société Française de Philosophie,* 54:3 (July-September). Contains Merleau-Ponty's contribution to a discussion.

1961

"L'Ontologie cartesienne et l'ontologie d'aujourd'hui: Philosophie et non-philosophie depuis Hegel," in *Annuaire du Collège de France* (Paris, Imprimerie Nationale), p. 163. Announcement of the course Merleau-Ponty was to have taught that year.

"L'Oeil et l'esprit," *Art de France*, 1:1 (January). Reprinted in *Les Temps Modernes*, 17:184-85 (November), 193-227; and in book form *L'Oeil et l'esprit* (Paris, Gallimard, 1964). The article as originally published and as reprinted in book form contains illustrations chosen by Merleau-Ponty. English translation by Carleton Dallery in *The Primacy of Perception and Other Essays* (1964), pp. 159-90.

"Cinq notes sur Claude Simon," *Mediations*, Winter, pp. 5-9.

1964

Le Visible et l'invisible suivi de notes de travail. Texte établi par Claude Lefort accompagné d'un avertissement et d'une postface. Paris, Gallimard. Posthumous publication of parts of a book on which Merleau-Ponty was working at the time of his death.

Secondary Sources

Acton, H. B. "Philosophical Survey: Philosophy in France," *Philosophy*, 24:88 (January, 1949), 77-81.

Alquié, Ferdinand. "Etude sur le comportement," *Cahiers du Sud,* 31:267 (August-September, 1944), 48-54. Review.

—— "Une Philosophie de l'ambiguité: L'Existentialisme de Maurice Merleau-Ponty," *Fontaine*, 11:59 (April, 1947), 47-70.

"Der Andere Mensch in der Phänomenologie Merleau-Pontys," *Evangelische Ethik*, I (1960), 10-26.

Anzeiu, Didier. "Thèse et diplômes d'études supérieures de philosophie," *Essais et Etudes Universitaires* (1946), pp. 115-21. On *Phénoménologie de la perception*.

Arendt, Hannah. *Eichmann in Jerusalem.* Rev. ed., New York, The Viking Press, 1964.

Aron, Raymond. *The Opium of the Intellectuals.* Translated by Terence Kilmartin. New York, W. W. Norton, 1958.

Audry, Colette. "La Vie d'un philosophe," *L'Express*, May 11, 1961, pp. 34-35. In memoriam.

"Les Aventures de la dialectique," *L'Express*, May 28, 1955, p. 13. Review.

Bainton, Roland. *Christian Attitudes Toward War and Peace.* Nashville, Abingdon Press, 1960.

Bakker, R. "De Leer van 'de ander' in de fenomenologie van Merleau-Ponty," in *Handelingen v. h. 25e nederl. filologencongres, 1958* (Groningen, 1958), pp. 86-88.

Ballanti, Graziella. "L'Esistenzialismo di Maurice Merleau-Ponty," *Rivista di filosofia neo-scolastica*, 44:5 (September-October, 1952), 458-61.

Ballard, Edward G. "On Cognition of the Precognitive—Merleau-Ponty," *Philosophical Quarterly*, 11:44 (July, 1961), 238-44.

—— "The Philosophy of Merleau-Ponty," *Tulane Studies in Philosophy*, 9 (1960), 165-87. Studies in Hegel

Bannan, John F. "Philosophical Reflection and the Phenomenology of Merleau-Ponty," *Review of Metaphysics*, 8:3 (March, 1955), 418-42.

Barral, Mary Rose. *Merleau-Ponty: The Role of the Body-Subject in Interpersonal Relations*. Pittsburgh, Duquesne University Press, 1965.

Bataillon, M. "Eloge prononcé devant l'Assemblée des Professeurs du Collège de France, 25 juin 1961," *Annuaire du Collège de France* (Paris, Imprimerie Nationale, 1961), pp. 37-40.

Bayer, Raymond, editor. *Manuel de la recherche documentaire en France, Tome II: Philosophie*. Paris, Vrin, 1950.

—— "Merleau-Ponty's Existentialism," *The University of Buffalo Studies*, 19 (1953), 95-104. The article was later published in French under the title "Merleau-Ponty et l'existentialisme," *Revue Philosophique de la France et de l'Etranger*, January-March, 1962, pp. 107-17.

de Beauvoir, Simone. *The Ethics of Ambiguity*. Translated by Bernard Frechtman. New York, Philosophical Library, 1948. Reprinted in paperback by the Citadel Press, 1962.

—— *La Force des choses*. Paris, Gallimard, 1963.

—— "Merleau-Ponty et le pseudo-Sartrisme," *Les Temps Modernes*, 10:114-115 (April-May, 1955) 2072-2122. Reprinted in *Privilèges* (Paris, Gallimard, 1955).

—— "La Phénoménologie de la perception de Maurice Merleau-Ponty," *Les Temps Modernes*, 1:2 (November, 1945), 363-67. Review.

—— *The Prime of Life*. Translated by Peter Green. New York, The World Publishing Co., 1962.

—— *She Came To Stay*. Translated by Yvonne Moyse and Roger Senhouse. New York, The World Publishing Co., 1954.

Bell, Daniel. *The End of Ideology*. Glencoe, The Free Press, 1960. Reprinted in paperback by Collier Books, 1961.

Bendix, Reinhard. *Max Weber: An Intellectual Portrait*. Garden City, Doubleday and Co., 1962.

Bergson, Henri. *An Introduction to Metaphysics*. Translated by T. E. Hulme. New York, G. P. Putnam and Sons, 1913. Reprinted in paperback by the Liberal Arts Press, 1949.

—— *Matter and Memory*. Translated by Nancy M. Paul and W. Scott Palmer. New York, Macmillan Co., 1911. Reprinted in paperback by Doubleday and Co., 1959.

Berl, Emmanuel. *De l'Innocence*. Paris, René Julliard, 1947.

Boring, Edwin G. *A History of Experimental Psychology*. New York, Century, 1929; rev. ed., 1950.

Boring, E. G., H. S. Langfeld, and H. P. Weld. *Foundations of Psychology*. New York, John Wiley and Sons, 1948.

Borne, Etienne. "Les Aventures de la dialectique de Maurice Merleau-Ponty," *La Vie Intellectuelle*, 26:7 (July, 1955), 6-19. Review.

Bouet, Michel M. "Le Problème de l'interiorité objective dans la psychologie phénoménologique de M. Merleau-Ponty," *Etudes Philosophiques*, 3:3-4 (July-December, 1948), 297-314.

Brus, B. "De Tall by Merleau-Ponty," *Ned. Tijdschrift v. Psychologie* (1958), pp. 268-80.

Burns, Emile. *Handbook of Marxism*. New York, International Publishers, 1935.

Caillois, Roland. "De la perception à l'histoire," in *Deucalion II* (Paris, Editions de la Revue Fontaine, 1947), pp. 57-85.

—— "Destin de l'humanisme marxiste (à propos d'Humanisme et terreur)," *Critique*, 4:22 (March, 1948), 243-51.

—— "Le Monde vécu et l'histoire," in *L'Homme, le monde, l'histoire* (Paris, Arthaud, 1948), pp. 7-24. Reflects the influence of Merleau-Ponty's philosophy of history.

—— "Note sur l'analyse réflexive et la réflexion phénoménologique," in *Deucalion I* (Paris, Editions de la Revue Fontaine, 1946), pp. 125-39.

Cairns, Dorian. "Phenomenology," in Vergilius Ferm, editor, *A History of Philisophical Systems* (New York, Philosophical Library, 1950), pp. 353-64.

Calvez, Jean-Yves. *La Pensée de Karl Marx*. Paris, Editions du Seuil, 1956.

Campbell, Robert. "Monsieur Merleau-Ponty et ses lecteurs," *Paru*, 37 (December, 1947), 49-51. On *Humanisme et terreur*.

—— "Sens et non-sens," *Paru*, 51 (February-March, 1949), 66-67. Review.

Carew Hunt, R. N. *The Theory and Practice of Communism.* New York, The Macmillan Co., 1960. Reprinted in paperback by Pelican Books in 1963.

Centineo, Ettore. *Una Fenomenologia della storia; L'Existenzialismo di M. Merleau-Ponty.* Palermo, Palumbo, 1959.

Chisholm, Roderick M., editor. *Realism and the Background of Phenomenology.* Glencoe, The Free Press, 1960.

Christianus. "Sainte Antigone," *La Vie Intellectuelle,* 15:1 (January, 1947), 1-4. On *Humanisme et terreur.*

Collins, Larry, and Dominique Lapierre. *Is Paris Burning?* New York, Simon and Schuster, 1965. Reprinted in paperback by Pocket Books in 1966.

Cornu, Auguste. *Karl Marx: l'homme et l'oeuvre.* Paris, Felix Alcan, 1934.

—— *The Origins of Marxian Thought.* Springfield, Illinois, Charles C. Thomas, 1957.

Deguy, Michel. "Maurice Merleau-Ponty," *La Nouvelle Revue Française,* 9:102 (June, 1961), 1118-20. In memoriam.

Delfgaauw, B. "De Inaugurale rede van Maurice Merleau-Ponty," *Studia Catholica* (1953), pp. 137-39.

Desan, Wilfrid. *The Marxism of Jean-Paul Sartre.* New York, Doubleday and Co., 1965.

Desgroupes, P. "Le Phénomène Koestler," *Fontaine,* 11:59 (April, 1947), 112-30.

Dondeyne, Albert. *Contemporary European Thought and Christian Faith.* Translated by Ernan McMullin and John Burnheim. Pittsburgh, Duquesne University Press, 1963.

Douglas, Kenneth. *A Critical Bibliography of Existentialism (The Paris School).* New Haven, Yale French Studies, Special Monograph No. 1 (1950), items 201-29.

Dreyfus, H. L., and S J. Todes. "The Three Worlds of Merleau-Ponty," *Philosophy and Phenomenological Research,* 22:4 (June, 1962), 559-65.

Dufrenne, M. "Maurice Merleau-Ponty," *Les Etudes Philosophiques,* 36:1 (January-March, 1962), 81-92.

Earle, William. "Phenomenology and Existentialism," *The Journal of Philosophy,* 52:2 (January 21, 1960), 75-84.

Ecole, Jean. "Rentrée au Collège de France avec M. Merleau-Ponty," *Revue Thomiste* (1953), pp. 193-96.

Edie, James M. "Expression and Metaphor," *Philosophy and Phenomenological Research,* 23:4 (June, 1963), 538-61. Reflects in part the influence of Merleau-Ponty's view of language.

—— "Recent Work in Phenomenology," *American Philosophical Quarterly*, 1:2 (April, 1964), 115-28.

Farber, Marvin. *The Foundation of Phenomenology*. New York, Paine Whitman Publishers, 1962.

—— editor. *Philosophic Thought in France and the United States*. Buffalo, University of Buffalo Publications in Philosophy, 1950. Published simultaneously in French by Presses Universitaires de France.

Fontan, Pierre. "Le Primat de l'acte sur l'énoncé, à propos de la Phénoménologie de la perception," *Revue Philosophique de Louvain*, 53:37 (February, 1955), 40-53.

G., Y. "La Phénoménologie de la perception," *Paru*, 14 (January, 1946), 99-101. Review.

de Gandillac, Maurice. "Maurice Merleau-Ponty," *Revue Philosophique de la France et de l'Etranger*, January-March, 1962, pp. 103-6. In memoriam.

Garaudy, Roger, et al. *Mésaventures de l'anti-marxisme*. Paris, Editions Sociales, 1956. Marxist critique of *Les Aventures de la dialectique*.

Gilson, Etienne. *The Philosopher and Theology*. Translated by Cécile Gilson. New York, Random House, 1962.

—— *The Spirit of Medieval Philosophy*. Translated by A. H. C. Downes. New York, Charles Scribner's Sons, 1940.

—— et al. "La Notion de philosophie Chrétienne," *Bulletin de la Société Française de Philosophie*, 31:2-3 (March-June, 1931), 37-93.

Grenier, Jean. "La Philosophie," *L'Arche*, 3:10 (October, 1945), 135-36. Review of *Phénoménologie de la perception*.

Gurwitsch, Aron. "Discussion: The Last Work of Edmund Husserl," *Philosophy and Phenomenological Research*, 16:3 (March, 1956), 380-99; 17:3 (March, 1957), 370-98. Summaries of the central group of Husserl's *Krisis* lectures.

—— *The Field of Consciousness*. Pittsburgh, Duquesne University Press, 1964.

—— "Quelques aspects et quelques développements de la psychologie de la Forme," *Journal de Psychologie Normale et Pathologique*, 33 (1936), 413-71.

Hayen, André. "La Phénoménologie de M. Merleau-Ponty et la métaphysique," *Revue Philosophique de Louvain*, 50:25 (February, 1952), 102-23. Discussion of Alphonse de Waelhens' book on Merleau-Ponty, *Une Philosophie de l'ambiguité*.

Heidegger, Martin. *Being and Time*. Translated by John Macquar-

rie and Edward Robinson. New York, Harper & Brothers, 1962.
—— "The Way Back into the Ground of Metaphysics," in Walter
Kaufmann, editor, *Existentialism from Dostoevsky to Sartre*
(New York, Meridian Books, 1957), pp. 206-21. Introduction to
the fifth edition of the essay, "What Is Metaphysics?".
—— *Kant and the Problem of Metaphysics*. Translated by James
S. Churchill. Bloomington, Indiana University Press, 1962.
—— "Letter on Humanism," translated by Edgar Lohner, in H.
D. Aiken and William Barrett, editors, *Philosophy in the Twen-
tieth Century*, Volume III (New York, Random House, 1962),
pp. 270-302.
—— "What Is Metaphysics?" in *Existence and Being*, edited by
Werner Brock (Chicago, Henry Regnery Co., 1949), pp. 325-61.
Reprinted in paperback by Henry Regnery, 1962.
Hoffer, Eric. *The True Believer*. New York, Harper and Brothers,
1951. Reprinted in paperback by New American Library, 1958.
Husserl, Edmund. *The Cartesian Meditations*. Translated by Dorian
Cairns. The Hague, Martinus Nijhoff, 1960.
—— *Ideen zu einer reinen Phänomenologie und phänomenolo-
gischen philosophie*. Edited by M. and W. Biemel in *Husserliana*,
Volume III. The Hague, Martinus Nijhoff, 1952. Critical edition
of *Ideen I*, 1913. French translation: *Idées directrices pour une
phénoménologie*, by Paul Ricoeur. Paris, Gallimard, 1950, Eng-
lish translation: *Ideas*, by W. R. Boyce Gibson. New York, The
Macmillan Co., 1958; reprinted in paperback by Collier Books,
1962.
—— *Die Krisis der Europäischen Wissenschaften und die
Transzendentale Phänomenologie*. Edited by Walter Biemel in
Husserliana, Volume VI. The Hague, Martinus Nijhoff, 1954.
Contains the three central lectures of the *Krisis* group, as well
as related lectures dating from the same period. French trans-
lation of the first two lectures in the central *Krisis* group, "La
Crise des sciences européennes et la phénoménologie transcen-
dentale," by Edmond Gerrer in *Les Etudes Philosophiques*, 4
(1949), 127-57; 229-301. French translation of the Vienna lecture, "La Crise de l'humanité européenne et la philosophie," by
Paul Ricoeur in *Revue de Métaphysique et de Morale*, 55:3
(July-September, 1950), 225-58. English translation of the
Vienna Lecture, "Philosophy and the Crisis of European Man,"
by Quentin Lauer in *Phenomenology and the Crisis of Philosophy* (New York, Harper and Row, 1965), pp. 149-92.
—— "Personliche Aufzeichnungen," *Philosophy and Phenomeno-*

logical Research, 16:3 (March, 1956), 293-302.

—— "Phenomenology," translated by C. V. Solomon, in Roderick Chisholm, editor, *Realism and the Background of Phenomenology* (Glencoe, The Free Press, 1960), pp. 118-28. Originally published in the 14th edition of the *Encyclopedia Britannica* (1929).

—— "Phenomenology and Anthropology," translated by Richard G. Schmitt, in Roderick Chisholm, editor, *Realism and the Background of Phenomenology* (Glencoe, The Free Press, 1960), pp. 129-42.

—— *The Phenomenology of Internal Time-Consciousness.* Edited by Martin Heidegger. Translated by James S. Churchill. Bloomington, Indiana University Press, 1964.

—— "La Philosophie comme prise de conscience de l'humanité," translated by Paul Ricoeur, with introduction by Walter Biemel. *Deucalion III* (Paris and Neuchâtel, Editions de la Baconnière, 1950), pp. 109-27. Daily meditations dating from the period of the *Krisis* lectures.

—— "Philosophy as a Strict Science." Translated by Quentin Lauer in *Phenomenology and the Crisis of Philosophy* (New York, Harper and Row, 1965), pp. 71-147. Originally published in *Logos*, I (1910-11), 289-341.

Hyppolite, Jean. "Existence et dialectique dans la philosophie de Merleau-Ponty," *Les Temps Modernes*, 17:184-85 (October, 1961), 228-44.

—— *Sens et existence dans la philosophie de Maurice Merleau-Ponty.* The Zaharoff Lecture for 1963. Oxford, The Clarendon Press, 1963.

—— "Les Travaux de jeunesse de Hegel d'après des ouvrages récents," *Revue de Métaphysique et de Morale*, 42:3 (July, 1935), 399-426; 42:4 (October, 1935), 549-78.

"Il Faut lire le polonaise pour savoir où en est Sartre," *L'Express*, June 21, 1957, pp. 24-25. An account of Sartre's critique of Marxism, published in Polish; the critique itself was later published in French.

Jeanson, F. *Le Problème moral et la pensée de Sartre.* Preface by Jean-Paul Sartre. Paris, Editions du Myrte, 1947.

Jolivet, R. "Le Problème de l'absolu dans la philosophie de M. Merleau-Ponty," *Tijdschrift v. Philosophie*, 19:1 (March, 1957), 53-100.

Kaelin, Eugene. *An Existentialist Aesthetic: The Theories of Sartre and Merleau-Ponty.* Madison, The University of Wisconsin Press, 1962.

Kaufman, Fritz. "La Phénoménologie de la perception," *Erasmus,* 2:7-8 (January 15, 1949), columns 202-6. Review.

Kingston, F. Temple. *French Existentialism: A Christian Critique.* Toronto, University of Toronto Press, 1961.

Kockelmans, J. A. "Merleau-Ponty's Phenomenology of Language," *Review of Existential Psychology and Psychiatry,* 3:1 (Winter, 1963), 39-82.

—— "Merleau-Ponty's View on Space-Perception and Space," *Review of Existential Psychology and Psychiatry,* 4:1 (Winter, 1964), 69-105.

—— "Ruimtewaarneming en ruimte volgens Merleau-Ponty," *Tijdschrift v. Philosophie,* 19:3 (1957), 372-427.

Koestler, Arthur. *Darkness at Noon.* Translated by Daphne Hardy. New York, The Macmillan Co., 1941. Reprinted in paperback by New American Library, 1961.

—— *The Yogi and the Commissar, and Other Essays.* New York, The Macmillan Co., 1945. Reprinted in paperback by Collier Books, 1961.

Koffka, Kurt. *Principles of Gestalt Psychology.* New York, Harcourt, Brace and Co., 1935.

Kojève, Alexandre. *Introduction à la lecture de Hegel.* Paris, Gallimard, 1947; 2d rev. ed., 1962.

Koyré, Alexandre. "Rapports sur l'état des études hégéliennes en France," *Revue d'Histoire de la Philosophie,* 5:2 (April-June, 1931), 147-71.

Kuhn, Helmut. "Existentialismus und Marxismus. Zu Merleau-Pontys Philosophie der Zweideutigkeit," *Philosophisches Jahrbuch,* 62 (1953), 327-46.

Kwant, Remy C. "In Memoriam M. Merleau-Ponty," *Streven* (1960-61), pp. 946-60.

—— *The Phenomenological Philosophy of Merleau-Ponty.* Translated by Henry J. Koren. Pittsburgh, Duquesne University Press, 1963.

Lacan, Jacques. "Maurice Merleau-Ponty," *Les Temps Modernes,* 17:184-85 (October, 1961), 245-54.

Landgrebe, Ludwig. "The World as a Phenomenological Problem," *Philosophy and Phenomenological Research,* 1:1 (September, 1940), 38-58.

Langan, Thomas. "Maurice Merleau-Ponty: In Memoriam," *Philosophy and Phenomenological Research,* 23:2 (December, 1962), 205-16.

Le Blond, Jean-Marie. "Le Sens de l'histoire et l'action politique,"

Etudes (November, 1955), pp. 209-19. Review of *Les Aventures de la dialectique.*

Lefebvre, Henri. "M. Merleau-Ponty et la philosophie de l'ambiguité," *Pensée*, 68 (July-August, 1956), 44-58; 73 (May-June, 1957), 37-52.

Lefort, Claude. "De la Réponse à la question," *Les Temps Modernes*, 9:104 (February, 1954), 157-84. Article written June, 1953.

—— "L'Idée d''etre brut' et d''esprit sauvage,'" *Les Temps Modernes*, 17:184-85 (October, 1961), 255-86.

—— "Le Marxisme et Sartre," *Les Temps Modernes*, 8:89 (March, 1953), 1541-70.

de Lubac, Henri. *The Drama of Atheist Humanism.* Translated by Edith M. Riley. New York, Sheed and Ward, 1950. Reprinted in paperback by Meridian Books, 1963.

Luethy, Herbert. *France Against Herself.* Translated by Eric Mosbacher. New York, Frederick A. Praeger, 1955. Reprinted in paperback by Meridian Books, 1959.

Luijpen, William A. *Existential Phenomenology.* Translated by Henry J. Koren. Pittsburgh, Duquesne University Press, 1962.

Lukacs, Georg. *Existentialisme ou marxisme?* Paris, Nagel, 1948; 2d ed., 1960.

Lyotard, Jean -F. *La Phénoménologie.* Paris, Presses Universitaires de France, 1956.

Malraux, André. *The Voices of Silence: Man and His Art.* Translated by Stuart Gilbert. New York, Doubleday and Co., Inc., 1953.

Marcel, Gabriel. *Being and Having.* Translated by Katherine Farrer. Westminster, The Dacre Press, 1949; Boston, The Beacon Press, 1951. Reprinted in paperback by Harper Torchbooks, 1966.

—— *Metaphysical Journal.* Translated by Bernard Wall. Chicago, Henry Regnery Company, 1952.

—— *The Philosophy of Existentialism.* Translated by Marya Harari. New York, Philosophical Library, 1956. Reprinted in paperback by The Citadel Press, 1961.

Marcuse, Herbert. *Reason and Revolution.* New York, Oxford University Press, 1941; 2d ed., New York, Humanities Press, 1954; paperback edition with a new preface, Boston, The Beacon Press, 1960.

Maritain, Jacques. *True Humanism.* Translated by Margot Adamson. New York, Charles Scribner's Sons, 1938.

Martinet, J.-D. "Les Intellectuels et le goût du pouvoir," *La Révolution Prolétarienne*, 303 (May, 1947), 43-45. On *Humanisme et terreur*.

Martins, Diamantino. "O communismo existencialista de M. Merleau-Ponty," *Revista portuguesa di filosofia*, 9:3 (July-September, 1953), 225-50.

Marx, Karl. "Economic and Philosophical Manuscripts of 1844," translated by T. B. Bottomore, in Erich Fromm, editor, *Marx's Concept of Man*. New York, Frederick Ungar Publishing Co., 1961.

Marx, Karl, and Frederick Engels. *The German Ideology*, edited and with an introduction by R. Pascal. New York, International Publishers, 1947. Comprises Parts I and III (written in 1846).

—— *The Holy Family*. Moscow, Foreign Languages Publishing House, 1956. Written in 1844.

Marxisme et Existentialisme: controverse sur la dialectique, Jean-Paul Sartre, Roger Garaudy, Jean Hyppolite, Jean-Pierre Vigier, and J. Orcel. Paris, Plon, 1962.

Matson, Floyd W. *The Broken Image: Man, Science, and Society*. New York, George Braziller, 1964.

McCleary, R. C. *Ambiguity and Freedom in the Philosophy of Maurice Merleau-Ponty* (Master's Thesis). University of Chicago, 1954.

Meyer, Rudolf W. "Merleau-Ponty und das Schicksal des französischen Existentialismus," *Philosophische Rundschau*, 5:3-4 (1955), 129-65. The article was the first in a series, but the series was never continued.

Michalson, Carl. *The Rationality of Faith*. New York, Charles Scribner's Sons, 1963.

Millet, Louis. "Sur la Leçon inaugurale de Maurice Merleau-Ponty dans la chaire de Bergson au Collège de France," *Les Etudes Bergsoniennes*, 4 (Paris, Albin Michel, 1956), 230-33. On *Eloge de la philosophie*.

Monnerot, Jules. "Liquidation et justification," *La Nef*, 4:27 (February, 1947), 8-19. This and the two following articles concern *Humanisme et terreur*.

—— "Réponse aux *Temps Modernes*," *La Nef*, 4:37 (December, 1947), 32-44.

—— "Du Mythe à l'obscurantisme. Réponse aux *Temps Modernes* II," *La Nef*, 5:39 (February, 1948), 3-21.

Moreau, Joseph. *L'Horizon des esprits, Essai critique sur la phénoménologie de la perception*. Paris, Presses Universitaires de

France, 1960.

Murchison, Carl, editor. *Psychologies of 1925*. Worcester, Clark University Press, 1927.

—— *Psychologies of 1930*. Worcester, Clark Univeristy Press, 1930.

Murphy, Gardner. *Historical Introduction to Modern Psychology*. New York, Harcourt, Brace and Co., 1949.

Natanson, Maurice. *A Critique of Jean-Paul Sartre's Ontology*. Lincoln, University of Nebraska Press, 1951.

—— *Literature, Philosophy, and the Social Sciences*. The Hague, Martinus Nijhoff, 1962.

Paci, Enzo. "Introduzione," to *Saggio sulla natura (An Essay on Nature)*, by F. J. E. Woodbridge, translated by Francesco Tato. Milan, Bompiani, 1956. Paci shows how Woodbridge's concept of nature is similar to the existential and temporal structure of reality found in Husserl and Merleau-Ponty.

Papi, Fulvio. "Libertà e marxismo in Merleau-Ponty," *Atti del XII Congresso intern. di Filosofia, 1958*, 12 (Florence, 1961), pp. 361-68.

Pariente, J.-C. "Lecture de Merleau-Ponty," *Critique*, No. 186 (November, 1962), pp. 957-74; No. 187 (December, 1962), pp. 1067-78.

Patri, Aimé. "Bibliographie," *Paru*, 37 (December, 1947), 51-52. Bibliography of the material dealing with Merleau-Ponty's *Humanisme et terreur*; not complete.

—— "Humanisme et terreur," *Paru*, 42 (May, 1948), 61-62. Review.

—— "La Philosophie de la police politique," *Masses*, 7-8 (1947).

Pavlov, I. P. *Conditioned Reflexes: An Investigation of the Physiological Activity of the Cerebral Cortex*. Translated by G. V. Anrep. London, Oxford University Press, 1928.

"La Phénoménologie de la perception," *Revue de Métaphysique et de Morale*, 51:2 (April, 1946), 183-84. Review.

Philippe, M.-D. "Exposé de la phénoménologie de M. Merleau-Ponty," *Nova et Vetera* (1951), 132-46.

—— "Réflexions sur la phénoménologie de M. Merleau-Ponty," *Nova et Vetera* (1951), 198-209.

Pickles, Dorothy M. *France Between the Republics*. London, Love and Malcomson, Ltd., 1946.

—— *France: The Fourth Republic*. New York, Barnes and Noble, Inc., 1954.

de Plinval, Georges. "Quand la vérité passe à travers M. Merleau-

Ponty," *Ecrits de Paris* (February, 1953), 37-44. On *Eloge de la philosophie.*

Podlech, Adalbert. *Der Leib als Weise des In-der-Welt-Seins: Eine systematische Arbeit innerhalb der phänomenologische Existenzphilosophie.* Bonn, Bouvier and Co., 1956.

Pontalis, J.-B. "Note sur le problème de l'inconscient chez Merleau-Ponty," *Les Temps Modernes,* 17:184-85 (October, 1961), 287-303.

Pos, H.-J. "Phénoménologie et Linguistique," *Revue Internationale de Philosophie,* 1:2 (January 15, 1939), 354-65.

Puente Ojea, G. "Existencialismo y Marxismo en el pensamiento de Merleau-Ponty," *Cuadernos Hispano-Americanos,* 30 (1957), 41-88.

—— "Fenomenologia y marxismo en el pensamiento de M. Merleau-Ponty," *Cuadernos Hispano-Americanos,* 26 (1956), 295-326; 29 (1959), 221-56.

Report of Court Proceedings in the Case of the Anti-Soviet "Bloc of Rights and Trotskyites." Moscow, People's Commissariat of Justice of the U.S.S.R., 1938.

Ricoeur, Paul. "Analyses et problèmes dans 'Ideen II' de Husserl," *Revue de Métaphysique et de Morale,* 56:4 (October-December, 1951), 357-94; 57:1 (January-March, 1952), 1-16.

—— "Appendice: Quelques figures contemporaines," in Emile Bréhier, *Histoire de la philosophie Allemande* (Paris, Vrin, 1954,) pp. 181-258.

—— "Etude sur les 'Meditations Cartesiennes' de Husserl," *Revue Philosophique de Louvain,* 52:33 (February, 1954), 75-109.

—— *Finitude et culpabilité.* 2 vols. Paris, Montaignes, 1960. English translation of Vol. I: *Fallible Man.* Translated by Charles Kelbley. Chicago, Henry Regnery Co., 1965.

—— *Histoire et vérité.* Paris, Éditions du Seuil, 1955.

—— "Hommage à Merleau-Ponty," *Esprit* (June, 1961), 1115-20. Published also in *Nouvelles Littéraires,* May 11, 1961.

—— "Husserl et le sens de l'histoire," *Revue de Métaphysique et de Morale,* 54:3-4 (July-October, 1949), 280-316.

—— "Phénoménologie existentielle," *Encyclopédie Française: Philosophie-Religion,* Vol. 19. Paris, Librairie Larousse, 1957, 19.10.8-12.

—— "Sur la Phénoménologie," *Esprit,* 21 (1953), 821-38.

Robinet, A. *Merleau-Ponty: Sa vie, son oeuvre, avec un exposé de sa philosophie.* Paris, Presses Universitaires de France, 1963. A brief analysis with selections from the works.

Rouart, Julien. "'La Structure du comportement' de Maurice Merleau-Ponty," *L'Evolution Psychiatrique année 1947*, No. 1. (Paris, Desclée de Brouwer, 1947), pp. 333-50.

Sartre, Jean-Paul. *The Age of Reason.* Translated by Eric Sutton. New York, Alfred A. Knopf, 1947. Reprinted in paperback by Bantam Books, 1959. Volume I of *Les Chemins de la liberté*, originally published, 1945.

—— *Anti-Semite and Jew.* Translated by George J. Becker. New York, Schocken Books, 1948. Reprinted in paperback by Grove Press, 1962. Originally published, 1946.

—— *Being and Nothingness.* Translated by Hazel Barnes. New York, Philosophical Library, 1956. Originally published, 1943.

—— "Les Communistes et la Paix," *Les Temps Modernes:* I: 7:81 (July, 1952), 1-50; II: 8:84-85 (October-November, 1952), 695-763; III: 9:101 (March, 1954), 1731-1819.

—— *Critique de la raison dialectique, précédé de Question de méthode.* Paris, Gallimard, 1960. The first part has appeared in English translation: *Search for a Method.* Translated by Hazel Barnes. New York, Alfred A. Knopf, 1963.

—— "Existentialism Is a Humanism," in Walter Kaufman, editor, *Existentialism from Dostoevsky to Sartre* (New York, Meridian Books, 1957), pp. 287-311. Originally published, 1946.

—— *Imagination.* Translated by Forrest Williams. Ann Arbor, University of Michigan Press, 1962. Originally published, 1936.

—— *Literature and Existentialism.* Translated by Bernard Frechtman. New York, Philosophical Library, 1949. Reprinted in paperback by The Citadel Press, 1962. Translation of parts of *Situations I* and *III*.

—— "Materialism and Revolution," in *Literary and Philosophical Essays.* Translated by Annette Michelson. New York, Criterion Books, 1955. Reprinted in paperback by Collier Books, 1962. All essays in this volume are from *Situations II*. This article, first published in *Les Temps Modernes* in 1946, is a critique of Marxism.

—— "Merleau-Ponty vivant," *Les Temps Modernes*, 17:184-85 (October, 1961), 304-76. Reprinted in *Situations IV*; translated in *Situations*.

—— *Nausea.* Translated by Lloyd Alexander. New York, New Directions Press, 1959. Originally published, 1938.

—— *The Psychology of Imagination.* Translation anonymous. New York, Philosophical Library, 1948. Reprinted in paperback by The Citadel Press, 1961. Originally published, 1940.

—— "Réponse à Lefort," *Les Temps Modernes*, 8:89 (March, 1953), 1571-1629.

—— *The Reprieve*. Translated by Eric Sutton. New York, Alfred A. Knopf, 1947. Reprinted in paperback by Bantam Books, 1960. Volume II of *Les Chemins de la liberté*, originally published, 1945.

—— *Sketch for a Theory of the Emotions*. Translated by Philip Mairet. London, Methuen and Co., Ltd., 1962. Originally published, 1939.

—— *Situations I, II, III, IV*. Paris, Gallimard, 1947, 1948, 1949, 1964.

—— *Situations*. Translated by Benita Eisler. New York, George Braziller, 1965. Translation of *Situations IV*.

—— *The Transcendence of the Ego*. Translated by Forrest Williams and Robert Kirkpatrick. New York, The Noonday Press, 1962. Originally published, 1937.

—— *Troubled Sleep*. Translated by Gerard Hopkins. New York, Alfred A. Knopf, 1950. Reprinted in paperback by Bantam Books, 1961. Volume III of *Les Chemins de la liberté*, originally published, 1949.

—— "Une Idée fondamentale de la phénoménologie de Husserl: L'Intentionnalité," in *Situations I* (Paris, Gallimard, 1947), pp. 31-35. Originally published, 1939.

de Saussure, Ferdinand. *Course in General Linguistics*. Translated by Wade Baskin. New York, Philosophical Library, 1959.

Scharstein, Ben-Ami. "Bergson and Merleau-Ponty," *Journal of Philosophy*, 52:4 (July 7, 1955), 380-86.

Scheler, Max. *Ressentiment*. Translated by William W. Holdheim. Glencoe, The Free Press, 1961.

Schopenhauer, Arthur. *The World as Will and Idea*. 3 volumes. Translated by R. B. Haldane and J. Kemp. London, Routledge, and Kegan Paul, 1948.

Schutz, Alfred. *Collected Papers I: The Problem of Social Reality*. Edited by Maurice Natanson. The Hague, Martinus Nijhoff, 1962.

—— Discussion: Edmund Husserl's *Ideas*, Volume II," *Philosophy and Phenomenological Research*, 13:3 (March, 1953), 394-413.

—— "Discussion: Die Phaenomenologie und die Fundaments der Wissenschaften (*Ideas III*, by Edmund Husserl)," *Philosophy and Phenomenological Research*, 13:4 (June, 1953), 506-14.

Scotti, Guiseppina. "Originarieta e relazione in Merleau-Ponty," *Aut aut*, 7:38 (March, 1957), 172-84 (Discussion of *The Struc-*

ture of Behavior); 7:39 (May, 1957), 295-309 (Discussion of *Phenomenology of Perception*).

—— "Originalita e relazione nella 'Phénoménologie de la perception'," *Aut aut*, 7:41 (September, 1957), 436-42.

—— "Sulla percezione in Merleau-Ponty," *Aut aut*, 7:42 (November, 1957), 512-23.

Semerari, Guiseepe. "Critica e projetto dell'uomo nella fenomenologia di Maurice Merleau-Ponty," *Il Pensiero*, 5:3 (September-December, 1960), 329-59.

—— "Esistenzialismo e marxismo nella fenomenologia della percezione," *Revista di filosofia*, 52:2 (April, 1961), 167-90; 52:3 (July, 1961), 330-53.

Sérant, P. "Maurice Merleau-Ponty et la pensée de gauche," *Revue des Deux Mondes*, July 1, 1955, pp. 117-27.

Spiegelberg, Herbert. "French Existentialism: Its Social Philosophies," *Kenyon Review*, 16:3 (Summer, 1954), 446-62.

—— "Husserl's Phenomenology and Existentialism," *The Journal of Philosophy*, 52:2 (January 21, 1960), 62-74.

—— *The Phenomenological Movement: A Historical Introduction*. 2 volumes. The Hague, Martinus Nijhoff, 1960.

Strasser, Stephan. *Phenomenology and the Human Sciences*. Translated by Henry J. Koren. Pittsburgh, Duquesne University Press, 1963.

"La Structure du comportment," *Revue de Métaphysique et de Morale*, 50:4 (October, 1945), 307-8. Review.

Thévenaz, Pierre. *What Is Phenomenology?* Edited with an introduction by James M. Edie. Translated by James M. Edie, Charles Courtney, and Paul Brockelman. Chicago, Quadrangle Books, Inc., 1962.

Thody, Philip. *Jean-Paul Sartre: A Literary and Political Study*. New York, The Macmillan Co., 1960.

Tilliette, Xavier, S. J. *Le Corps et le temps dans la "Phénoménologie de la perception."* Basel, Verlag für Recht und Gesellschaft, 1964.

—— "Merleau-Ponty ou la mesure de l'homme," *Archives de Philosophie*, 24:3-4 (July-December, 1961), 399-413.

Touron del Pie, Eliseo. *El hombre, el mundo en la fenomenologia de Merleau-Ponty*. Madrid, 1961.

Trotsky, Leon. *Terrorism and Communism*. Translated by Max Schachtman. Ann Arbor, University of Michigan Press, 1961.

Tymieniecka, Anna-Teresa. *Phenomenology and Science in Contemporary European Thought*. New York, Noonday Press, 1962.

Ullmo, Jean. "Une Etape de la pensée politique (A propos des *Aventures de la dialectique*)," *Critique*, 11:98 (July, 1955), 625-43.

Uranga, E. "Maurice Merleau-Ponty: Fenomenologia y existencialismo," *Filosofia y Letras*, 15:30 (1948), 219-42.

Van Breda, H. L. "Maurice Merleau-Ponty et les Archives-Husserl à Louvain," *Revue de Métaphysique et de Morale*, 67:4 (October-December, 1962), 410-30.

Van Lier, Henri. "A propos des *Aventures de la dialectique*, Philosophie et politique," *La Revue Nouvelle* (1955), 222-32. Review.

——— "L'Existentialisme de Jean-Paul Sartre," *Encyclopédie Française: Philosophie-Religion*, Volume 19. Paris, Librairie Larousse, 1957. 19.12.14-16, 19.14.1-2.

Viano, Carlo. "Esistenzialismo e umanesimo in Maurice Merleau-Ponty," *Rivista di filosofia*, 44:1 (January, 1953), 39-60.

Virasoro, Manuel. "Merleau-Ponty y el mundo al nivel de la percepcion," *Ciencia y Fe* (1957), pp. 147-55.

de Waelhens, Alphonse. "In Memoriam Maurice Merleau-Ponty," *Tijdschrift v. Philosophie*, 23:2 (June, 1961), 340-47. Text in Dutch.

——— "Merleau-Ponty philosophe de la peinture," *Revue de Métaphysique et de Morale*, 67:4 (October-December, 1962), 431-49.

——— *Phénoménologie et vérité: Essai sur l'évolution de l'idée de vérité chez Husserl et Heidegger*. Paris, Presses Universitaires de France, 1953.

——— *Une Philosophie de l'ambiguité: L'Existentialisme de Maurice Merleau-Ponty*. Louvain, Publications Universitaires de Louvain, 1951.

——— "La Philosophie du langage selon M. Merleau-Ponty," in *Existence et signification* (Louvain, Editions E. Nauwelaerts, 1958), pp. 123-41.

——— *La Philosophie et les expériences naturelles*. The Hague, Martinus Nijhoff, 1961. Dedicated to the memory of Merleau-Ponty.

——— "Sartre," in Merleau-Ponty, editor, *Les Philosophes célèbres* (Paris, Lucien Mazenod, 1956), pp. 344-50.

——— "Situation de Merleau-Ponty," *Les Temps Modernes*, 17:184-85 (October, 1961), 377-98.

——— "De Taalphilosophie volgens M. Merleau-Ponty," *Tijdschrift v. Philosophie*, 16:4 (1954), 402-8.

Wahl, Jean. "A propos de l'introduction à la phénoménologie de

Hegel par A. Kojève," in *Deucalion V* (Neuchâtel, Editions de la Baconnière, 1955), pp. 77-99.

——— "A propos d'une conférence du Maurice Merleau-Ponty sur les aspects politiques et sociaux de l'existentialisme," *Renaissances*, 51 (1946), 678-79.

——— *A Short History of Existentialism.* Translated by Forrest Williams and Stanley Maron. New York, Philosophical Library, 1949.

——— "Brève introduction aux philosophies françaises de l'existence," *Encyclopédie Française: Philosophie-Religion*, Volume 19. Paris, Librairie Larousse, 1957. 19.12.3-8.

——— "Cette Pensée," *Les Temps Modernes*, 17:184-85 (October, 1961), 399-436.

——— *Le Malheur de la conscience dans la philosophie de Hegel.* Paris, Rieder, 1929.

Watson, John. *Behavorism.* New York, W. W. Norton & Co., 1925.

Weber, Max. *From Max Weber: Essays in Sociology.* Edited and translated by H. H. Gerth and C. Wright Mills. New York, Oxford University Press, 1958.

——— *The Protestant Ethic and the Spirit of Capitalism.* Translated by Talcott Parsons. New York, Charles Scribner's Sons, 1958.

Werth, Alexander. *The de Gaulle Revolution.* London, Robert Hale, Ltd., 1960.

——— *The Destiny of France.* London, Hamish Hamilton, 1937.

——— *France 1940-1955.* London, Robert Hale Ltd., 1956.

——— *Lost Statesman: Pierre Mendès-France.* London, Abelard-Schuman, 1958.

Wild, John. "Existentialism as a Philosophy," *The Journal of Philosophy*, 52:2 (January 21, 1960), 45-62. This article reflects the strong influence of Merleau-Ponty upon the author.

Wolman, B. B. *Contemporary Theories and Systems in Psychology.* New York, Harper and Brothers, 1960.

Zaner, Richard M. *The Problem of Embodiment: Some Contributions to a Phenomenology of the Body.* The Hague, Martinus Nijhoff, 1964.

Zani, L. "Fenomenologia dell'essere in Maurice Merleau-Ponty," *Rivista di filosofia neo-scolastica*, 49:5-6 (September-December, 1957), 542-49.

Zuidema, S. U. "Een confrontatie tussen Barths theologische theologie en Merleau-Pontys filosofische filosofie," *Philosophia reformata* (1959), pp. 90-96.

Index

leau-Ponty on, 12, 21 ff., 38-39, 212-13, 247-48; Sartre on, 73, 118-19
Freud, Sigmund, the unconscious and, 28, 160-61, 290n20
Galileo, 55-56
de Gaulle, Charles, 89 ff., 104
Gilson, Etienne, 227, 228
God: Marcel on, 64-65, 65-66; Merleau-Ponty on, 218, 219-21, 224-25, 230-31, 233-35

Harnack, Adolf, 256
Hegel, G. W. F., 47, 240; French interpretations, 75-81, 273n85
Heidegger, Martin, 47, 52, 60, 65, 69-70, 74, 80, 160, 240-41; on being-in-the-world, 39-41; Husserl and, 67-68; Kojève's interpretation, 79; Merleau-Ponty and, 69, 179-80; phenomenology, 67-69
Hervé, Pierre, 219 ff.
History of philosophy, Merleau-Ponty in relation to, 174-87
Horizon, see Lebenswelt; World
Hume, David, 71, 72, 240
Husserl, Edmund, 47, 54-69, 74, 77, 135, 152, 153; on Descartes, 56-57; egology, 51-52, 266n14, criticized by Merleau-Ponty, 60, by Sartre, 70-71; and existential phenomenology, 270n45, 292n6; on Galileo, 55-56; on Greek philosophy, 54-55; and Heidegger, 67-68; on Hume, 57; on intentionality, 50, 52; on Kant, 57; Kojève's interpretation, 78-79; on Lebenswelt, 54-60, 269n39, 270n41; and Merleau-Ponty, 53, 60-63, 158-60, 166-72, 268n21, 292n6; on phenomenological reduction, 51-52, 54 ff.; idea of reason, 53-59; and Sartre, 72; on science, 58-59, 268n26, 270n41; on subject-object di-

chotomy, 56-57; on transcendental phenomenology, 51-52, 59; on world, 270n40
—— Works: Cartesian Meditations, 51-52; Idee der Phänomenologie, 51; Ideen I, 51, 52; Krisis lectures, 52-59; Logische Untersuchungen, 49-51; Philosophie der Arithmetik, 49
Hyppolite, Jean, 3, 224; on Bergson, 294n23; on Hegel, 273n85

Idealism, see Intellectualism
"Institution," Merleau-Ponty on, 156-57, 289n14
Institutions, integrity of, 149, 217-18, 222-23, 254-57
Intellectualism, Merleau-Ponty on, 4, 18-19, 42, 209
Intentionality: Husserl on, 50, 52; Merleau-Ponty on, 7, 12, 22, 33, 61-62; Sartre on, 266n16
Intersubjectivity, see Being-in-the-world; Body; Temporality
Interworld, Merleau-Ponty on, 11-12, 42-43, 132, 135, 168, 213, 242; see also Being-in-the-world; World

Jaspers, Karl, 66, 69, 234, 241

Kaelin, Eugene, 44, 45, 188
Kant, Immanuel, 57, 152, 153
Kierkegaard, Søren, 64, 220, 234, 240, 246
Koestler, Arthur: discussed, 100-2; Darkness at Noon, 95-100, 278n14; The Yogi and the Commissar, 95-96, 278n13
Kojève, Alexandre, Introduction à la lecture de Hegel, analyzed, 76-81
Korean War, importance for Merleau-Ponty, 105-6, 108
Koyré, Alexandre, 75, 76
Kravchenko, Victor A., 92
Kwant, Remy, 45, 190